Yale Western Americana Series, 33

BIG GAME IN ALASKA
A History of Wildlife and People

MORGAN SHERWOOD

NEW HAVEN AND LONDON
YALE UNIVERSITY PRESS

Published with assistance from the foundation established in memory of
William McKean Brown.

Chapters 2 and 4 and the Afterword contain in revised form material that originally appeared in two articles by the author, "Specious Speciation in the Political
History of the Alaskan Brown Bear," *Western Historical Quarterly* 10 (1979):
49–60, and "The Great Duck Egg Fake," *Alaska Journal* 7 (1977): 89–94.

Designed by Nancy Ovedovitz and set in Baskerville type.
Printed in the United States of America by Halliday Lithograph,
West Hanover, Mass.

Library of Congress Cataloging in Publication Data
Sherwood, Morgan B.
  Big game in Alaska.

  (Yale Western Americana series ; 33)
  Bibliography: p.
  Includes index.
  1. Wildlife management—Alaska—History. 2. Big game
hunting—Alaska—History. I. Title. II. Series.
SK367.S53   333.95′4   81-3005
ISBN 0-300-02625-0   AACR2

10   9   8   7   6   5   4   3   2   1

For Jeanie

Contents

Illustrations

(following p. 102)

1. George Folta with one of his smaller bears. Courtesy of Claire Folta Wipperman.
2. Big game hunter Dall De Weese with record Kenai moose horn. Courtesy of Simon and Seaforth's Saloon and Grill, Anchorage.
3. Thomas C. Riggs, Jr., on the Boundary Survey, 1907. Courtesy of the Library of Congress.
4. Edward W. Nelson, architect of Alaskan game management. USDA Photograph.
5. Sam O. White, who pioneered the use of the airplane in wildlife management. Courtesy of the University of Alaska Archives, Fairbanks.
6. Some Alaska Game Commission staff members photographed in Fairbanks, 1939. Courtesy of James G. King, USF & WS, Juneau.
7. Hosea Sarber with bear skull. Courtesy of USF & WS, Anchorage.
8. Andrew Simons, famous big game hunter's guide. Courtesy of Mr. and Mrs. Robert Reeve.
9. Naturalist Olaus Murie. Photograph by James Gilligan. Courtesy of The Wilderness Society.
10. Game Warden Jack O'Connor. Courtesy of Lois Irvin.
11. Lieutenant General Simon Bolivar Buckner, Jr. Portrait by Edwin Chapman. Photograph courtesy of William C. Buckner.
12. U.S. District Court Judge Simon Hellenthal. Courtesy of Mr. and Mrs. John S. Hellenthal.
13. Dr. Romig's Wild Game Feast, 1941. Courtesy of Mr. and Mrs. John S. Hellenthal.

Acknowledgments

I am indebted to several archivists for their expert and courteous help: Renee Jaussard of the National Archives in Washington, D.C.; Phillip Lothyan and staff at the Federal Archives and Records Center, Seattle; Phyllis DeMuth and the staff of the Alaska State Historical Library, Juneau; Paul McCarthy of the University of Alaska Archives in Fairbanks and his staff, especially Renee Blahuta; Diane Brenner of the Anchorage Historical and Fine Arts Museum; and the staff of the Manuscript Division, Library of Congress.

A number of private citizens deserve my special thanks too. Robert De Armond, of Juneau, provided several important leads and loaned me part of his clipping file. Mrs. S. B. Buckner, of San Francisco, and William C. Buckner, of Kansas City, Missouri, kindly sent me references and useful newspaper clippings. The late Emory Tobin of Vancouver, Washington, and the late Ira N. Gabrielson of Oakton, Virginia, also responded promptly and informatively to my inquiries. Mr. and Mrs. John S. Hellenthal and Mrs. Warren Cuddy, of Anchorage, James J. O'Connor, of Juneau, and the late Sam O. White, of Fairbanks, all kindly consented to discuss the subject with me. My Alaskan friends and relatives, in informal conversations, gave me ideas and information about how to handle the subject. Thomas Larsen, of Halibut Cove, emphasized a point that should have been obvious to me as an Alaskan but was not: humans *fear* brown bears. Of the many others who contributed data, several are mentioned in the footnotes and bibliography.

So many scholars read parts of the manuscript that it would serve no useful purpose to mention them in a long list. They know who they are and I will express my gratitude to each personally. If, as a result, they are not thanked publicly, neither are they likely to be blamed for my own errors. I must also thank my editors at Yale University Press, Charles Grench and Sharon Slodki, for the close attention they gave my manuscript.

A number of people aided my search for appropriate illustrations; some of their names appear in the photo credits. John S. Hellenthal, Sam Kimura, and Claire Wipperman, of Anchorage, Lois Irvin and Jim Rearden, of Homer, Conner Sorensen, of Juneau, Malcolm Greeney, of

Hood River, Oregon, and Maj Laughrun, Robert Boyd, and Fielding Woods, of Washington, D.C., went out of their way to help in the search. Despite all the assistance, I failed to find many photos of the wardens. Most were camera shy, whether from modesty or to pursue their enforcement duties more effectively I hesitate to guess.

Finally, I want to mention the small and big game animals of Alaska, whose company I have enjoyed off and on for more than forty years. They inspired this book.

Big Game in Alaska

1

The General and
the Game Wardens

The people and big game animals of Alaska lived together successfully until the dawn of the twentieth century. Before the gold rushes, the human population was minuscule and the country's vast size—586,000 square miles—and varied landscapes provided ample living room for beast and man. The gold fever was a temporary aberration in the evolution of man-animal relationships. The significant changes came near mid-century, with the arrival of military and civilian defense personnel before the Second World War. Demographic, technologic, and economic growth triggered by the military buildup marked the beginning of the end of Alaska's frontier innocence and endangered the most fragile part of the wilderness—the big game animals. Subsequent changes were a matter of degree, not kind.

Between the gold rushes and the war, the history of wildlife and people in Alaska was a story of adaptation to the realities of frontier life, the rhetoric of economic development, American colonial policy, and the ideology of American conservation. Conservation was tested and survived. The earliest game laws were a national, not an exclusively Alaskan, response to the decimation of wildlife during the stampedes for gold. Later attempts to acquire local control of all of Alaska's natural resources focused on game animals. Not until the early 1930s, with the maturation of the Alaska Game Commission, was a balanced game management program implemented. But the program was hindered by flawed science, the menace of new technologies, environmental imperatives, pressures from a uniquely structured population, the traditional hostility of farmer and fisherman toward animal predator, and an atavistic belief in man's democratic right to shoot wild animals whenever he chose.

The most dramatic challenge came late in 1941, when Major General Simon Bolivar Buckner, Jr., took the game commission to court for the right to hunt on the same terms as any resident Alaskan and according

1

to regulations written for a few frontiersmen. The game wardens were convinced that his action threatened the animals and the pioneer life-style as well. In August of that year Buckner had walked into the Anchorage headquarters of the Alaska Game Commission requesting an application for a one-dollar resident big game hunting license; he claimed he was qualified because he had lived in Alaska longer than one year, off the military base. When Jack O'Connor, the game warden for the district of Anchorage, denied Buckner's claim to legal domicile in Alaska, Buckner asked him to telegraph Frank Dufresne, of the Alaska Game Commission in Juneau, with whom the army had been conferring about the whole question of hunting by military personnel. According to O'Connor, just before Buckner left the office he said he was going to the Arctic and would kill a polar bear if he saw one; he asked if he could purchase his license later. O'Connor told him that he could not legally take any game animals unless he held a fifty-dollar nonresident license and that he would get the same treatment as any other violator if he were caught.[1]

Immediately after Buckner's departure from the Federal Building, two army officers from the new military base in Fairbanks, Lieutenant Colonel L. V. Gaffney and a captain, walked into the commission office. The same issues—the rights of military personnel in Alaska to hunt big game—were discussed again. Gaffney bought a nonresident small game hunting license for ten dollars; he said that he "didn't care" to buy the license from the wardens in Fairbanks, with whom he had had a spat the month before.[2]

That same day, August 25, O'Connor complied with Buckner's request and sent a radiogram to Juneau. It closed: "INTEND STANDING PAT ON RULING AND GO TO JAIL IF ORDERED IN CONTEMPT OF COURT IF ACTION TAKEN STOP PLEASE ADVISE."[3] In Juneau Frank Dufresne tried to prevent an embarrassing public confrontation by informing Buckner that Juneau was continuing to draft changes in the game laws for Congress, in response to the discussion between Buckner and the commission.[4] Unsatisfied, Buckner, on the shrewd political advice of his army attorney, Major Justin Harding, enlisted the aid of a local civilian lawyer named Warren Cuddy.[5] On September 5, all three men—Buckner, Harding, and Cuddy—marched into the commission office in Anchorage with a completed application and an affidavit supporting the general's claim to Alaskan domicile.

The papers were forwarded to Juneau. With remarkable speed, considering the distance, normal bureaucratic inertia, and the gravity of the issues, General Buckner's application was denied "without prejudice to submission of further proof if applicant wishes." It was the opinion of George Folta, Alaskan counsel-at-large for the Department of the Interior (who had set down the legal guidelines for the issuance of licenses to military personnel), that Buckner's affidavit was insufficient "to meet the burden which rests upon him to prove the acquisition of a domicile under the Alaska Game Law."[6]

In mid-September Buckner wrote a précis of his position for Dufresne. He had tried to keep quiet the controversy over hunting by the military until the game commission made some meaningful compromises. Now his men felt the commission was insincere. Buckner himself had "already lost one month of hunting privileges in what appears to be dilatory tactics." Worse still, he added, the controversy had come to the attention of the secretary of war in Washington, who wanted a full report. For that report the general asked for a commitment by the game commission to support residential hunting privileges for soldiers who had completed one year of service in Alaska. In the meantime, he had "taken recourse to the courts . . . as a matter of principle and aside from the general subject of revision of the game laws."[7]

On September 19, 1941, General Buckner formally initiated proceedings in the Third District Court, Territory of Alaska, Judge Simon Hellenthal presiding. Buckner asked for a writ of mandamus ordering Frank Dufresne and Jack O'Connor, as agents of the Alaska Game Commission, to issue him a resident big game hunting license for one dollar. The stage was set for the most dramatic episode in the history of game management by the commission, a symbolic turning point in the history of Alaska, a case that indirectly raised serious questions about the proper relationship of man to his natural environment, and a controversy that excited Alaskans as it sent aftershocks all the way to Washington, D.C.

Buckner's action challenged a way of life in Alaska by threatening to alter the northerners' relationship with their natural environment. Buckner wanted to hunt for recreation; most Alaskans hunted for food. Buckner's soldiers, all armed, and the civilians who followed them north to build defense facilities, could increase dangerously the hunting pressure on Alaskan game animals. The economic growth that would accompany a larger population promised to encroach on wildlife habitats. The military buildup also brought new prosperity to the Territory and the technologies to pursue big game more efficiently, particularly improvements in transportation.

Buckner may have been the first general O'Connor ever met. In 1940 Alaskans were unaccustomed to rubbing elbows with celebrities of any kind. They had no congressmen, although they had seen enough senators and representatives pass quickly by on junkets. Warren Harding had been the only American president to visit the Territory. Will Rogers stopped in Anchorage before his airplane, piloted by Wiley Post, crashed in the Arctic and killed them both, but no movie stars paraded regularly to previews at Cap Lathrop's little theaters. A yacht freighted with English nobility on a hunting trip had anchored at the head of Cook Inlet in 1939. The sight was a curiosity. Since the completion of the Alaska Railroad in 1923 few large ships had challenged the forty-foot tidal range of the inlet, not even during the summer, when no gray ice floes litter the wide mud flats below Anchorage.

Buckner brought to Alaska an old family name, along with his title. He was the son of Confederate Lieutenant General Simon Bolivar Buckner, Sr., who had surrendered unconditionally to U. S. Grant in the Civil War, an action that gave Grant his nickname. Buckner, Sr., was nominated for the vice-presidency of the United States on the Gold Democrat ticket during the hotly contested campaign of 1896. He polled very few votes. At the splinter party's convention young Buckner (then ten years old) was introduced to the delegates, who were so charmed by the youngster that they called him the "Child of the Democracy." In later years Simon Junior preferred to forget the honor. Other memories of his childhood were more pleasant to him.[8]

Buckner was marked early for an army career. He entered West Point in 1904 and graduated in 1908, in the middle of his class of 107 cadets. After service on the Texas border and in the Philippines (he hunted wild game in both places), he was attached to the Army Air Corps during the First World War and stationed in the States. Then he served at West Point, the General Staff School, the Army War College, and as chief of staff of the Sixth Division. Despite the pedagogical and administrative appointments, and no combat record, Buckner's reputation as a "driving apostle of the vigorous life" remained intact. According to a journalist writing in 1943, all the legends about him dealt somehow with either his physical hardness or his hunting prowess.

General Buckner brought to Alaska more than a numerically powerful constituency, rank, and a respected name. He brought a commanding physical presence and personality too. He was almost six feet tall, stocky, weighing 185 pounds, with a ruddy, weather-beaten complexion. The impressive appearance was complemented by an outgoing temperament. He was articulate, and his vocabulary could stretch from the academy to the saloon. In polite company he had "the gentle accent and courtly manners of a Kentucky colonel." And he was witty. After the Japanese bombed Pearl Harbor in 1941, Admiral Kimmel and General Short, commandants in Hawaii, were replaced and called back to Washington for an explanation. Said Buckner, "There, but for the grace of fog, go I."[9]

With all these institutional, social, and personal credits, Buckner's presence in Anchorage added a special aura to what the newspapers are pleased to call "society," such as it was at that time in this frontier town, where class lines were nonexistent or blurred. It was a new city in the wilderness, founded in 1915 as a construction center for the Alaska Railroad; it served later as headquarters for the line.[10] Anchorage had no ghettoes, golden or otherwise. An isolated town (Seattle was 1,400 air miles away, but no airline made regular flights between the cities and travel by ship could take the better part of a week) with a population in 1939 of only 4,200, where reputations were new and where family backgrounds were dim (sometimes kept so deliberately, for distant Alaska was a second chance for some Americans who had not always observed the letter of the law), such a place could not support the social stratification of established communities. In this fluid milieu Buckner made friends quickly, but his day in court raised serious questions in the minds of many Alaskans about the future of their unique way of life. It was a matter of logistics.

Before his arrival and the military expansion that began in 1940, there were about 500 servicemen in Alaska: a handful of Signal Corps personnel, who operated the telegraph system, wore civilian clothes, and were considered Alaskan by the Alaskans; a handful of coast guardsmen; and a token detachment of soldiers (most of the 500) stationed at Fort Seward, or Chilkoot Barracks, in southeastern Alaska. By October 1941, when Buckner went to court, there were nearly 23,000 officers and enlisted men in Alaska, all of hunting age, and all having some familiarity with firearms. Even worse news for the Alaska game commissioners, if they did their sums (and apparently they did, without the benefit of official, public, War Department statistics): servicemen in 1941 constituted 50 percent of the non-Native* Alaskan males over fifteen years of age and more than twice the number of big game hunters then licensed in the Territory.[11] In other words, the number of new migrants and potential hunters under the direct authority of the commanding general threatened to rise dramatically, possibly to double or even triple the hunting population for which the Alaskan game laws were designed.

These data worried Jack O'Connor that fall of 1941, and explain why a local game warden chose to tilt with an army general. O'Connor was an ardent utilitarian conservationist and a dedicated law-enforcement officer. If in the Buckner case he dodged a court order, it was because the order represented an opinion at variance with another legal interpretation, which came down from his superiors and was more consistent with his own views of the purpose of the game laws.

---

* The term *Native* will be used interchangeably with *indigene* and *aborigine* to refer to Alaska's Eskimos, Aleuts, Athapaskan Indians, and Tlingit Indians, individually and collectively. The four major Alaskan Native groups have subdivisions, to which specific reference is sometimes made in the text. To avoid confusion, the term *native* to identify anyone born and raised in Alaska, regardless of race, is not used.

The commanding general of the U.S. Army in Alaska and Federal District Judge Hellenthal were not the first influential citizens to be confronted by the stubbornly honest warden. When a cannery owner whom he had arrested was released on orders from Washington, D.C., O'Connor expressed his disgust openly.[12] In 1933 he apprehended two men at Kasilof, in south-central Alaska, for killing moose during the closed season and left the culprits overnight with the U.S. marshal at Kenai. The next morning his prisoners told him that he had no warrant, there was no commissioner (that is, magistrate) in Kenai, and suspects could not be held longer than twenty-four hours. Apparently the poachers learned all this from the deputy marshal, who was also charged by the law to enforce game regulations. O'Connor's superior reported the warden's reaction: he "promptly made a decision and without preliminary explanation demanded his prisoners from the U.S. marshal, put them ahead of his dog team and snowshoed through to Seward in two days where he immediately filed a complaint. Upon pleas of guilty, one of the men he had arrested was sentenced to six months and the other two months in jail."[13] Such stories of O'Connor's almost evangelical dedication spread rapidly throughout underpopulated Alaska (where there were 72,500 people in 1940), despite the great distances (the Territory covered 586,000 square miles), especially stories about his willingness to shoot down the big shots who illegally hunted the animals he was expected to protect.

Charles John O'Connor was born in Montreal in 1884 and came to Alaska when he was in his early teens. After working as a miner, he served in several government positions. For a time he was chief of police and fire chief of Fairbanks. In 1930 he received his first independent assignment as a warden, at Holy Cross, on the Yukon River, where he put his wilderness experience to work on frequent dogsled and motorboat patrols. In the fall of 1931 he was transferred to Anchorage, a town with fewer than 3,000 people situated at the head of Cook Inlet and the toe of the Chugach Mountains. An urban island whose main economic supports were the Alaska Railroad, two seasonal fish canneries, and a collection of stores and saloons, Anchorage was a supply and watering center for the south-central Alaskan bush.

Unlike Simon Buckner, Jack O'Connor was probably considered neither an unusually striking person nor an "outsider" with status and rank. (Alaskans then and now refer to the rest of the United States as "outside," an ethnocentric but geographically justifiable conceit.) He was short, about five-foot, seven inches—barely within the commission's height requirement—weighed perhaps 165 or 170 pounds, and was round. Seen full-front, even his face was round. He wore round, steel-rimmed eyeglasses and, in winter, a round beaver hat that failed to add the horizontal and vertical planes needed to sharpen the circularity of his appearance. Usually he wore a green Filson or whipcord field-type jacket with numerous pockets, and trousers to match—what the locals called an "Alaskan tuxedo." The familiar outdoorsman's costume did not correct a first impression that he was only a plump, inactive townsman.

Actually, there were probably not two pounds of untoughened flesh on the warden. The round torso was in fact a hard barrel chest. What typed O'Connor as a sourdough was his walk, or more accurately, his sway and roll from side to side, his short legs slightly bowed with feet placed widely apart at each step. It was the gait of a man unaccustomed to flat land and pavement, the movement of a man with years of experience traveling on snowshoes and hiking over Alaska's spongy tundra, muskeg, and moss. It was a distinctively Alaskan stride and very unmilitary. O'Connor would not have qualified for General Buckner's drill team.

The warden's physical endurance was coupled with a quick mind. His colleague Sam O. White, of Fairbanks, recalled when he and O'Connor were mushing down the frozen Toklat River in temperatures around minus fifty degrees Fahrenheit. The lead dog failed to turn as ordered and tumbled into an overflow, plunging itself and White into the murderously cold water. In one swift movement O'Connor raced by the sled, snatching an ax, innersoles, and socks, and before White got to shore O'Connor had a fire going and dry clothes waiting nearby.[14]

O'Connor's jurisdiction included the Matanuska Valley. During the Great Depression, President Franklin Roosevelt's New Deal resettled 200 unemployed ruralists from the north-central United States on public land in the valley, about fifty miles from Anchorage. They were expected, with the help of donated labor and tax money, to establish farms where the moose and bear browsed on the natural vegetation. The highly publicized colony was a harbinger of problems and conflicts to come six years later with the more disruptive immigration of military personnel and construction workers.

Before the arrival of the would-be farmers and during the same year that O'Connor moved to Anchorage, M. D. Snodgrass, who promoted colonization for the Alaska Railroad, had asked the game commission to waive the nonresident hunting license fee for new colonists, and also the requirement that nonresidents be accompanied by a guide. "With such plentiful stocks of wild game it would seem that this added inducement might well be offered to assist in encouraging permanent settlers to come to the Territory." In effect, Snodgrass hoped to use Alaskan game to promote settlement that, if successful, would ensure the game's disappearance. Another problem was bureaucratic. The commission's federal, administrative arm was the Bureau of Biological Survey, an agency of the Department of Agriculture until 1940. The commissioners told Snodgrass that they could not change the law, and would not even if they could.[15] The commission's decision was reiterated when the New Deal colonists arrived.

More than a few of the colonists considered the wildlife a part of their federal subsidy, and they illegally killed big game and small game for meat, fur, or fun. One resident of Palmer, headquarters of the colony, wrote to the game commission, pleading for more wardens: "I have sent for Jack O'Connor so often that I am ashamed of myself. Jack covers a lot of ground, but it isn't humanly possible to keep an eye on these fellows and patrol the other districts also. . . . I have never known people to whom the right to get out and kill anything at any time is quite so important."[16] O'Connor must have found it difficult to maintain his reputation for fairness in such a setting, particularly when he had to handle violations like the one at nearby Willow, in early 1941. Henry Chilligan and a friend were hunting moose out of season when Chilligan mistook his partner for a moose and shot him. The official report reads: "There was no action taken against Chilligan for killing his partner, but he was given ninety days for hunting moose out of season."[17]

O'Connor's codefendant in the general's legal action was Frank Dufresne, the boss warden in Juneau; his official title was executive officer of the Alaska Game Commission. He too was considered a conservationist by the definition of those days; both men believed in the careful management of natural resources to ensure their continued use. Dufresne was also a veteran wildlife officer. He went to work as a "fur warden" for the Bureau of Biological Survey before the establishment of the game commission and soon after the bureau acquired (in 1920) from the Department of Commerce jurisdiction over fur-bearing land animals. In exchange for this jurisdiction the bureau gave the Department of Commerce the jurisdiction over walruses and sea lions that it had exercised as a result of one of those illogical bureaucratic arrangements that Alaskan politicians often complained about. (Other terrestrial wildlife was under the authority of Alaska's governor—an agent of the Department of the Interior—who had his own squad of game wardens between 1908 and 1925, and who reported to the secretary of agriculture.)[18] Dufresne, also like O'Connor, had wide experience in Alaska's wilderness. All told, Dufresne had traveled seventeen thousand miles by dog team.[19] But here the similarities in any comparison of the two men should probably end.

Jack O'Connor was short and stocky; Dufresne was wiry. O'Connor went by the book; Dufresne, a transplanted New Hampshire farm boy with a prior interest in natural history, had an urge to write a book.

Eventually he wrote three. O'Connor shied from publicity; Dufresne seemed to bask quietly in it. One of Dufresne's books is an autobiography, and his wife wrote an autobiography too. O'Connor's behavior suggests that he thought rigorous but fair enforcement of the law was the best way to teach people the importance of wildlife conservation. Dufresne eventually perceived that laws, to be effective, needed the public's support, and he therefore appreciated the value of public relations work.[20] O'Connor was a cop, Dufresne a naturalist.

"Most of my life has been spent in watching, and watching over, wild animals," Dufresne wrote in his autobiography.[21] He preferred watching to watching over, observing and giving entertaining reports of the observation to arrests and convictions, education and public relations to handcuffs and incarcerations. He soon developed a standard thirty-minute lecture that he delivered in Eskimo villages in the Nome district. The first ten minutes were "devoted to throwing the fear of the law into them"; in the following five minutes he explained the history of the game law and the need for it; the next five minutes were spent explaining how easy it was to apprehend them; he then used wrongdoers "as a horrible example to the rest"; and the performance closed with a ten-minute debate among the chiefs and old men, who were given the responsibility for compliance.[22] "The Eskimo mind is a peculiar one and it is the sort of mind that is rarely or never false to a trust," he told his Washington chief of the Biological Survey.[23]

In 1923 Bureau Chief Edward W. Nelson congratulated Dufresne on his missionary work among the Eskimos and on his educational campaign in general, but he suggested that Dufresne do a little more police work. Dufresne said he would begin to enforce the laws vigorously, but more than a year later his immediate supervisor, Ernest P. Walker, still believed that Dufresne should exercise his police powers more forcefully, do less science, and deliver fewer lectures. It was not until the fall of 1925 that Walker could report Dufresne's new belief that scientific work should be conducted by wardens in a way incidental to enforcement.[24]

The dispute between Dufresne and his supervisors does more than illustrate the different temperaments of O'Connor and Dufresne. It represents in microcosm a persistent problem in game management that has plagued attempts to save the animals in Alaska and elsewhere. The question was (and is): what should be the proper balance between law enforcement and scientific investigation on which the laws should be based? Eventually—in Alaska about 1950—the "enforcement versus biology" issue would fuse with another problem in the history of science, technology, and public policy: the conflict between the self-educated or apprenticed specialists and the formally trained, degree-holding wildlife agents without much field experience but with plenty of theory and institutional prestige. The latter preferred scientific investigation to enforcement. In Alaska, until the Second World War, almost all wildlife specialists were apprenticed and self-educated game managers. Mid-century Alaska was a place of rapid institutional change, as well as demographic, technologic, and economic adjustment.

Dufresne probably thought that he was hired mainly to undertake natural history investigations, though he had no formal training in biology. After his appointment Nelson assigned him to L. J. Palmer and Olaus Murie to learn scientific techniques. Palmer and Murie were the only bona fide biologists on the payroll in Alaska; they also acted as wardens. Whatever Dufresne thought he was doing or was expected to do, few if any enforcement officers or scientists contributed poetic reports to regulatory or scientific agencies the equal of his early communiqués to the Bureau of Biological Survey. The following is dated January 1924.

There comes a peculiar uncanny, deathly stillness in the air at 70 below zero. No wild thing seems to stir. . . . The heavy breathing of our dogs, the squealing of the sled runners and the crackling of our own breaths in the air sound loud and harsh and seem to be violating this brooding silence of the north woods. It seems we are the only things that dare move—But no! there in the riffling shallows of an open waterhole a tiny, gray bird dashes and flits about with all the grace of a flycatcher. . . .

Our map tells us we are forty miles north of the Arctic Circle; our thermometer tells us it is seventy below zero, yet there is a frail little bird seemingly unsuited to cold weather having the very time of its life. It is, of course, the Water Ouzel, or Dipper. . . .

It required considerable steeling of one's conscience to blast that little life into eternity for the cause of science.[25]

Dufresne's accumulation of such intimate knowledge about Alaska's natural resources, and his way with words, did not disturb his superiors too much. Ira N. Gabrielson, his Washington chief in the fall of 1941, remembered Dufresne as a knowledgeable traveling companion with a dry New England wit.[26] Dufresne was cut from the same literary pattern as John Muir, the high priest of wilderness conservation, but Dufresne enjoyed hunting, was a utilitarian conservationist rather than a preservationist, and was willing to undertake wildlife administration, although he lacked enthusiasm for office work and disliked the police side of game management. In his autobiography he described in his woodsy-folksy style how he often threw his jacket over a stream that was difficult to cross, or up a slope that was difficult to climb, as an inducement to cross the stream or climb the slope. He did not, however, throw his jacket into Anchorage when General Buckner filed suit. Dufresne did not even arrive there until after the proceedings ended, and did not reveal what the commission's reaction to the court's decision would be until he was interviewed while boarding an airplane for Fairbanks.

Ira Gabrielson was in Anchorage when Buckner's complaint was in litigation. He had come to conduct fishery hearings. In 1940 the Bureau of Biological Survey and the Bureau of Fisheries were moved into the Department of the Interior, as the Fish and Wildlife Service. Gabrielson, the director, spent five weeks in Alaska busily collecting the opinions of fishermen, industry representatives, and his own employees. The 1942 fishing regulations would be based on such data. The director had too long an agenda of sensitive matters to discuss with Alaskans to enter the dispute over military hunting.

Gabrielson was a cautious science administrator up from the ranks. He was an Iowan who graduated from Morningside College in Colorado, taught public school for a while, and joined the Bureau of Biological Survey in 1915. His specialty was ornithology. He was a portly person who once claimed to have climbed "more mountains than any other fat man in the world."[27]

Gabrielson (searching his memory in 1976) maintained that Interior Secretary Harold Ickes did not interfere in the military controversy either. Ickes let Gabrielson run the service and participated only when the director needed special help. More than once the secretary said that he would not want Gabrielson's job even if it paid $100,000 a year, because the director's constituents were "the biggest bunch of nuts" Ickes knew. "Any person," the secretary repeated several times, "who liked to fish and hunt for fun was a perennial juvenile."[28] Whether he exercised any influence in the Buckner affair or not, some Alaskans were bound to suspect him of turning the military issue into another bureaucratic power play, for Ickes's Department of the Interior virtually owned and ran Alaska before the army arrived. Alaskan politicians considered the secretary more perniciously autocratic than the Russian czars and czarinas who formerly governed the Territory.[29]

In the hierarchy of wardens, between Harold Ickes and Jack O'Connor, were four men who sat with Dufresne as the Alaska Game Commission. Established in 1925, the commission recommended rules, regulations, and policies for the management of big game, small game, land fur-bearing animals, and sport fish; the commercial fishery was not under its jurisdiction. Its recommendations were almost always accepted in Washington, by the secretary of agriculture until 1940 and after 1940 by the secretary of the interior. The commissioners, one from each of Alaska's four judicial divisions, were supposed to represent the opinions of Alaskans and thus to provide a measure of local control, or home rule, for which Alaskan politicians and aspiring officeholders were forever clamoring. Appointments to the commission were made through Washington and were advertised as "nonpolitical," but in fact commissioners tended to agree that only the surplus population of a species could be killed each year, to assure the preservation and continued use of the animal. This philosophy was itself "political," though not necessarily the exclusive viewpoint of one of the major parties.

Of the fifteen commissioners who served without compensation between 1925 and 1959, most were men with years of experience in Alaska before their appointment. The law required at least five years of prior residence. A surprising number of appointees were connected directly to natural resource industries—big game, fish, or fur. It was a time when "conflict of interest" was not interpreted strictly; of the first four commissioners, one was a logger, one a miner, one a physician who also collected wild animals for zoos, and one a dentist. Of the four commissioners on duty when General Buckner filed his complaint, one was Earl Ohmer, a seafood processor and mink farmer from Petersburg; he was called the "shrimp king." Frank P. Williams, of St. Michael, operated a trading post. John Hajdukovich, of Fairbanks, was a guide, trapper, and prospector. Andrew A. Simons, of Lake View on the Kenai Peninsula, was Alaska's most famous big game guide. All had a direct interest in the perpetuation of Alaska's game. All were old-timers, with a combined total of almost 150 years of Alaskan residence. Two were particularly colorful characters.

Ohmer was born in Ohio, attended college in Manitoba, and left an Oregon cattle ranch to process seafood and raise mink in southeastern Alaska. For many years he served as mayor of Petersburg. He was bearded and liked to wear wide-brimmed cowboy hats and buckskin shirts draped with a gold nugget watch chain. His office was decorated with elk horns, pictures of big game he had shot, Indian totems, and animal skins, all dominated by a stuffed bald eagle over his desk.[30]

"Andy" Simons was a cheerful, short, wiry Finn who came to Nome in 1903 as a miner. He settled permanently on the Kenai Peninsula around 1908 and became a guide almost by accident, when he helped an Englishman, previously unsuccessful, to get a trophy. By the Second World War he had guided what one writer has described as a "who's who of hunters." Simons thought the wisest use of game was as food for Natives and settlers. Trophy hunting was acceptable to him (provided the meat was not wasted) because it tended to take only the biggest heads, that is, the oldest males. According to Frank Dufresne, Simons asked of any new regulation under consideration by the game commission, "Is it right for the animals?"[31]

Simons and all the wardens wanted to protect Alaskan game. General Buckner wanted to hunt and wanted his men to hunt. The wardens did not object to hunting by any particular group of people, provided it was regulated to ensure the continuation of healthy animal populations. Buckner's intention was not to exterminate Alaska's wildlife; the rules of hunting behavior that he promulgated later were in large part the old "sportsmen's code." Despite the agreements, by September 1941 the general and the wardens had become so alienated that the imbroglio could not be untangled until the attorneys had had their day in court. The advocate of recreational hunting called upon the lawyers to challenge regulations established to support subsistence hunting. It was another sign that frontier conditions were fading in Alaska.

The Buckner case lured many attorneys into the courtroom gallery because of the personalities involved and the unique circumstances, not because the legal conversation was an exercise of principled judgment or because precedents were being set. There was no attempt to examine critically the basic definition of wildlife, its ownership and regulation, the constitutionality of licensing, or the interpretation of domicile. Game remained "birds and beasts of a wild nature, obtained by fowling and hunting," the "community property of all mankind" (except when on posted private property); to be owned, game must be reduced to possession, and the taking of game could be regulated by the state "for the benefit of all its people in common"; the state could also make regulations that discriminated in favor of its own citizens.[32]

The Buckner case did not even settle any conflict between citizens, and doubtless would have created new discord if a more significant historical development had not blunted the issues and diverted the adversaries. During October, American ships were torpedoed in the Atlantic Ocean, Adolf Hitler's *Wehrmacht* marched on Moscow, and Japanese Emperor Hirohito asked his minister of war, General Tojo, to form a new cabinet. Those events must have given Buckner's cause an edge in the minds of many Alaskans, including some lawyers, because it might be considered unpatriotic to deny recreational hunting to soldiers when the nation was on the brink of war.

To increase the psychological advantage, Buckner hired a civilian attorney, Warren N. Cuddy, in whose bridge-playing circle the Buckners moved. Cuddy, originally a Marylander, came to Alaska in 1914. He was a banker, Elk, Mason, Rotarian, and Republican. Noel Wennblom, assistant U.S. attorney, handled the defense. The district attorney was out of town, and Wennblom was young and inexperienced. Working with him on O'Connor's behalf was a more complicated character, George W. Folta, Alaskan counsel-at-large for the Department of the Interior. Folta was born in Pittsburgh, educated in Beutel's Business College at Tacoma, Washington, and came to Alaska in 1913. He served as secretary of Alaska (1919–21), then as court stenographer, assistant U.S. attorney (1927), and Interior counsel (1940). In 1927 he was admitted to the bar after having studied law on his own, a practice not uncommon among lawyers as well as biologists during these years of Alaskan history.

Folta began soon after his arrival in Alaska to express himself on wildlife issues. He corresponded with Washington representatives of the Biological Survey, and he enjoyed the company, in town and in the field, of bureau personnel.[33] When he was secretary of Alaska, he outlined his private opinions about the controversy then raging over the legal protection of bears. He mailed his viewpoint to Nelson, at the Biological Survey, in a letter marked "personal," because the opinion was contrary to that held by his superior, the governor. There should be no open season on bears at all, said Folta. Black bears, he asserted, are "absolutely harmless," and after hunting brown bears for eight years, seeing perhaps 150, and being attacked by only one (who had provocation), Folta did not think that browns should be exterminated as a threat to human life.[34]

It may be that George Folta wanted to protect the bears from himself, and later, to preserve them for himself rather than for army hunters. What makes his role in the history of Alaskan wildlife so enigmatic is that he was a confirmed hunter who took special delight in shooting bears of every variety. Frank Dufresne once quoted a newspaper story from Juneau dated June 5, 1932: "This is Mr. Folta's two hundredth bear or thereabouts, as he kills a number each year, being one of the most successful of the local hunters."[35] Folta's "affinity" for bears was a local joke. A story in the *Alaska Daily Empire* reported how he went hunting in 1949 for moose and shot a brown bear instead, to nobody's surprise. Less than a year later, the *Empire* could report that Folta had gotten number 129, which brought his average bag, since arriving in Alaska, to three and one-half bears per year, "to hang up the world's record in that department."[36]

Federal District Judge Simon Hellenthal, who presided over the Buckner case, knew about Folta's predilection for shooting bears. They had both lived in Juneau for many years and had practiced law there. To Hellenthal it may have appeared ludicrous for Folta, with 100 notches on his bear rifle, to pose as a protector of Alaskan game by frustrating the general's attempt to hunt the big animals for one dollar. Some of the unique courtroom antics that amused Anchorageites in the fall of 1941 may have been motivated by old memories, animosities, rivalries, or jealousies from the Juneau years, but the judge was convinced that his objectivity was unassailable.

"I feel that I went into the trial of this case absolutely without prejudice either for or against the parties. I did not know the facts and had paid little attention to the law. . . . The only time I remember discussing the game laws . . . was one time at Fairbanks when they arrested some high Army officials for shooting game out of season. And, I expressed my approval of this procedure without qualification."[37]

Simon Hellenthal was born in Michigan, attended Hope College, and studied law at the University of Michigan. He entered Alaska in 1909, to practice law at Juneau in partnership with his brother, Jack. Simon was a tall, slender, sober man who disliked publicity and flamboyance. In 1933 Alaska's congressional delegate, Anthony Dimond, a Democrat, recommended Hellenthal's appointment as judge of the First Judicial Division, with headquarters in Juneau.[38] The incumbent was unfit, said Dimond, after learning that he was in Yakutat on a two-week bear hunt, ignoring court business.[39] The incumbent was Judge Justin W. Harding, General Buckner's army lawyer in 1941. (Harding, as U.S. attorney in Juneau in 1927, had recommended George Folta to fill the vacancy of assistant U.S. attorney; it was Folta's first job as a lawyer.)[40] Neither Simon Hellenthal nor any Alaskan got the Juneau appointment. The following year, however, Hellenthal was named judge of the Third Division, in south-central Alaska. In that position he would hear the Buckner case and hand down a decision that would help to cut short his judicial career.

Hellenthal's personal attitude toward game conservation is elusive. The evidence at hand is indirect. In the year prior to Hellenthal's try for the judgeship in Juneau, a plank in the platform of the Alaska Democratic party advocated the abolition of the game commission.[41] Earlier, Hellenthal had witnessed the controversy between Theodore Roosevelt's chief conservation adviser, Gifford Pinchot, and Richard Ballinger, President William Howard Taft's secretary of the interior. Pinchot and others had charged Ballinger with conflict of interest in the handling of certain Alaskan coal claims, and with anticonservation policies.[42] Precisely where Hellenthal stood on the central issues is unclear. He probably shared at least partially the bias against Pinchot's utilitarian conservation, which became a policy of the Progressive party, because it was the bias of his class, his political party, and his brother-in-law, Clarence Cunningham, who gave his name to the coal claims that triggered the Ballinger-Pinchot squabble. It was also the bias of his partner and brother, Jack Hellenthal, who unlike Simon, enjoyed exercising his oratorical abilities and was never reluctant to express publicly his distaste for Pinchotism.

John A. "Jack" Hellenthal's *The Alaskan Melodrama* was published in 1936. It was titled appropriately, engagingly written, and witty, in a homemade, satirical way. As nonfiction, it was not reliable; the geography, anthropology, geology, archaeology, biology, and history were quaint. Hellenthal's gustatory advice deserves even lower marks; he did not consider halibut very palatable. Nevertheless, his *Melodrama* was a typical expression (but with humor) of a point of view that dominated Alaskan political criticism for at least half a century, until statehood in 1959, and the remnants of which still linger.

Jack Hellenthal's heroes, his "men of genius," were the local industrialists, men like A. E. "Cap" Lathrop and E. A. Rasmuson, provided they did not become monopolists. Hellenthal's enemies were bureaucrats (though he conceded that Alaskan bureaucrats had been free from graft), absentee monopolists, and conservationists. "It is to be regretted that the Pilgrim Fathers were not Conservationists; for if they had been, they would still be sitting on Plymouth Rock admiring the beauties of the wilderness."[43]

Hellenthal's social philosophy was individualism, his economic religion, faith in the market mechanism. He thought the early American pioneers had developed a social system that eliminated waste by putting everything to the best use. He believed that self-interest would be more effective in preventing waste than any system of laws and bureaucratic interference. To Jack Hellenthal, unexploited resources meant waste and consumer prices kept high by stateside monopolists working hand in glove with conservationists. Conservation was an excuse to keep new competition at bay. It was even a disguise for monopolistic control of the fur seals, which the government should have allowed any Alaskan to hunt, according to Hellenthal. In 1941 he was still urging Alaskans to "ditch Pinchotism" for prosperity.[44]

Alaska's wildlife was to Hellenthal simply another natural resource governed by laws written for outside sportsmen and conservationists, not Alaskans, and administered by another group of bureaucrats. "The game laws are made for the sportsman. The aim is, not to make wild life serve the needs of mankind, but to gratify the desire to kill, possessed by the abnormal. It is, no doubt, a good thing to allow the killers to satisfy their craving in this way." The brown bear, "the ugliest and meanest brute on earth," said Hellenthal, "is conserved for the killers exclusively; it is unlawful for ordinary people to injure him or even to insult him."

"Now, it must not be supposed that the bureau officials have devoted all their time to the brown bear. Oh no, they have done their full duty. Even such useless brutes as the sea-lions have been given full protection. At the present rate of progress, it will not be long before an Alaskan will need a license signed by a cabinet officer to kill a mosquito."[45]

Change the time, the geography, some of the resources, and add a federal agency or ten, and Jack Hellenthal's viewpoint becomes a classic statement of the frontier, American, entrepreneurial philosophy, dating back at least to the Jacksonian era. Privilege of any kind but especially

private privilege protected by government was evil when it hindered local "men of genius" from acquiring property and privilege themselves.
Individual self-interest operating in a laissez faire atmosphere would use
natural resources in the best interest of society. It was the philosophy
that had dominated earlier American economic activity on the
advancing frontier and that supported the excesses that Pinchot's conservation was invented to hold in check.

Conservationists in the age of Theodore Roosevelt viewed Alaskan resources in the public domain as the property of all Americans, then and
in the future, and not just the property of local businessmen on the spot
and on the make. Alaskan wildlife belonged to all Americans. It represented a last chance to avoid the mistakes of the past. But Alaskan game
laws, though written by outsiders, were also administered to maintain a
renewable supply for Alaskans and only incidentally for stateside sportsmen. Many Alaskans did not realize the game laws were written to sustain subsistence hunting and were surprised when the game commission
would not accept General Buckner's application for a resident hunting
license.

How many, if any, of Jack Hellenthal's opinions were shared by his
brother, the judge, is a mystery. No doubt, some were. That Simon
Hellenthal "paid very little attention" to the game laws might indicate a
very human apathy toward a single, small corner of his professional
territory—which is not to say that legal precedents governing wildlife
were few or insignificant by 1941.

2

The Laws: Duck Eggs
and Provocative Bears

The laws and traditions that should have fascinated the Alaskan lawyers in 1941 reached back to the taboos and superstitions of primitive man, the hunter. In biblical times several injunctions were handed down. One urged humans to subdue and conquer the earth. Lynn White, Jr., an American scholar writing a few years ago, saw in that admonition "the historical roots of our ecologic crisis." But a conflicting enjoinder warned humans not to take the hen from the nest along with the young, and Noah was in the business of animal preservation, not extermination. Solon the Greek thought hunting interrupted more productive occupations, but Xenophon considered it excellent training for war, an opinion General Buckner might have endorsed. According to Aldo Leopold, a founder of wildlife management as a profession, Marco Polo described the great khan's game laws, in the latter half of the thirteenth century, as a well-rounded system of game management for conservation purposes. Spring and summer shooting of deer and large birds was prohibited, bird refuges were maintained, and food and cover were sometimes provided.

Feudal Europeans lagged behind the Mongols in providing food habitats, but they did regulate hunting for the benefit of the aristocracy, as anyone who has read the adventures of Robin Hood knows. Robin's political cause and his illegal hunting combined to make poaching respectable in democratic circles, and wardens early in their history were burdened with a reputation like the sheriff of Nottingham's. The first English laws set open seasons to coincide with the time the meat was in the best condition for eating, stipulated the type of deer that could be taken, and limited the equipment that could be used in the hunt. Only later, under the Tudors, were game laws enacted with conservation in mind, and laws passed to control predators—"ravening birds and vermin" that threatened other wildlife, fish, and crops. Game preserves were private, for the hunting pleasure of the nobility. Artificial propagation and some environmental controls were introduced. For example, in 1694 William and Mary forbade the burning of nesting cover in springtime.

Leopold sees in the history of game management a constant sequence of events, or historical pattern. First, various restrictions are placed upon hunting. Second, predator populations are controlled with, for example, bounties paid for killing animals that prey on game. Third, game lands are reserved as parks, forests, and refuges. Fourth, restocking and game farming, that is, artificial propagation, is undertaken. Fifth, environmental controls are introduced: food may be provided for game, its range controlled, its habitat improved, and animal diseases checked.[1] Events occurred in about the same sequence in the contiguous United States. In Alaska every step except the fifth was taken almost simultaneously.

In transferring the European tradition to America, the first need was to democratize game management. The democratization came naturally with the free land and a plentiful supply of game. Jenks Cameron has described the long-range effect of the impression of limitless resources upon the thought and behavior of the American.

In a word, it was inevitable that his environment should have bred in the early American settler a fixed idea and a trait. The fixed idea was a conviction that any such thing as the extermination of game was impossible. The trait was a prodigal disregard for not merely game but wild life of all sorts comparable to the solicitude which the boy with a stick in his hands feels for the weeds by the wayside. And both the trait and the idea were transmitted to the early settler's children and to his children's children. And along with them were transmitted the fierce conviction that the free-born American had the right to bear arms, and to "gun" pretty much where, when, and how he pleased.[2]

The results were predictable. By the time of the American Revolution, wildlife was already disappearing in the populated sections, and twelve of the thirteen colonies had game laws of some kind. There were closed seasons for certain animals used as food, laws against Sunday hunting, laws against hunting with fire at night, and licensing laws discriminating against nonresidents and "disorderly and dissolute" people engaged in wanton waste (in the words of a North Carolina statute). The nonresident licenses were to restrict hunting; the resident licenses—when they were adopted—were to regulate hunting.[3] Despite these early game laws, the opinion that an American had the "free-born right" to "gun" down animals that were the property of all mankind continued to govern the behavior of many, and the Robin Hood attitude remained more prevalent than the Franciscan. To break a game law has never been considered a great moral wrong in the United States. It has instead, until recently, been "a little like getting drunk in public," in the words of one student of the subject.[4]

The "prodigal disregard" lingered longer in Alaska, in part because of the abundance of game, in part because of the small population of hunters and the wilderness conditions, and in part because comprehensive game laws and a staff to administer them did not come to Alaska until two hundred years after they were introduced in the English colonies of North America. The Alaskan lawyers had very little game law to worry about until the dawn of the twentieth century. Earlier wildlife legislation for Alaska had aimed to control the hunting of fur seals only. The early history of this animal and that of the sea otter remain among the sadder examples of man's selfish efforts to rob his own nest of the last egg for some temporary advantage.[5]

The new laws were preceded by a quickening federal interest that came in response to a wider effort at national wildlife conservation. In the late nineteenth century, the movement was led mainly by easterners, by scientists, naturalists, and hunters such as George Bird Grinnell, the publisher of *Forest and Stream*. Though European precedents for game management needed democratization in America, the excesses of democracy could not be controlled by laws alone; an aristocratic social philosophy was needed. It was called "sportsmanship." It aspired to curb the harmful effects of democracy on wildlife, which were unavoidable with the population pressures, new technologies, and American commercialism appearing in the forty-eight states decades before they threatened game animals in Alaska.

The man historians credit as preeminent in the acceptance of "ethical" hunting was an English immigrant, Henry William Herbert, who wrote under the pen name "Frank Forester." To Herbert, sportsmanlike hunting was measured in direct proportion to "the difficulty of the capture, the degree of skill, science, courage, or endurance, called forth in the act of taking [the animal]."[6] The philosophy of the gentleman hunters was manifested in their own outdoor magazines and their own private game preserves, or hunting clubs. There was even an English "sporting conversation." The gentleman bird shooter referred to a "brace" of partridge, a "leash" of grouse, a "wing" of plover. A rougher side of the jargon labeled undesirable hunters. A "game hog" was just that; sportsmanlike conduct was not measured by the quantity of the game killed. "Pot hunters" shot grouse on the ground, ducks in the water, and game caught in the crusted snow. The "poacher" shot wildlife in violation of democratic laws. The "market hunter" slaughtered game willy-nilly for what money it would bring. A "meat hunter" shot game only to feed himself.[7]

Obviously, part of the sportsman's code needed still more "republican editing," as one New York hunter observed. In a democratic context the "meat hunter" could not be a serious enemy of the sportsman. Grinnell announced in 1884, "The day of wild game as . . . [a significant] economic factor in the food supply of the country has gone by," but he criticized so-called sportsmen who secured wild animals according to all the other provisions of the "code" and left the meat to rot—hunters who took the trophy only—as well as those who hunted only for food.[8] For Alaska (as it turned out) Grinnell's "editorial compromise" was not enough. Wildlife was still an important economic factor in the food supply of Alaskans and would remain so for a long time—a fact that not every outside sportsman, conservationist, and naturalist grasped.

The code was amended further. Another sportsman said: "We are all noblemen in Columbia. . . . Our game laws go for the protection of game, not for the benefit of corporations."[9] At the turn of the century the corporation was a popular target of reformers. Introducing it as an enemy of game law was to be expected. Charles Hallock, the founder of *Forest and Stream* and an early authority on Alaska, was especially vitriolic in his condemnation of America's blind pursuit of the almighty dollar. The worship of "progress" was to Hallock the "nation's secular religion." He preached a theological revisionism for every place except Alaska, which (he thought) needed natural resource industries, people, and development.[10]

With the organization of the Boone and Crockett Club by Grinnell and Theodore Roosevelt in 1887, the sportsmen and naturalists acquired some impressive political clout. The club was dedicated to the preservation of big game—bear, buffalo, mountain sheep, caribou, cougar, musk-oxen, mountain goat, elk, wolf (but not the outcast coyote), prong-horned antelope, moose, and deer.[11] Membership was limited to 100 sportsmen who had killed, in a fair chase, at least three of these animals, each of a different kind. When in Washington, D.C., the group usually met in the Metropolitan, a rich man's club. Most members were well-to-do college graduates, from old families, and from the older parts of the nation.[12]

At first the legislative gains in post–Civil War America, resulting from the influence of the sportsmen, were slight. On the local level game laws of one kind or another were put on the law books of the forty-eight states and territories. The states took the initiative in wildlife legislation, as they did also in social reform during the late nineteenth century; legally, the states owned the wild animals within their borders. Most of the measures were aimed at regulating destructive hunting with laws that prohibited spring shooting, with license laws, bag limits, and the like. Altogether the regulations were a jumble and their enforcement uneven or indifferent.[13]

At the national level the gains were even less spectacular. Yellowstone National Park had been established in 1872, but its wildlife was not protected by enforced laws until 1894. An act passed in 1891 allowed President Benjamin Harrison to reserve national forestland; among the thirteen million acres he withdrew was Afognak Island in Alaska's Kodiak group. Afognak has been called the "first federal wildlife refuge."[14] Such federal developments, however, were mere gestures. There were no federal laws to protect animals that crossed state or national boundaries, and most animals are not political geographers. By the turn of the century, private and commercial hunting on a large scale had all but exterminated the big game of the East, and had threatened all game in the West, south of the forty-ninth parallel.

Commercial, or "market," hunting of birds had been on the wane around the middle of the nineteenth century, until the railroad, cold-storage technologies, and more deadly guns appeared. The bison was only the most publicized victim. The passenger pigeon was hunted to extinction. A single New York dealer in game birds received in a single shipment twenty thousand prairie chickens. The hungry slaughter endangered hundreds of wild species. Then, in the 1880s, Parisian milliners "decreed" feathers to be fashionable, and the wildlife conservation movement coalesced around a campaign to save the birds. One writer, during two walks through downtown New York City in 1886, counted 542 hats topped with mounted birds representing forty different species. The Audubon Society and the American Ornithological Union were organized; Grinnell had a prominent role in their formation.[15]

With public sentiment aroused, a fear that profiteers might in fact take the last egg from the nests of every Alaskan game bird did more to promote the passage of general game laws than did concern about seals and otters. The Bureau of Biological Survey and the American Ornithological Union classified as game animals certain birds that nested in Alaska: swan, geese, brant, duck, snipe, oyster catchers, curlew, and grouse.[16]

Of central concern late in the nineteenth century was the future of waterfowl that nested in the great delta region of the Yukon and Kuskokwim rivers. The area is a vast lowland of rivers, streams, marshes, and lakes covering thousands of square miles. In the whole southwestern region the white population was less than 100 in 1880 and numbered fewer than 900 in 1890. The Native population varied from about 11,000 to 14,000 between 1840 and 1900, according to estimates. The region had been investigated by only a handful of reliable Russian and American scientists before the end of the nineteenth century.[17] In short, the area's waterfowl breeding grounds were huge, difficult to traverse, underresearched, and uninviting to Caucasians. It was a perfect setting for "the great duck egg fake," as one notorious incident was called by the outdoor magazine that reported the affair.[18]

"The greatest fake ever perpetrated in this line" was unmasked in an article in *Forest and Stream* dated 1895, two years after the historian Frederick Jackson Turner reported the disappearance of the western frontier, and what he thought that frontier had meant to the development of the American national character.[19] A sportsmen's club in the Pacific Northwest had claimed that millions of migratory waterfowl eggs were gathered each year in the great breeding grounds of southwestern Alaska and shipped to venal corporations in the eastern United States, where the albumen was sold to manufacturers. The sensational charge appeared in newspapers across the country, and Senator John H. Mitchell of Oregon joined officially in the protest.[20] The editors of *Forest and Stream* systematically demolished the story, exposing it as a complete hoax. In addition to the public outcry in defense of all birds, a number of conditions may have explained the general acceptance of the "duck egg fake," even after its exposure. *Forest and Stream* suggested only one motive for the fraud: the story was an attempt to distract people from the real reason for the decrease in game birds—spring shooting and sale in the United States. If so, the diversion failed. Broad legislation, at both the federal and state levels, was soon forthcoming.[21]

To the welcome spate of federal wildlife protection laws enacted around the turn of the century were added provisions for the protection of wild birds and their eggs. A tariff law passed in 1894 prohibited the importation of the eggs of game birds; another tariff act, in 1897, extended the prohibition to include the eggs of wild birds not used for food. Senator Lacey's act of 1900, the animals' Magna Charta, prohibited the transportation in interstate commerce of game killed in violation of local statutes, and empowered the Department of Agriculture to preserve and restore the populations of game birds. Section 463 of an Alaska civil government law, also dated 1900, made it a misdemeanor to "break, take from the nest, or have in possession the eggs of any crane, wild duck, brant, or goose." This section, along with the tariff laws, made it illegal to take eggs for scientific purposes or for propagation and transplantation; it was modified by a new bill passed on June 3, 1902.[22]

Four days later Alaska got its first comprehensive game law. The first sentence prohibited the wanton destruction of wild birds including game birds, the destruction of nests and eggs of such birds, and the killing of any wild birds including game birds to ship from Alaska. Regulations governing the hunting of game birds were also promulgated. The law was a tardy acknowledgment, prompted by the gold rushes, that

Alaskan wildlife should be protected too. Indians and Eskimos, miners, explorers, and travelers in need of food were exempted, but the birds they killed could not be shipped or sold.[23]

The law was needed, but Alaska was again out of step with national developments. T. S. Palmer, in his analysis of the chronological sequence in state legislation to protect wild birds, notes that game birds were protected first, then insectivorous birds of value to farmers, then songbirds and "harmless" birds, then seabirds and birds considered valuable for their plumage. English law traveled a similar path.[24] In Alaska every type of bird received some protection all at once—in print, on the pages of a law book. The game birds' real victory came later, when the Migratory Bird Treaty of 1916 and enabling legislation of 1918 assured federal regulation of migratory wildfowl that would ban spring killing and shooting for the market. The new regulations set a bag limit of twenty-five ducks and ten geese per hunter per day.[25] For most of the continent, the laws internationalized and federalized the killing of migratory game birds. For Alaska, however, these enactments too were in reality only a paper precedent. Although the spreading of false information about Alaskan waterfowl did help in a small way to get at least paper protection for the birds, erroneous information about Alaskan brown bears almost led to their extermination in some areas.

It is difficult to envision what the popular image of Alaska might be, or how Alaskans would see themselves, or what would happen to their unique sense of place, if there were no bears in the state. Elsewhere the bear is kept captive. In Alaska the bears are wild. Big brown bears are Alaskan in the same way that kangaroos are Australian, giraffes are African, camels are Muslim, and bulldogs are English. In Alaska, bear stories are a favorite form of parlor entertainment, oral history, and literature. The "cache," a miniature log cabin on stilts used to protect a trapper's or prospector's food supply from bears, is a cliché in Alaskan art.[26] Alaska's flag has eight gold stars on a background of blue: the North Star and the stars of the Big Dipper, in the constellation of Ursa Major, the Great Bear.

Bears were also in the constellation of enduring Alaskan political issues. Periodically Alaskan civic leaders advocated the extermination of the animals and made Ursus the symbol of an alleged colonialism that they claimed was inspired by conservationist sentiment and directed by bureaucrats in Washington, D.C., working in concert with vested absentee interests. This colonialism, they believed, prevented resident Alaskan entrepreneurs from exploiting the Territory's natural resources and prevented resident politicians from setting the terms of that exploitation. The bear question was effective bait to attract local support for home rule because it exposed the elements of a class issue: the struggling but hardy independent pioneer versus the effete eastern conservationist and the wealthy sportsman with the power of big government in his hands. Furthermore, Alaskans were often viewed by others and even themselves as a people courageous enough to live around brown bears, and the on-and-off advocacy by Alaskans of bear genocide was perhaps a kind of public reaffirmation of this image, which was in turn part of an unformulated and usually unconscious set of sometimes real, often mythical, human characteristics associated with frontier living. If the self-image were true, of course, the extermination of the bears would then have altered the character of the people, but rank and file Alaskans who rallied every ten years to support the systematic slaughter of bears rarely considered the logical results of their advocacy. For all these reasons and because the big bears are in fact dangerous animals that inspire fear in humans, the history of Alaskan game laws from about 1900 to 1941, the year of the Buckner case, and even later, can be written as the political history of Alaskan brown bears.

Before the Klondike–Alaska gold rushes at the end of the nineteenth century, there was little need for a comprehensive game law to protect bears or any other land animal or game bird. The human population was sparse, game was abundant with room to hide, and transportation and weapon technologies were primitive, except along portions of the coast. The number of indigenes varied from 32,000 to 41,000 between 1840 and 1890. During the Russian period the non-Native population never reached 1,000.[27] The Russians in Alaska wanted "tame" food —grain and livestock, called "Russian supplies"—not "colonial supplies" consisting of game, fish, and berries.[28] Under these conditions terrestrial wildlife was never threatened, except in the immediate vicinity of human settlements and transportation routes.

The same was true of the early American period. In 1890 there were 4,300 whites in all of Alaska, two-thirds of whom lived in the southeastern towns of Juneau and Sitka. Near those places the hunting pressure on deer and wildfowl had been serious. Sitka, the capital of Alaska at the time of its ceremonial transfer to the United States in 1867, had welcomed 300 soldiers, the crews of four naval and five private ships, and perhaps 600 new settlers, many of whom wanted to sample the deer, goat, and game birds. A correspondent for the *Boston Journal* had reported: "Deer, which three months ago could be bought for fifty cents, now sell for five and sometimes for eight dollars. The wild . . . [goat], duck and grouse also sell at rates which the Russians pronounce fabulous." But the population of Sitka dropped sharply after the first excitement of American ownership, and so did the demand for wild meat. By 1880 a grouse or a mallard fetched only "two bits," and part of a saddle of venison, one dollar, according to a writer in *Forest and Stream*.[29] Juneau was also a market for wild meat after its establishment as a mining camp in 1880. Elsewhere in Alaska, fish cannery and mine operators in the 1880s bought or shot wildlife to provide a change in the fish diet of their employees. This practice, a minor threat to game in the nineteenth century, was not halted effectively until after the foundation of the Alaska Game Commission.

Few trophy hunters ventured to Alaska before the gold rushes. The eastern sportsmen whose crusade for the legal protection of wildfowl and big game would soon arouse hostility among some Alaskans posed no danger to the animals. One popular guidebook to the world's best hunting in the 1880s did not recommend "wild and boggy" Alaska "as a sporting locality, as it rains incessantly nine months out of every twelve, and its inhabitants are the most degraded of aborigines."[30]

The gold rushes tilted the balance of nature dramatically. After George Carmack's strike on the Klondike River of Canada in 1896, thousands of would-be millionaires trekked northward to prospect the streams and rivers, mountains, and valleys of the Yukon Territory and Alaska. Between 1890 and 1900 the total population of Alaska increased 100 percent. The number of non-Natives increased 750 percent! There are no concrete figures to indicate how many prospectors arrived after 1896 and left before the census of 1900, but the number must be substantially higher than the 26,000 new whites counted in 1900. Each miner brought a gun, an outdoorsman's appetite, and perhaps a hungry sled dog to a place where food prices were exorbitant and domestic meat was scarce. Many did their own hunting. Others relied on white or Native market hunters.

The demographic, economic, and geographic conditions, the legal proposition that game was the community property of everyone until reduced to possession, and the acquired American trait of "prodigal disregard" for wildlife all combined to create a serious threat to Alaska's fauna at a time when the only pertinent law was the act of 1900 protecting wildfowl eggs. Sportsmen on the East Coast felt obliged to abandon their indifference toward the fate of faraway Alaskan animals. The Boone and Crockett Club resolved in 1901 to extend to Alaska its campaign for the protection of big game. The country's moose, caribou, deer, sheep, bear, and goats needed a legal shield as much as its birds did. Madison Grant, of the New York Zoological Society, began to collect evidence for the use of Congressman Lacey, also a member of Boone and Crockett.[31]

The evidence was not difficult to find. A national magazine reported 5,000 caribou killed in 1894 (before the first big stampede for gold) in the Fortymile mining region.[32] The big game hunter and outdoor writer, Dall De Weese, in 1897 counted 500 sheep within a six to eight-mile radius of a spot in the Kenai Mountains; the animals had declined drastically in number by 1901.[33] Wilfred Osgood, on a biological reconnaissance in 1900 along the Yukon River, reported that moose were rare, although several years earlier it had been commonplace for a party of miners to kill one or two while descending the river. The high price of moose meat, which sold for one or two dollars a pound in the camps, induced some men to abandon mining for work as professional hunters. The Natives also bartered and sold game meat. On one market hunt, forty-four moose were killed in one month.

Moose sold for only ten cents a pound in the Hope–Sunrise mining district of south-central Alaska, where access to imported meats and to big game was easier.[34] Two men at Chickaloon Bay, near Turnagain Arm, upper Cook Inlet, killed sixteen moose in two days and used little of the meat. A trader at Knik ordered twenty-four bull moose heads and skins; his Indian hunters filled the order promptly. Most of the meat was wasted. J. Alden Loring, a hunter-naturalist, reported that a single Native hunter killed fifty moose near Tyonek. In southeastern Alaska the carcass of a deer sold for one dollar—when there were buyers—and dead deer were often "piled up on the wharves like cord-wood." One team of five hunters came back to town after a week's work with more than 150 dead deer aboard their boat. The deer had been killed not primarily for their meat but for their hides, which brought ten cents to forty cents a skin.[35] Thousands were killed between 1900 and 1901, in a slaughter reminiscent of the buffalo's misfortune, but this time the Indians did most of the killing.

Those horror stories, along with national sentiment (some of it Alaskan) favoring the preservation of birds and wildlife in general, and the political influence of the Boone and Crockett Club, resulted in the passage of the Alaskan game law of 1902. The law prohibited the shipment from Alaska of any wild game except fur-bearing animals, scientific specimens, zoo animals, animals for propagation, and "specimens and trophies." Hunting seasons were set for each species, though regulations governing closed and open seasons could be modified by the secretary of agriculture. Bag limits for the season were set: two moose per hunter; four each of caribou, sheep, goat, and large brown bears; eight deer; ten grouse per day; twenty-five game birds per day. The killing of female or yearling moose, caribou, deer, and sheep was forbidden. Game killed legally could be sold during the open season and by dealers fifteen days after closure of the season. A few United States marshals and deputy marshals, collectors of customs, and coast guard officers were to act as wardens.[36] The weak provision for enforcement vitiated the law's effect in so vast a field. The law did curtail but not end completely the blossoming export trade in hides, heads, and horns.[37] Other than that, it did nothing to alter the hunting habits of Alaskans.

Vocal Alaskans rebelled anyway. The law seemed to discriminate against them in the matter of exporting trophies. The September 1 opening of the migratory game bird season was too late for citizens living in the high latitudes. The season for hunting moose and caribou was too short. Cow moose were tasty. A stateside bureaucrat would decide who got export permits and what regulations should be promulgated. Finally (enter the Alaskan pursued by a bear), brown bears would be protected as game animals. In the brown bear's power, size, and reputation Alaskan political figures found a potent issue. (Scientists have had trouble differentiating between brown and grizzly bears, and, as we shall see, the problem of classification created political confusion. I will use the terms "brown" and "grizzly" interchangeably, keeping in mind the confession of Andrew Simons, Alaska's famous hunter's guide, who said that after thirty years of hunting bear he could not "distinguish the difference between a Grizzly and a Brown Bear, of the same size, if seen walking side by side.")[38]

The grizzly's reputation for indestructibility and ferocity was gained early in the history of its contact with man in North America. Indians feared the animal and preferred not to go out alone in pursuit of it. Vaqueros of Spanish California caught the bears alive, with much difficulty, and staged gory public "bear and bull fights," complete with wagering. In 1805 the Lewis and Clark expedition had several violent confrontations with the big bear. Mindful of these stories, in 1814 Governor DeWitt Clinton of New York referred in a speech to "the white, brown, or grizzly bear, the ferocious tyrant of the American woods."[39]

The "tyrant" could not stand against the repeating rifle and human encroachment. For all practical purposes it disappeared from the southern half of the continent before the conquest of the Old West was complete. In Alaska it continued to thrive, and reached its most magnificent proportions as the Kodiak and Giant Peninsula brown. The bear's celebrity as a dangerous carnivore persisted too. Frank Dufresne, who was responsible for the bear's protection in the 1930s and 1940s and who later wrote a book advocating the establishment of a sanctuary for grizzlies, admitted in 1963 that Alaskan grizzlies were "grumpy, belligerent and subject to unpredictable outbursts of temper."[40]

Also from the beginning of the grizzly bear's recorded association with man, the bruin's fearful reputation was tempered by reports that it never attacked without provocation. One careful reader of the Lewis and Clark bear stories argues persuasively that the grizzlies were provoked. Explorer Zebulon Pike told Thomas Jefferson in 1808 that grizzlies seldom or never attack a man unprovoked.[41] In Alaska, to the present, everyone has agreed that the grizzly bear was tough. Whether it was aggressive when unprovoked remained a hotly debated question.

Apparently the bear's popular name referred to its light, hoary, grayish, "grizzly" color and not to its "grisly," or terrifying, notoriety and size. The Latin name for the grizzly, *Ursus horribilis*, translates "horrifying bear." Anyone who has seen a full-grown Kodiak bear or Peninsula brown in captivity could not have difficulty imagining why the grizzly was considered a fearsome beast when loose. It could weigh as much as three-quarters of a ton, be four to five feet tall at the shoulders, and stand nine feet high on its hind legs. Boone and Crockett records for 1939 describe one monster with a skull almost nineteen inches long and more than a foot wide, measuring, from the tip of its nose to the tip of its tail, two inches short of eight feet, with a hide more than ten feet by ten feet.

Dish-faced, humpbacked, solitary brown bears roam throughout Alaska, preferably at twilight, although they can be seen day or night in open or wooded country during the spring and summer months. The animal retreats to a den in the winter, sometimes one of its own excavation, but it cannot be counted upon to remain in the den all winter. Though omnivorous it subsists mainly on plants and fish. Favorite seasonal diets are early grasses, roots, and other vegetation in the spring, salmon—mostly spawned salmon and carrion—during the summer, and berries in the fall. In between, the brown bear will chase mice and squirrels and eat insects or miscellaneous available meats, wild and domestic, that are often carrion. The greater the supplies of protein in the form of fish, the larger the bears, which explains why grizzlies are smaller in the interior and immense along the coasts.

Every other year or every third year, during the summer, the male wanders widely in search of companionship. He mates by chance rather than by choice, which explains the physical variations that have puzzled mammalogists and confused conservationists. Mother brown gives birth to from one to four but usually two cubs in midwinter, after a gestation period of about six months. At birth the young provide no clues to their adult status as the largest of land-based carnivores. The cubs weigh from under a pound to a pound and one-half, are naked, and their eyes remain closed for days. They will stay with their mother for a year or more, and live twenty or twenty-five years (in captivity). Adults are powerful swimmers and remarkably speedy runners.[42]

The size of the Alaskan brown bear population was not much more than an educated guess until recently. Even with the use of more scientific techniques, the numbers are suspect. In 1937 Dufresne's estimate for the National Resources Committee was 10,000 "grizzlies" and 8,300 "large browns." In 1958 there were about 1,500 brown bears on the Alaska Peninsula and more than 2,200 on three islands in southeastern Alaska. The Kodiak bear population has apparently been stable, judging from the number killed each year, but stable at exactly what number is uncertain;[43] for purposes of social (not biological) analysis, 2,000 is a fairly safe figure.

The precise number is irrelevant. A dozen would have been too many to Alaskan opponents of the game law of 1902, who found in the protection of brown bears what they considered the ultimate absurdity of outside control over Alaskan resources, which the locals considered their own. These opponents found a willing spokesman in the person of United States Senator William P. Dillingham, of Vermont. Dillingham returned from a tour of Alaska "full of praise for the progressive people of Alaska and bursting with enthusiasm to free the new pioneers from the red tape of bureaucracy," according to the historian James Trefethen.

Among [Dillingham's] startling discoveries had been that the game laws were strangling the economy of the Territory. The brown bears, he had heard, had grown so numerous in the few months since the enactment of the law that they were killing all the sheep and cattle and were such a menace to human life that few people dared venture unarmed more than a few yards from their homes. He had been informed also that law-abiding settlers, prospectors, and natives were being deprived of fresh meat, to the detriment of their health, and risked fine and imprisonment if they dared take a single head of game to feed their families. Moreover, he had learned that sportsmen from the United States and Europe were aggravating the situation by slaughtering game that the natives depended upon for food, while residents of the Territory risked arrest if they killed a single head for sale. Such conditions could not prevail in a democratic nation. The game laws of Alaska had to go![44]

Dillingham's report was a whopper of a bear story, a tale worthy of the most talented spinner of sourdough yarns. Alaskan civic leaders applauded and named a town after him. His Senate bill to change the law was introduced in 1904.[45] Once again, Boone and Crockett members and other conservationists collected their own evidence for presentation to the lawmakers. James Kidder, of Boston, told the club that he had seen wanton destruction of game by Natives, white residents, and so-called sportsmen in south-central Alaska in 1900 and 1901. One of J. Alden Loring's Indian employees around upper Cook Inlet had admitted killing five moose and taking the meat of only one because the others "were bulls and tough." Andrew J. Stone reported that employees of one mining camp in the Panhandle consumed ten deer a week, on an annual average, although beef could have been shipped from Seattle. He wrote that the Natives and the white men married to Natives supplied the mines at Unga with caribou meat all year round. The mail boat on which the biologist Wilfred Osgood traveled in southwestern Alaska featured on its menu caribou chops, caribou roast, and caribou stew. Near Fairbanks, one white hunter killed sixty-two caribou in one day, and soon thereafter a party of Natives killed forty-two more. Another hunter, who arrived at the scene of the carnage a day later, followed a bloody trail for five miles, mercifully killing seven crippled caribou that had been left to hobble along and perish from their wounds.[46]

As for the brown bears, the president of the Boone and Crockett Club told Dillingham: "We cannot help but feel that you have been misinformed both as to its numbers and ferocity. On the Alaska Peninsula and on Kodiak Island, the Brown bears have been reduced to a small fraction of their former numbers. These bears are fish and vegetable rather than meat eaters."[47]

The bloody record compiled by opponents of Dillingham's proposal helped to bury his bill, as did the support of Senator John H. Mitchell, of Oregon, the guardian of wildfowl eggs. The victory gave the Bureau of Biological Survey time to modify, amend, and strengthen the old law, and also to permit a measure of local control. The act of 1908 removed protection from the American national bird, the bald eagle, changed certain bag limits, allowed regional management of species, and altered other details, but with one important exception the new law resembled the old. The exception permitted the employment of game wardens by the Territorial governor, who also registered game guides and issued nonresident hunting and export licenses. The power to set regulations and issue permits to collect specimens for science or exhibition in museums and zoos, or for propagation, remained with the secretary of agriculture and his Biological Survey, to whom the governor reported on game matters.[48]

Despite the continuation of hunting for the local markets and what Madison Grant of Boone and Crockett, a mammalogist, called the "havoc worked on game" by transient miners in many locations, Grant could write in 1907 that destruction of game had not yet gone far enough to permanently injure the fauna of the region, but that scientific protection of wildlife should be undertaken immediately. He added that neither the white settlers nor the Natives had any inherent right to the game; it did not belong to them alone, and it was in the interest of all Americans to preserve forms of animal life that have come down through years of slow evolution. Further, "Any legislation that gives Indians privileges superior to the whites is based, not on scientific, but on sentimental considerations," now that the Natives had rifles. The Federal Government should preserve and control the wild game of the national domain, he asserted. "In Alaska we have our last chance to preserve and protect rather than to restore."[49]

Grant's opinion (though not his objection to special privileges for Natives) remained the operational philosophy of federal control of Alaskan game. Ownership of the wildlife did not reside exclusively with Alaskans who reduced the animals to possession. Alaska was "public domain," and the "public" included Americans at large and their children, not just living Alaskans. The policy was a departure from practices and traditions that had existed before the states erected their own framework of game laws. It came about in an attempt to learn from past mistakes. The Territory was one final chance, the last frontier for wildlife as well as man. Federal control angered ambitious Alaskans because it blocked local attempts to control land and resources, especially the fishery, coal, and timber, the economics of which concerned those Alaskans more than did the economics of game. Yet big game, particularly the bear, remained at the center of the controversy.

Almost immediately after the law of 1908 was enacted, the appointed governor of Alaska complained about the birds and the bears. In 1911 Governor Walter Clark asked for a twelve-month open season on brown bears, which he said were dangerous animals. Another governor in 1915 said that the brown bear was "a savage beast." He added that the black bear was more likable, but unless the Kodiak brown could be practically exterminated, cattle and sheep-raising would probably be abandoned. Furthermore, the new law did not contain any hunting season for game birds north of sixty-two degrees latitude; the "inadvertence" was a bureaucratic oversight corrected in 1911. Then began a long struggle by Alaskan governors to move the opening date of the waterfowl season to August 15, because (the argument went) the birds were gone from many parts of Alaska by September 1.

To the governors, such "absurdities" in the management of game argued for complete local control of wildlife by the new Territorial legislature, created in 1912.[50] Outsiders thought differently. Big game hunters and naturalists in the northeastern United States, bureaucrats in Washington, D.C., and fish cannery interests on the West Coast lobbied successfully for the retention of federal control over all of Alaska's wild creatures.[51] The cannery people probably had the most influence, and the conservationists appear not to have recognized the incongruity of their alliance with an oligopolistic wildlife industry.

By then Madison Grant had lost some of his patience and more of his tact. The new Territorial legislature should not have total authority over game, he contended, because Alaska's population remained unstable. Further, "The jealous consideration of our legislators for the poor Indian and the honest miner has gone too far." Grant thought game refuges were the only remedy. As for Governor Clark's scientific advice, he "consulted a local bar-room bear hunter" and then, said Grant, called for an end to the protection of brown bears.[52]

More than Madison Grant and the Katmai volcano erupted during these years. William T. Hornaday, of the New York Zoo and the Permanent Wildlife Fund, was in a permanent state of eruption over the preservation of game, but he had not paid much of the energetic attention for which he was famous to Alaskan wildlife issues. Before he became America's best-known opponent of hunting, Hornaday was himself a professional headhunter. As a taxidermist he was also a buyer of trophies obtained by market hunters. At one time he said that the peregrine falcon (now on the endangered list) should be shot on sight. In 1904, after the presence of black mountain sheep had been reported, he urged people in the Alaskan and Canadian mountains near the sheep's range "to bring out all the large horns they can get; for they will be worth fully twice as much money, if not three times as much, as the same amount of meat."[53] Nine years later he entered the discussion of Alaskan game with a vigorous diction that some other, more politic, conservationists thought intemperate and maybe even harmful to the cause of wildlife preservation.

Wrote Hornaday in his book, *Our Vanishing Wild Life*, published in 1913:

It is no longer right nor just for Indians, miners and prospectors to be permitted by law to kill all the big game they please, whenever they please. The indolent and often extortionate Indians of Alaska—who now demand "big money" for every service they perform—are not so valuable as citizens that they should be permitted to feed riotously upon *moose, and cow moose at that*, until the species is exterminated. Miners and prospectors are valuable citizens, but that is no reason why they should forever be allowed to live upon wild game, any more than that hungry prospectors in our Rocky Mountains should be allowed to kill cattle.[54]

Hornaday's polemic was the kind of talk that Alaskan civic leaders could label cheechako arrogance. (A *cheechako* is a person new to Alaska, a word Alaskans use for "greenhorn.")

Until the First World War, however, Alaskan politicians did not do much to alter relations between man and wild beast in the Territory, except to recommend annually the removal of protection from bears and the transfer of all authority over wild animals to Juneau. Outside, the demands of war created new dangers to American wildlife. Ostensibly to prevent food shortages, a game refuge was abolished in one state, and closed seasons were opened. The commercial hunting of game was advocated in another state, and bills and proposals were heard to abolish game laws for the duration of the conflict.

Conservationists became alarmed and allied to form the Committee for the Protection of Wildlife in War Time. Charles Sheldon was one member. He had hunted, traveled, and studied in Alaska, and had successfully promoted the establishment of Mount McKinley National Park in 1917. As the new Alaskan specialist in the Boone and Crockett Club, he wrote a statement for Herbert Hoover, of the U.S. Food Administration, warning against relaxation of the game laws when "no emergency has as yet arisen sufficiently acute to warrant the Food Administration advocating the destruction of game."[55] The conservationists won this campaign. The war did no serious damage to American wildlife. In Alaska, however, it indirectly stimulated a political squabble that unnecessarily increased the friction between stateside conservationists and Alaskans.

The Territory's supply lines were few, long, and fragile, and ships were needed elsewhere. Alaskans in the interior found themselves the victims of profiteering and soaring prices. Beef, if it was available at all in Fairbanks, sold for sixty cents a pound—at that time, a high price. Wild meat sold for less than half the cost of domestic meat. Sheldon reported that northerners were "at the mercy of the beef monopoly." The game warden in Fairbanks told his supervisor, the governor, that no "exceptional action" was needed; a shipment of domestic meat was due soon, and there was plenty of canned meat in town. Nevertheless, in response to a suggestion by A. J. Nordale of the Fairbanks Commercial Club, Alaska's delegate to Congress, Charles Sulzer, introduced a bill in 1917 to permit the year-round sale of game killed north of sixty-two degrees, for the duration of the war. (The sixty-second parallel bisects Alaska about sixty miles north of present-day Anchorage.)

Edward W. Nelson, of the Bureau of Biological Survey, and Sheldon recognized in the proposal an opportunity to win over Alaskans to the support of at least some game laws, without sacrificing animals or changing the de facto condition of wildlife in Alaska. Both men knew that Alaskans would take whatever wild meat they wanted, when they wanted, if they could find the animals. Both men knew that existing law permitted Alaskans to sell game during the open season if it were shot legally. And both men knew that even this liberal allowance to market game, which did not exist in any other place under the flag, was violated regularly with impunity. A failure in the original Sulzer bill to set bag limits was corrected, a tagging system was added to ensure that game was legally killed, and after this and other patching, the two men lobbied for the measure.[56]

What Nelson and Sheldon knew, other conservationists did not know, or would not accept as adequate cause for undermining the basic pillar of wildlife preservation. The *idea* of market hunting was too repugnant. The historic campaign by sportsmen and naturalists against commercial hunting had been the foundation of wildlife protection, and wildlife protection was perhaps the basis of the entire American conservation movement, as one modern historian argues convincingly.[57] Grinnell and a few others joined Sheldon and Nelson. Hornaday led the opposition with "deliberate lies and malicious misrepresentation," Sheldon told Theodore Roosevelt. As a final blow, the American Game Conference joined Hornaday in condemnation.[58]

The Sulzer bill was not passed, proving to the satisfaction of Alaskans whom Hornaday was fond of calling "malcontents" that eastern sportsmen and conservationists would ally with war profiteers and beef monopolists to smother a mere legislative gesture designed to keep wild meat legally on Alaskan tables. The meat would be there, legal or not, because Alaskan court officials and juries were not all wealthy beef eaters, and because the game wardens were supervised by a new governor, Thomas C. Riggs, Jr., who was not intimidated by eastern wealth, money, and power.

Riggs got a warm welcome when he arrived in Juneau in 1918. At a reception for Mrs. Riggs attended by 160 ladies of the town, Klondy Nelson—later Mrs. Frank Dufresne—played the violin.

Governor Thomas Christmas Riggs was a rare bird in Alaskan politics. He had both eastern connections and impressive "bush" credentials. He was related to a Washington banking family, was a graduate of Princeton, and was married to the daughter of a prominent New York expert on international law who had been a United States commissioner during the Bering Sea controversy. Young Riggs had prospected the Yukon regions for three years at the height of the Klondike-Alaska gold rushes. Beginning in 1906, he worked for half a dozen years as a civil engineer surveying the Canada-Alaska boundary. Before he was appointed governor, he engaged in location and construction activities as a member of the Alaska Engineering Commission, the organization that became the Alaska Railroad. He was on speaking terms (though sometimes, just barely) with leaders of several big game conservation organizations in the East. When he was a candidate for governor, he supported the Sulzer bill and testified in Washington on its behalf. The support endangered his nomination, but he managed to deflect opposition by helping to persuade Roosevelt to change his mind, and by writing to one senator: "I suppose that I am one of the most consistent game conservators in the north and have done more personally than almost any other single man in Alaska to keep down illegal hunting."[59]

But when Riggs sat down in the governor's chair, the Sulzer fiasco and local demands for control of natural resources combined to turn his wrath on the sportsmen, whom he attacked through their favorite "pet," the brown bear. The grizzly was not mild-mannered and harmless, he said. That was the "ignorant propaganda" of "eastern conservationists." The animal was vicious and dangerous. In the promotion of that opinion Riggs was assisted by the death in 1918 of a youthful hunter in southeastern Alaska. The man wounded a grizzly; it then charged and mortally mauled the young nimrod.[60]

Riggs's attack on the bear was aided also by an Alaskan employee of the Department of Agriculture who disagreed with the department's Bureau of Biological Survey. C. C. Georgeson came to Alaska soon after the first gold rush to investigate the country's agricultural potential, and he stayed to establish and direct several agricultural experiment stations. One was at Kodiak. When bears prevented employees of the station there from doing their work, and killed three-fourths of the sheep and several head of cattle, Georgeson declared verbal war on the bruins. His views inspired governors Clark and Strong.[61] The belief of Americans that every new wilderness frontier must eventually reach a Jeffersonian, agrarian stage increased Georgeson's strength as a witness in the governor's case against the brown bear.

The case was dramatically reinforced by Riggs's decision to collect evidence of bear attacks on humans. Edward Nelson, in an effort to determine how true all the stories were, received reports of bear encounters from the naturalist Alfred Bailey, who had arrived in Alaska in 1919 as the Biological Survey's northern representative. Considered together, the bear incidents recounted by the governor, his agents, and Bailey are one of the most sanguinary collections of "bear stories" ever assembled outside the pages of the *Alaska Sportsman* magazine. Two examples will suffice here.

In the governor's office in Juneau, Riggs displayed photographs taken of "Wabash" Bill after a violent confrontation with a grizzly. (Nelson probably saw the photos when he visited Juneau in 1920.) A few years earlier, Bill's motorboat quit and he used the coil spring from his 30–30 to fix the gas engine, thereby converting the rifle to a single-shot. He then killed a deer and forgot to reload. While he was packing the deer out of the forest he stumbled onto a female bear with cubs. The old bear charged, knocking him down unconscious. The cubs, alarmed, climbed a tree while Mother Bruin chewed on Wabash Bill. Every time Bill regained consciousness, she attacked. He remained in this perilous position for three days, until the cubs descended and the family departed. With sixty-seven wounds, Bill crawled to the beach. On the seventh day the captain of a passing steamer spotted Bill on the shore, eating raw salmon. He finally recovered after medical treatment in Sitka.

One of the governor's officers reported how a man at Klutena Lake in Canada was attacked by a bear and severely injured. "His face bones were all smashed, and the flesh of the face terribly lacerated[;] the wound soon healed and the bones knit together in a distorted form." In New York City doctors rebroke the bones and "patched him up." Two years later the officer saw him in the city and did not recognize him, saying, "I believe he was better looking than before the encounter with the bear."[62]

Rex Beach, the novelist whose popular books were often set in Alaska, and who was no third-rate tale-teller himself, entered the bear story competition with an essay entitled "The Chronicle of a Chromatic Bear Hunt." He and a companion were told by their wives to bring back bear skins that matched the decor of their homes. A week before they arrived in south-central Alaska, said Beach, "a party of native hunters had been chased into camp by a herd of grizzlies," an unlikely happening. Toward the end of the "Chronicle," he claimed that a female brown bear without cubs deliberately attacked two hunters who had passed her and were walking away; she even forded a stream to get at them. Beach said that he repeated the last story "at the risk of arousing the ire of every peaceful naturalist and nature singer" who might read it.[63]

Beach had highlighted a central issue: did the brown bear attack without provocation? "Peaceful naturalists and nature singers" claimed the bear did not; Governor Riggs and company said that it did. Most of the stories were either too short on detail or suggested provocation. Riggs's subordinate, Secretary of Alaska George Folta (who took Riggs's brother-in-law and two nephews hunting on the Kenai Peninsula about this time), told Nelson confidentially that provocation was present in the episodes cited by the governor. A hunter with the unbelievably appropriate surname of Bonebrake wrote to the *Journal of Mammalogy* describing what he believed to be an unprovoked attack on him in Yukon Territory. Bonebrake shot a moose and returned later for the meat. Within fifty yards of the moose carcass, which a female brown had sampled and then buried, the bear attacked. Charles Sheldon and George Bird Grinnell could not let the claim pass without comment. Sheldon said there was no intentional provocation on the part of Bonebrake, but he did have dogs with him and the bear was protecting its cache from interlopers. Grinnell said pointedly, "The mildest mannered domestic dog does not submit to having food taken from it by a stranger without making some protest."[64]

The issue of provocation may never be resolved to everyone's satisfaction—bear and man alike—because the problem arises from a conflict between two species over the same territory and resources. A mother grizzly will charge humans if she thinks her family or food is in danger. Any grizzly may charge if it decides that its next meal is threatened or if it is deliberately goaded. The ownership of the food may be in dispute. Edibles may be an abandoned carcass, as in Bonebrake's case, or food in an abandoned outdoorsman's cache or cabin that the bear has claimed in an ursine version of the legal doctrine of adverse use. Or a person may simply stumble onto a bear's own kill or quarry. Starving bears who have learned that human habitations are a source of food can be dangerous. In the absence of food or family, a sudden, surprise encounter in thick brush or dense forest may startle the bear sufficiently to make it attack. Grizzlies may very well charge if wounded, or if they carry an old wound and remember its source. One bear in the Panhandle with a nasty reputation was found at its death to have lived most of its life with a rifle slug in the brain.[65] Man calls such a creature a "rogue," yet the most forgiving human who has been scarred by a bear (whatever the circumstances) is not likely to remain kindly disposed toward the animal thereafter. The point is, bears and humans when living together need management. Their relationship was not managed adequately in pioneer Alaska, and regardless of where any individual stood on the question of provocation, all Alaskans knew that the brown bear was dangerous when aroused and difficult to kill. Very likely it was *fear* more than any other emotion or reason that made the grizzly a usable political issue.

Another ploy of the governor in the First Bear War was to encourage a sympathetic Alaska Fish and Game Club of Juneau to send out questionnaires on which selected Alaskans could register their opinions about controversial wildlife questions. Earl Ohmer received one, and his response, in 1920, was more or less typical. He said he knew of cases where bears had attacked people and he thought that brown bears should be exterminated.[66]

For all Riggs's efforts—his recommendations, his questionnaires, his bear stories—he never convinced the easterners.[67] He failed to persuade the influential conservationists because they knew the real reason for his war against the bear. He stated it himself flatly and officially in 1919: "The brown bears have no place in the economic development of the Territory any more than the herds of wild buffalo would have in the wheat fields of Minnesota and the Dakotas."[68] The bear was only a plaything of so-called sportsmen and should go the way of the buffalo because it impeded "development." Unfortunately for the governor's case, by that date there were few if any people outside Alaska calling themselves conservationists who would justify the extinction of any spectacular animal for vaguely defined economic reasons, and no self-styled conservationist outside Alaska who would do so by invoking the buffalo's fate, the knowledge of which was perhaps the most powerful emotional prop under the whole conservation movement.

When persuasion failed, the governor played a trump card that almost won the contest as it threw sportsmen, biologists, bureaucrats, politicians, and lawyers into a state of confusion. The trump was a discrepancy in the 1908 game law, which had been written and administered in large part by the natural historians. That such a loophole could have existed in the law and could have been ignored for so long was a clue to the state of the mammalogist's art.

In 1918 C. Hart Merriam, formerly chief of the Biological Survey and probably the nation's leading mammalogist, published a monograph on the grizzly and big brown bears. In it he identified eighty-six species on the continent. Only a handful had been recognized twenty years earlier. Approximately one-third of his bear species were Alaskan.[69] Edward Nelson hailed the monograph as an important contribution to scientific mammalogy. That same year the National Geographic Society published Nelson's own *Wild Animals of North America*, first in its magazine and then as a book. The foldout frontispiece was a painting of a huge Alaskan brown bear. In the section of the volume devoted to bears, one article was on grizzlies and another on brown bears. Governor Riggs found in the Nelson and Merriam books an opportunity to intensify his inroad on the bears while making the eastern naturalists who designed Alaskan game policy look foolish.

The comprehensive Alaskan game law of 1908 permitted the brown bear, by name, to be shot at any time north of sixty-two degrees of latitude; south of that parallel, hunting was restricted by a closed season during the summer, and by a three-bear limit. The naturalists knew that it was not these hunting regulations that protected the bear. Even William Hornaday came around to favor open season on brown bears, every place in Alaska, at any time. He may have been shaken into agreement partly as a result of vitriolic attacks by an Alaskan press that called him an "unbalanced," "assinine fakir," who represented a few sentimentalists, "most of whom are women and children."[70]

What did protect the big bears was a requirement that Alaskan residents buy a five-dollar license to ship the head or trophy of a single brown bear. The price for exporting two, which was the limit, was forty dollars. The purpose of export control was to prevent market hunting and commercial traffic in hides, heads, and meat, for which there was a demand in the United States. (The total "production" of bear skins in North America in the years 1923–1924 was estimated at 25,000; most were probably black bears.) Wildlife conservationists who influenced Alaskan game legislation realized that if market hunting for export were prohibited, the small number of Alaskans and nonresident sportsmen would not endanger a species, even if they hunted commercially for a local market. Alaskans would be particularly reluctant to stalk a tough grizzly for no profit. On these propositions the conservationists had usually agreed; the split in their ranks during the Sulzer imbroglio was the exception, to that date. Riggs argued disingenuously that hunting for a wider market was unlikely because brown bear skins sold for only twenty dollars apiece in St. Louis. He knew that an export trade in bear hides was already under way in 1919, when at least one stateside furrier had agents in Alaska collecting grizzly trophies.[71] Apparently he hoped the trade would expand. So he showed his trump card.

The law of 1908 not only failed to list all of Merriam's Alaskan species of big bears, it neglected even a mention of the grizzly. The governor, as local supervisor of the game statutes, ruled in 1919 that a grizzly was not a brown bear, was therefore not protected, and the shipment of a grizzly's head and hide did not require an export license. He was overruled by the departments of agriculture and commerce but did not let the issue die there. He contended correctly that Merriam and Nelson had differentiated in print between the grizzly and brown bear and that a judge in Juneau had also made the distinction. The governor asked Nelson to withdraw his veto of the Riggs ruling or face a court challenge to uphold the judge's decision and Merriam's and his (Nelson's) own opinion that browns and grizzlies were different.[72]

Nelson was in a quandary. He asked Congressman W. E. Humphrey what the intention had been behind the amendments that Humphrey had introduced in 1908. The obvious reply was that Humphrey, T. S. Palmer of the Bureau of Biological Survey, Charles Sheldon of the Boone and Crockett Club, and Merriam had intended "brown bear" to include grizzlies (but not the brown phase of the black bear). The news did nothing to mollify Riggs.[73] In early 1920 he advised the attorney general of Alaska to bring suit for the issuance of a shipper's manifest on a grizzly bear hide. The customs collector had refused to allow shipment of the hide without a permit from Riggs's own office and payment of the five-dollar fee. Riggs cited Merriam once again, as well as Nelson's *Wild Animals of North America*. Then, with a mock display of objectivity, Riggs asked the attorney general of the Territory for a trial in chambers because trial by jury "would be too easy for us," given the sentiment in Alaska toward bears. In a letter to Nelson, Riggs gloated, "I don't know, but I think I have got you."[74]

Indeed he had. Nelson learned from the acting solicitor for the Department of Agriculture (who was an ornithologist, a former employee of the Bureau of Biological Survey, and "a good friend of conservation")[75] that "there appears to be no way in which the Department can appear in court in defense of the bears."[76] It was disheartening, Nelson reflected, because brown bear hides would be exported as grizzly skins. George Bird Grinnell consulted his own lawyers in New York City, others testified as to the intent of the law, and the Biological Survey's case was prepared for the U.S. attorney general.[77] The case pleaded that "brown" was used in the law only as a color designation, not to identify a type of bear. But it conceded that scientists could not draw the bear line with any precision and that scientific classifications change.[78] The bureau, Nelson, the sportsmen, and the naturalists were in a legal box of their own construction from which they would not have escaped if this early, dramatic mandamus action had been completed. It was not.

Riggs backed off. He was never incurably hostile toward the eastern conservationists. At a conference with Grinnell and Madison Grant in Washington's exclusive Cosmos Club, Riggs agreed to delay the suit if the eastern wildlife establishment could come up with a reasonable concession on the brown bear question.[79] But soon thereafter the American political timetable intervened to preserve the bears.

The year 1920 was a presidential election year and the future of Riggs's party was not bright. In November, Republican Warren Harding walked away with the United States presidency. In this setting it may be that Riggs, most of whose life was spent in appointive posts, thought it unwise and unnecessary to alienate influential easterners by pressing the case. In mid-1921 Harding appointed a new governor; the bears were saved by a political coincidence.

If the governor's mandamus action had been completed, he would have won, and the Kodiak bear and Alaska Peninsula brown would almost certainly have been threatened with extermination, except in their special refuges. They were easy to reach and to see and there were not many of them. It was a close call. The southeastern and interior grizzlies might have held out longer because they were not as accessible and were protected by rugged terrain and thick vegetation.

The American frontier has had five main, measurable characteristics: (1) a sparse population, measured by a low man / land ratio; (2) the existence of wilderness and wildlife; (3) some subsistence hunting; (4) few and uncomplicated technologies; (5) few effective institutional constraints. At the end of the First Bear War, frontier life was still intact in Alaska, although it had been threatened by the earlier search for gold. Rapid modernization was still a generation away. In the meantime, a new institution on the horizon, the Alaska Game Commission, was designed to preserve frontier conditions—the proximity of wildlife and subsistence hunting by a small population—by introducing some minimal restraints on freedom, including attempts to keep the tools of the hunt uncomplicated.

3

The Laws: Nelson's Victory and More Provocative Bears

In addition to the regulations for game animal export, protection, though not well-enforced protection, was given to wildlife and wilderness on special refuges. Riggs had played an important part in the refuge movement. Before he was governor, when his railroad construction crews advanced toward the Mount McKinley area, Riggs had joined the eastern conservationists in a drive to establish Mount McKinley National Park. Land was withdrawn for that purpose in 1917.[1] The following year another significant refuge was created. Its function as a bear refuge was kept quiet deliberately.

In the Katmai region of the Alaska Peninsula opposite Kodiak, a series of violent volcanic disturbances in 1912 created almost overnight a new natural wonder dubbed by a National Geographic Society expedition, "the valley of ten thousand smokes." The Society's spectacular reports stimulated a movement to create Katmai National Monument, and Charles Sheldon was asked for his advice. He shrewdly recommended boundaries that would protect the big brown bears, but he cautioned Grinnell that the word *bear* should never be mentioned in connection with the establishing of the monument. Grinnell relayed the warning to members of Boone and Crockett.[2] Katmai Monument was created in 1918, before the furor over the Sulzer bill had subsided, and when Riggs, as the new governor, was launching his attack on the grizzlies. Since then, most of the fumaroles of Katmai have cooled and most of its volcanoes are dormant, but within its boundaries (which have been enlarged) the Giant Peninsula brown cannot be hunted.[3]

As far as Governor Riggs was concerned, other wildlife refuges were "for the birds" in both meanings of that phrase. Of the ten (excluding the Pribilof Islands) withdrawn in 1909, 1912, and 1913, most were small areas aggregating approximately one hundred square miles. Most were designated bird sanctuaries. Fire Island, at the head of Cook Inlet, was reserved as a breeding ground for moose that was easy to police yet near population centers. Riggs alleged that the island was only a nesting place for fish-killing sea gulls, saying, "I would like to see them exterminated." Although Nelson moved to cancel the Fire Island reservation, the governor was not pacified; the island was, he said, the most insignificant game refuge, but he hoped Nelson would "keep up the good work of reducing other foolish reserves."[4]

Two of the ten refuges were anything but modest in size. Together their boundaries enclosed thousands of square miles. The Aleutian Islands Reservation "for the protection of indigenous birds, the propagation of reindeer and fur-bearing animals, and the development of fisheries"[5] included all the Aleutians from Attu to Unimak. Riggs thought it was "iniquitous."[6] In still another move to please Alaskans, the Bureau of Biological Survey sponsored development on the islands by turning some of them over to fox farmers. The birds became a major source of food for the foxes. On Amchitka the Aleutian Canada goose disappeared. Elsewhere on the islands, naturalist Olaus Murie reported in the 1930s that foxes and native birds were not compatible, and the bureau began to phase out fox farming.[7]

The second large bird refuge had a short life. In 1909 the Yukon Delta region—the setting for the duck egg scandal—was declared a sanctuary for birds, probably on the advice of Nelson; it was familiar to him from earlier and extensive explorations that made his reputation as a naturalist.[8] Said Riggs, the reservation "gets my goat." Yet the governor admitted in his official report: "I doubt if a printed proclamation has changed the customs of the inhabitants."[9] Because of the difficulty of policing such a large area, Nelson recommended revocation of the Yukon reserve, and it was abandoned.[10]

The Bureau of Biological Survey's retreat from the delta was only a recognition of reality that carried with it the tactical advantage of humoring Alaska's political establishment. Nelson needed to make friends for his own solution to the "Alaska problem"—a new game law. To find support among Alaskans for his plan, he needed to calm the excited and largely meaningless talk about bears and unsympathetic Washington bureaucrats and eastern sportsmen and federal domination of the Territory by land withdrawals to protect birds.

The wildlife withdrawals were, like the bears, only symbolic. The reservations that upset Alaskan entrepreneurs were mineral and timber withdrawals. Riggs thought such withdrawals, made in 1906 and 1910, were almost criminal, and he wrote to Nelson in 1921: "I wish you could have taken some of the trips which I have, and seen wharves, built in high hopes, rotting down; mines, caving in; the grave of a suicide; railroads abandoned. These withdrawals have been the real cause of Alaska's decline," along with other governmental restrictions and bureaucratic inefficiency.[11]

Alaska's problems, Nelson replied, had very little to do with governmental inefficiency. Self-government for Alaska, Nelson argued, was not a remedy for the loss of the young men who had emigrated during the First World War and had not returned, not a remedy for high freight rates, or for the exhaustion of the large mines and bonanza placers.[12] Nelson agreed with his man in Alaska, Ernest P. Walker, who charged the politicians and newspapers with the whole campaign to "swat the bureaus." In one paper an editorial had appeared with that very title, while elsewhere in the same edition there was a plea to establish two more federal agency branches in Alaska and a "clamor" for a federal building. Walker pointed out the inconsistency.[13]

On such issues, with slight variations, the debate over self-government spun its wheels until Alaskan statehood was granted in 1959. The odd picture of a hardy, courageous, self-reliant frontiersman facing Washington with one hand clenched into a fist and the other outstretched, palm up, had been a common sight on earlier American frontiers too. Usually Alaskan territorial governors, to the last, adopted the posture. Although they were appointed in Washington and were themselves federal bureaucrats, more often than not they joined the Alaskan business community's criticism of Washington. Meanwhile, Edward Nelson had a homegrown Alaskan bureaucracy on which he could pick—the governors' wardens. Nelson believed that their dismal record was the best available argument for a new game law.

During a visit to Alaska in 1920 Nelson had found "common agreement [among Alaskans] as to the purely political character of the administration of the game law." He told the secretary of agriculture that Governor Scott Bone's report of growing animal populations and few violations of the game laws was an absurdity. One of Bone's game wardens resided in Anchorage, yet the sale of game meat, which was against the law there, took place in all the hotels and restaurants of the town, without any interference on the part of the game warden. Moose meat was listed on the menu as "top serloin [sic] steak hunter style" or "stew hunter style." The governor's administration of game, said Nelson, was "negligent and incompetent."[14]

There was more than a little evidence to support the indictment. A warden stationed at McCarthy, in the Chitina River basin, was a "fine, old fellow" (according to one complaint) who did not get around much any more. He had made one arrest in two years. A warden at Kenai used a Native to pose as a guide and collect guide fees which were shared with the warden; twenty-five persons signed a petition asking for the warden's removal.[15] Another of the governor's game wardens was accused of encouraging "side hunts" of small animals, to see who could kill the most in the shortest time, for excitement, when big game was not immediately available. A resident of a camp called Woodchopper, in the interior, said of the wardens he saw, "If they got 100 yards off the trail they could not find it." They were, complained the disgusted pioneer, "rummies."[16] After fur warden and biologist Olaus Murie made an arrest in Fairbanks, the governor's game warden was too drunk to testify.[17] Mr. A. F. Stowe told visiting congressmen that both game and fur wardens rode the Alaska Railroad to the end of the line and returned on the next train, but he did "verily believe" they would arrest anyone who killed a moose, sheep, or caribou that climbed aboard.[18]

Some complaints were spiteful. Two eight-month residents of "Nininiltchik" (Ninilchik) charged that certain citizens of that village were "killing the mooses like the musketes." The governor's warden thought the allegations were exaggerated by a grudge. An informant in the same region wrote to the governor: "Our game warden, who I am told is a nice fellow and a dancing man, does not pay much attention to his job." The "dancing man" responded: "The inhabitants of . . . Cook Inlet . . . have a reputation for . . . feuds and petty grievances."[19]

The governors may also have misjudged the reliability of their sources of information. In 1913 one zealous (and unemployed) citizen of McCarthy claimed that butcher shops in the Chisana district, on a tributary of the upper Tanana River, refused to import beef and sold big game meat for fifty or sixty-five cents a pound; the class of men who operate the shops "does nothing, but hunt, Kill, and distroy and smokes Cigarettes." The informant was appointed temporary warden. He began by entering and searching caches and cabins, and he would stop prospectors on the trails and search their sleds without a warrant. Seventy residents petitioned U.S. Commissioner Anthony J. Dimond to have Governor Strong remove the warden from office, alleging (among other things) that he had collected damages from the Copper River and Northwestern Railway after he received a blow on the head that "unbalanced him." He was replaced. A new warden reported two years later that everyone in the area agreed that game was fifty percent of the food supply there.[20]

The admission from Chisana pointed to a serious defect in the enforcement system. The governors and their wardens thought prospectors and trappers had a special right to take game beyond the emergency use permitted in the law. In 1913 a Fairbanks warden even recommended that hunting near mining operations be restricted: "This seems to me to be the only effectual way of maintaining a meat supply for these men who are giving their time and money to open up a vast mineral belt in the face of many obstacles." In effect, the warden was recommending game preserves for a privileged class of hunters as a social overhead cost of developing the country. Violation of the game laws could also be perceived as a form of charity, as well as a subsidy for mining and fur trapping. The warden at Eagle, in 1917, caught one miner with illegal caribou but did not arrest the man because he had "about gone the limit of his credit at the stores and has a wife and five children out there, so if any one in this country is in need of food, I would say that he is."[21]

Other "pioneers" (as defined by the wardens) were also given special treatment. Nellie Neal Lawing sold moose meat at her roadhouse on Kenai Lake, explaining that a washout of the railroad tracks prevented her from obtaining domestic meat from the seaport of Seward, a short twenty miles away. In Seldovia, on lower Cook Inlet, a Native boy confessed to killing a cow moose and two calves, and leaving the meat to rot in the woods. His fine of fifty dollars was suspended because he was young and because he had had enough trouble recently. Earlier that year he had killed his father, mistaking him for a moose while they were both market hunting on the Chickaloon Flats.[22]

Apparently, residents of Fairbanks continued to take advantage of their pioneer prerogatives well after 1902, when Felix Pedro's discovery of gold started a rush to the vicinity. Governor Riggs, who was forever defending the right of the prospector and trapper to take game for food at any time, decided by 1921 that some people in Fairbanks wanted to make their region an abattoir of game. It was no secret (Olaus Murie told Nelson) that cow caribou were killed and moose were hunted for the market.[23] Market hunting was perfectly legal if the game were taken lawfully and sold during open season only. Frequently it was not. Some professional hunters took more than their legal limit, hunted during closed seasons, and killed cow moose and yearlings.

Stephen Capps, of the Geological Survey, reported in the *National Geographic Magazine* of January 1917 that each winter since 1914, from 1,500 to 2,000 mountain sheep had been taken from the basin of the Toklat and Teklanika rivers, in the proposed Mount McKinley Park. Governor Strong asked his Fairbanks warden for an explanation. The warden, in rebutting Capps's evidence, naively painted a verbal scene of sheep slaughter that was only numerically less appalling than Capps's report. In no year during the previous four years, said the warden, had more than twenty tons of sheep, or 700 sheep, been marketed in Fairbanks and vicinity, and of that number only a fraction came from Capps's rivers.[24] Rephrased, only 2,800 sheep were killed for the market during four years within an area radiating two hundred miles from Fairbanks. Only about 500 were from the proposed park. (In 1950, estimates placed the total population of mountain sheep in the Alaska

Range and the Brooks Range at 9,000; there may have been 800 sheep in the park at that time.)[25]

"Prodigal disregard" for the future of wildlife, the belief that prospectors and trappers had a civil right to kill game when they wished, and widespread disdain for the game laws were attitudes matched by the reluctance of officials to prosecute violators even on those rare occasions when the governors' wardens acted. In 1912 the warden in Fairbanks brought a test case and was accused by the district attorney of "persecuting" the subject, who pleaded guilty. In 1916 the government attorney told Riggs that his engineering commission was not a "dealer" under the law and could therefore serve wild game in its mess halls—where food was bought with meal tickets. The district attorney was not even certain that restaurants should be considered "dealers." In 1917 a Fairbanks warden investigated reports that a storekeeper and fox farmer at Circle Hot Springs was selling illegal game and feeding it to his foxes. The suspect did indeed have game in his possession more than fifteen days after the close of the season, but the federal district judge, Charles Bunnell, dismissed the charge. The law, Bunnell ruled, did not state specifically that it was a crime for a dealer to have game in his possession after the deadline; it only permitted him to dispose of game legally within fifteen days after the close of the season![26]

In other parts of the Territory the intention of officials to enforce the laws and the willingness of juries to convict the offender were not much more in evidence. A citizen of Anchorage charged that deputy U.S. marshals in that town outfitted aliens who went to the Kenai Peninsula to shoot moose, including cow moose, which were then shipped to Anchorage and served to prisoners in the federal jail. A mine at Funter Bay, in southeastern Alaska, served deer in its mess hall, including does and fawns, but the owner escaped conviction; while the trial was under way, some of the deer meat to be used as evidence was stolen from the courthouse.[27] It was all a good joke—on everyone except the animals, people who might genuinely need the meat, and future generations of other animals or humans, some of whom might wish to have the deer around for dinner, or just as company.

In further defense of the governors' wardens, appropriations to enforce the game laws were minuscule ($15,000 or $20,000 annually), the wardens were asked to patrol huge areas, and there were very few wardens. Fur Warden Walker, the Bureau of Biological Survey's second Alaskan supervisor, could not have had too low an opinion of the game wardens; half were retained and transferred to the bureau when the new law was passed in 1925 (although as a group they seem not to have stayed with the agency very long). Game Warden J. F. McDonald, of Juneau, made twenty-nine arrests in 1916 and got twenty-five convictions. He arrested the superintendent of the Sheldon Jackson School in Sitka for one violation. McDonald learned and reported that C. C. Georgeson had bought illegal venison on Thanksgiving Day, but the warden could not get enough evidence to indict the chief salesman of agrarian development in Alaska.[28] Another warden followed two men who had boasted of their intention to take any Alaskan game they wanted. The two men, when confronted by the warden, turned out to be undercover Internal Revenue officers trying to entrap Alaskan violators of the liquor laws. The governors' game wardens were expected also to police the liquor traffic, after ratification of the Prohibition Amendment in January 1919. The additional duty did nothing to increase their efficiency or popularity.[29] Also in defense of the governors' wardens, some reports of game conditions in Alaska were erroneous. One, entitled "The Moose Butchers of Kenai," appeared in *American Forestry* and was reprinted in the *Literary Digest*. The Hoquiam, Washington, chapter of the Loyal Order of Moose protested to the Department of the Interior. Governor Bone assured the Hoquiam Moose that their four-legged Kenai brethren were increasing in number and in no danger of extinction.[30]

All in all, Edward Nelson was right. A reading of the governors' correspondence with their wardens leaves the unmistakable impression that wardens were selected and retained for political reasons, that they performed partisan political jobs while in office, that they were often unqualified—sometimes barely literate—and reluctant to arrest violators. Game law violations were widespread. The system was, as charged, "negligent and incompetent" between 1908 and 1925, and Alaskans who paid attention knew it.

Nelson wanted to unify the management of fur and game animals under his Bureau of Biological Survey, remove the appointment of wardens from the influence of local politics, hire experts, and cater to the cry for local control with a commission system, the commissioners to come from Alaska and represent Alaskan sectional opinion, although they would be appointed in Washington. Nelson got what he wanted because of the salutary coalescence of large and small historical events and personalities.

The most important element in his victory was a modicum of stability in the population, the ingredient essential for obtaining local support of utilitarian conservation, which "cropped" the surplus wildlife only (to borrow Aldo Leopold's agricultural metaphor). The total number of people in Alaska at this time was not large—30,000 Natives and 30,000 whites in 1930—but sometime during the 1920s permanent white residents probably began to outnumber transients unconnected to the summer fishery.[31] The days of the individual prospector and the one or two-man placer mine were not over, but wage earners employed in more or less permanent, large, quartz, hydraulic, or dredge mining were more numerous (4,000 to 5,000 in 1920 and 1930) than the few hundred lonely, wandering, gold seekers about whom so much printer's ink has flowed. After 1920 coal produced in Alaska exceeded the amount imported, and coal mines now employed a couple hundred people also. Copper mines in the Kennicott district, in the Chitina River basin, were in operation during the First World War and provided employment for several hundred other miners until just before the Second World War. The Copper River and Northwestern Railway provided institutional employment. The construction of that line and of the Alaska Railroad occupied a large temporary population during these years. By 1925 the Alaska Railroad was operating between Seward and Fairbanks, via Anchorage, with permanent personnel. At the same time the commercial fishery, dominated by outside capital, cannery labor, and fishermen numbering about 20,000 seasonal workers, was increasingly infiltrated by fishermen who made their homes in Alaska and who were critical of wasteful or privileged use of the country's marine resources. Fur trapping was another natural resource industry dependent upon wildlife management for sustained yields. Trappers were often recruited from the ranks of unsuccessful prospectors. Winter trapping and summer fishing were a popular combination for Alaskans who made their homes in the bush. Perhaps the two best indicators of a stabilizing population are the number of teachers and sex ratios. There were 76 teachers in 1910 and 330 in 1920. The ratio of males to females declined dramatically between 1910 and 1920, and gradually to 1940. The permanence of the white population is also suggested by stability in its geographical distribution after 1930.[32]

The growing number of Alaskan residents tended to appreciate the importance of maintaining a supply of game for their continued use. They were not as a group politically vocal, though some of them did express their views aloud.[33] A mining engineer in Cordova, on Prince William Sound, wrote to Governor Riggs: "I say lets [sic] not exterminate anything just for the sake of doing it. . . . People have been killed by dogs, yet that is no reason why we should exterminate dogs." Other arguments for wildlife protection took even more befuddling twists. A citizen of McCarthy who had been a buffalo hunter on the Great Plains was convinced that the buffalo had to go to "make room for civilization," but he thought Alaska was a different case, with land fit only for wildlife that should be protected from the Indians.[34]

The ex-buffalo hunter outfitted and guided nonresident hunters, another new service industry in Alaska upon which Nelson could call for political support of better game laws. After 1908, nonresident hunters on the Kenai Peninsula were required to hire a guide. Visiting big game hunters in other Alaskan locales often employed guides, packers, and outfitters also, to make the hunt more comfortable, safer, and to increase the possibility of success. Big game hunting in certain areas was a big business. To determine just how big—and to counter Riggs's charge that hunting by outside sportsmen had no significant impact on the economics of Alaska—the Bureau of Biological Survey sent out questionnaires to nonresident sportsmen who had hunted in Alaska between 1914 and 1922. The results helped Nelson to muster local support for his new law.[35]

During these years the local equivalent of the gentleman hunter and sportsman, and his club, also appeared. By the early 1920s game clubs could be found in Ketchikan, Juneau, Hoonah, Sitka, Nome, Seward, Chitina, Wrangell, Petersburg, and two in Cordova. They were sometimes dominated by wardens—either fur wardens or the governors' game wardens. Frank Dufresne helped to found the Nome game association. Nelson worked diligently to enlist the clubs' aid, and many eventually endorsed his bill.[36]

The local support helped Nelson to beat back attempts to place full authority over game in the hands of Alaskan politicians. One proposal to transfer all federal activities in Alaska to a board of Alaskans died in Congress.[37] At one point the Alaska legislature and Governor Riggs wanted a commission system under the full control of the Territory and financed by license fees, including licenses for market hunters, a tax on game meat sold in the Territory, and a heavy levy on hunters from outside. The only result of Riggs's plan was the passage by the Territorial legislature of a high-priced, additional nonresident big game license; it was ignored, and soon repealed.[38] On the eve of Nelson's victory in Congress, the Territorial House of Representatives denounced the "Nelson Game Bill" in a resolution that failed to clear both chambers and was replaced by a memorial favoring the bill but asking for local election of the commissioners. The Progressive tradition of administration by experts free from political pressures prevented acceptance of the election idea.[39]

Along with the demonstrably poor record of the governors' wardens and the growth of local backing for a better system, Nelson's achievement rested also on the support of two other groups: the federal bureaucracy and the eastern sportsmen-naturalists. The latter were consulted and they advised, and with minor objections they accepted Nelson's approach. Apparently every animal conservation organization in the country supported the new legislation. Even the erratic William Hornaday, of the New York Zoo, voted "aye," took Alaska Delegate Daniel Sutherland to lunch, and told Nelson that it was "our duty to stand by the frontiersmen of Alaska who really are out of reach of the cold storage houses and butcher shops of civilization [and] cannot be ignored."[40]

Nelson's Alaskan bureaucracy—his fur wardens—mobilized support for the commission bill introduced by Sutherland, organized public meetings to discuss the measure, and kept Nelson informed about local conditions. In Washington the bureaucracy's aid was easily recruited. Both the secretary of the interior and the secretary of agriculture favored an end to overlapping jurisdictions. At a meeting of the House of Representatives Committee on Agriculture, no one appeared in opposition to Nelson's bill.[41] Ex-governor Riggs confessed, "In all fairness . . . the law is designed to be as unobnoxious as possible, and it may work."[42]

It did work. Nelson has been accused of being old and ill and politically ineffective as chief of the Biological Survey during this period.[43] That may be a correct evaluation of some of his activities and policies; it is not true of his Alaska Game Commission law. Carefully conceived and guided skillfully through to passage, it was Nelson's monument to common sense in the management of game animals. He was ill when his campaign to change the law was under way, having been in delicate health since his Alaskan explorations between 1877 and 1881. In 1927 he resigned, after shepherding the early implementation of his bill.

Missing from the Alaska Game Commission law of January 1925 was any specific authority to end the closed season on brown bears. It appeared that no concession on the bear question came out of the East after all, but the appearance was misleading. The new commissioners could recommend changes in the regulations and they began to do exactly that, with the secretary of agriculture's approbation. Summer remained a closed season on browns, but anybody could kill the animal if it attempted "to inflict injury" to person or property; it could be killed within half a mile of a residence if there were "just cause to fear injury" or by a pursuit begun within two days of an attack. The phrasing was simplified in 1928 to state that brown bears could be killed at any time "when such animal is about to attack or molest persons or property, or when found within half a mile of a residence or human habitation." The distance was stretched to one mile in regulations promulgated the following year, and residents engaged in agriculture on Kodiak Island, Afognak Island, and three smaller islands nearby could kill a brown bear at any time if the animal were "considered a menace to persons, livestock, or property."[44]

The Kodiak group of "emerald islands," whose lush, summer vegetation leaves a visual impression of tropical fertility, became the regional focus of the second decennial assault on Ursus. Unfortunately for the agrarian dreams of a handful of aspiring farmers lured north by another branch of the Department of Agriculture, the verdant islands are not as naturally fruitful as they appear, and the world's largest bear enjoyed the green vistas too.

Although Alaska's agricultural potential to this day has been limited almost entirely to garden variety vegetables, a few hardy grains, some sheep, and dairy cattle and chickens, Kodiak's landscape attracted agriculturists soon after its discovery by Europeans. It was the center of agricultural activity in Russian America, the main one being livestock husbandry. But it never amounted to much. There were never more than about three hundred head of cattle on Kodiak during the Russian period of Alaskan history.[45] Some survived in a wild state into the American period, after 1867.

In 1878 a settler of Swedish extraction lost all his cows to grizzlies, according to one report.[46] The Frye-Bruhn Company of Seattle shipped 9,000 sheep to Kodiak during the first years of the next century; 80 remained in 1904. Of 200 head of beef cattle imported by the same company in 1903, 140 died when they fell over steep cliffs. Investigator C. V. Piper, of the Department of Agriculture, said in 1905 of predators: "Destructive wild animals are no menace to sheep raising on the islands. Eagles may destroy a few lambs, but these birds are easily exterminated. Kodiak bears are too scarce and too easily destroyed to merit consideration. On the mainland, however, both wolves and brown bears may prove troublesome."[47]

The contemptuous reference to North America's mightiest carnivore drew the battle lines between potential farmer and bruin. Piper assumed without question that if the bears (or the eagles) became a problem for cattlemen, they would be destroyed. Institutionally, it was a reasonable assumption. The Bureau of Biological Survey was in the Department of Agriculture, and much of the bureau's money was spent controlling predator enemies of the farmer.[48]

The bears and the bureau's preservation function, however, had allies off the farm, in the city, and in the halls of government. Agricultural scientist C. C. Georgeson appreciated that reality more than did Piper. Georgeson began to impress Alaska's governors with the need to promote agricultural development by removing the bears, which had become an excuse for the failure of Alaskan agriculture. The sheep lost to bears at the experiment station in 1914 numbered, in two separate reports of Governor Strong in 1915, forty percent of forty-two sheep, and forty sheep.[49] As in all good bear stories, details fluctuated.

The controversy might not have made much difference in the history of wild animals and people in Alaska if another agency, the General Land Office of the Department of the Interior, had not begun to implement a law passed in 1927 that created grazing districts, "for the protection, development, and utilization of the public lands of Alaska." The "development" was undertaken in accord with congressional policy "to promote the conservation of the natural resources of Alaska." Grazing was to be subordinate to higher priority land uses: mineral use, timber, water resource use, agricultural use, and "such other resources as may be of greater benefit to the public."[50] Wildlife was not mentioned. The ranking was a fair statement of American values in the 1920s, and the way in which the term "conservation" was used is a fair sample of continuing confusion in the American mind over what the word meant.

Under the law, twenty-year leases were authorized, and all or part of the leaseholds could be transferred. A single lease might cover thousands of acres, and some were so huge that they were measured more conveniently in square miles. Although few permits were actually granted, the grazing law created a new interest group intent upon urging an end to the Kodiak bear's existence. The group's spokesman in 1928 was Jack McCord.

Before McCord encamped on Kodiak as a cattleman, he had been involved in the construction of the Copper River and Northwestern Railway, fictionalized in Rex Beach's novel *The Iron Trail*; he was later called "Lightfoot Mac, the Copper River Scout." Though his own livestock on Sitkalidak Island in the Kodiak group were not molested by brown bears, he told the game commission that browns were the greatest obstacle preventing the establishment of a large livestock and agricultural industry on Kodiak Island.[51] A petition presented by McCord to lift the protection of Kodiak bears contained 500 signatures. At that time the population of the town of Kodiak was approximately 400.[52] "Lightfoot Mac" and his cattlemen's association must have beaten the brush to get 500 legitimate signatures. The number of ranchers actually engaged in raising cattle was not more than a handful, and the number of cattle no more than a few dozen head. Yet the political pressure applied by this small constituency undoubtedly explains the regulations of 1929, allowing Kodiak cattlemen to kill bears at any time they were considered a menace to livestock or property. Pressure for the extermination of the animal continued, despite the concession, and other Alaskans petitioned the game commission to remove the protection of brown bears.

But the drive to exterminate the big bruins needed more than petitions to succeed. As in 1918, it needed a cause célèbre. An obliging bear in southeastern Alaska killed a man named Thayer in 1929, and provided the cattlemen and other enemies of the brown bear with their most effective argument. In the mind of editor Harry McGuire of *Outdoor Life*, however, the tragedy was no excuse to send the brown bear the way of the passenger pigeon. The real reason for the new bear regulation, McGuire argued, was clear from the opening phrase in the game commission statement published in the Juneau newspaper: "In order not to stand in the way of an increasing industrial development in many parts of Alaska. . . ."[53]

The regulation introduced by that phrase ignited the stateside conservationists once again. The commission had decided to allow Alaskan residents a year-round open season on brown bears, except in certain areas, for example, part of the Alaska Peninsula; in these areas the bag limit was two bears. For nonresidents there was still a closed season during the summer, and the limit was lowered to two animals taken anywhere. The right to kill bears in self-defense remained legal in all parts of the Territory.[54] And restrictions on market hunting and export remained. The new regulation was the old concession Riggs had expected from Grant and Grinnell, a change that most Washington bureaucrats and eastern sportsmen and naturalists familiar with Alaska and its small population knew would do nothing to endanger the bear's existence. But the reaction of a few writers again catapulted the brown bear into a highly visible trajectory.

McGuire's article was one response. John M. Holzworth, who had spent most of the summers and autumns of 1927, 1928, and 1929 in southeastern Alaska, wrote a book about the Territory's brown bears. He had observed 200 browns and photographed most of them from five to fifty yards away. He reported only two isolated charges.[55]

The publicity that did the most to stir up opposition to the new regulation came from the pen of the renowned nature writer Stewart Edward White and appeared as an article in the April 12, 1930, issue of the *Saturday Evening Post*. White was certain that a year-round open season for Alaskans, together with a Territorial law appropriating $40,000 to clean salmon-spawning streams of trout "and other predatory enemies of the salmon," meant "our unique brown bear of Alaska is doomed to as complete extinction as the California grizzly." A lumber company cutting wood in the national forest had hired hunters to kill bears to protect loggers; said White, "Any man so sunk in timidity as to fear such a bugaboo should not be in the woods at all." Apparently (White wrote), those in favor of exterminating the grizzlies realized that protection of the cattle was a little flimsy as the only reason to eliminate the bears, and therefore intoduced Thayer, spawning salmon, and endangered lumberjacks as additional evidence against the bear.

"Man's genius apparently cannot even contemplate living side by side on an equality of tolerance with anything whatever in Nature." Maybe mankind should "spend a little time in examination of the way God and Nature made the planet, before concluding that the whole original scheme must be scrapped." White urged his readers to write letters to Alaskan politicians, federal bureaucrats, and their own congressmen.[56]

Letters poured into official channels. The game commission received fifty-four in 1930, many "written for purely sentimental reasons," the executive officer explained. No letters to the commission or to the governor came from anyone who had hunted in Alaska, and only two or three came from people who had visited the Territory. Letters came to the commission from a number of conservation and scientific organizations with members who knew Alaska firsthand. During the first half of 1932, more than 122 American newspaper editorials endorsed a refuge for bears on Admiralty Island, in the Panhandle.[57]

The reaction of big game guides was mixed. The manager of the Juneau Guides called White's article "hysterical ballyhoo." A spokesman for the Alaska Guides Incorporated of Anchorage pointed out that in 1929, 130 brown bear trophies were taken out of the region at an average cost of $550 each; he did not know of any form of livestock that could be raised in Alaska and "bring that return per head." The economics of guiding argued against exterminating the bear.[58]

Other Alaskan newspapers began to appreciate the monetary value of the brown bear, or so Frank Dufresne thought in 1932: "In a way I believe we owe something to the ultra-conservationists, who, by the very un-reasonableness of their demands have rationalized the press of Alaska to assume the middle ground." Still other Alaskans who were asked to choose between the brown bear and the salmon cannery interests chose the bruin. One said that all the bears in Alaska could not eat the salmon wasted by canneries.[59]

The game commission had five reactions to all the fuss. First, it reminded supporters of the new regulations who objected to the excepted areas that a bear could be killed anywhere at any time if it were deemed a menace to person or property. Second, opponents of the open season for residents were reminded that it did not apply to Mount McKinley Park, the Katmai region, and certain special areas where most of the bears were and where the old regulations, with a lower bag limit, still applied. Third, the commission added to its excepted regions the major coastal haunts of the brown bear. By 1933 most of Kodiak and all of Afognak Island, Admiralty Island, and the Kenai Peninsula had a closed season on brown bears in the summer for resident and nonresident alike.[60] Fourth, while the commission was extending its excepted areas where special regulations applied, it was discouraging offers and recommendations from outside to create permanent refuges, because feeling in Alaska regarding the withdrawal of public lands made it impolitic. The commissioners did, however, approve the assignment of national park status to Glacier Bay National Monument, and its enlargement. It was created in 1925 at the northern reach of the Panhandle despite objections from the *Alaska Weekly*, which declared the region was adaptable to agricultural pursuits. To increase the size of the monument would increase the protection of brown bears, as well as increase the number of scenic features within the monument.[61] Neither park nor monument status was recommended for Admiralty Island, in southeastern Alaska.

Admiralty, located in the Tongass National Forest, is nearly 100 miles long and about 30 miles wide at the widest. It has 678 winding miles of coastline and covers more than one million acres. Impressive mountains tower over streams and lakes and coves, green meadows, and dense forests of spruce and hemlock trees underlain by the almost impenetrable brush common to a rain forest. There were perhaps 1,000 brown bears on the island and 2,500 American bald eagles. Black-tailed deer are present but no black bears, as though the latter did not care to mix in such close quarters with the fearsome grizzly. The bears outnumber the members of the Kootznahoo branch of the Tlingit people, a Northwest Coast Indian group.[62]

In 1932 a park service naturalist had found on Admiralty "little . . . that is of National Park caliber." He concluded after consulting the regional forester that only 30 percent of the island would be logged and not more than 1/75th cut in a single year; logging therefore presented no threat to the bears. If they were in danger, said the naturalist, the obvious solution was to reduce the bag limit to one animal. Frank Dufresne could find no one in the area who thought the bears were being depleted. Allen Hasselborg, the hermit guide who lived on the island, thought logging would improve the bear's range. A Senate committee held hearings on the issue; there was no enthusiasm for the creation of a national park on Admiralty Island.[63] Opinion on the Admiralty issue from all official perspectives was that brown bears were in no danger and could be conserved through continued, careful game management.

Stewart Edward White kept the drive for a bear sanctuary on the island alive anyway, because he feared the effect of legal loopholes and lumbering and perhaps because he shared with the chief of the Biological Survey a belief that publicity (much of which had been engendered by White's own article) had increased the number of sportsmen who planned to visit Alaska and get a bear trophy. If so, the concern was not borne out by the data on license sales.[64] In support of his cause White had those 122 editorials and specific endorsements by the eastern organizations on record with the game commission. In 1934 he submitted a formal proposal to create a sanctuary for grizzlies on the island. Interior Secretary Harold Ickes told White that President Franklin Roosevelt was also interested in increased protection for Alaskan bears. But the proposal remained only a proposal. An attempt to revive it in 1941 was vetoed by Ickes on the advice of his staff. Ernest Gruening's explanation, that the debate over Admiralty's status was little more than interagency rivalry, is oversimple.[65] No government agency had advocated a permanent refuge for the island's bears. The safety of their relatives on the islands of the Kodiak group was another matter.

The fifth reaction of the game commission to the brown bear controversy was the practical decision to determine the facts in the Kodiak bear-cattle dispute. Warden Homer Jewell's first report was encouraging. The open season, he said, had made no difference one way or the other to the survival of Kodiak bears. He considered their population safe and healthy in 1931. The report of Warden Hosea Sarber for 1933 was not as reassuring. By then Kodiak and Afognak had been reassigned a closed season during the summer, and by then the commission had discouraged an attempt to make Afognak a permanent bear sanctuary. The latter compromise apparently did not please all citizens. Sarber, who became the commission's principal authority on the big bears reported a great deal of wanton slaughtering of bears on both islands.[66]

The brown bear remained a local political issue despite the attempt of the game commissioners to satisfy all parties. Anthony J. Dimond campaigned in 1932 against the commission in his bid for election as delegate to Congress. In February 1935 the Territorial legislature passed a joint memorial condemning the game commission as expensive, oppressive, "repugnant to a large majority" of Alaskans, and asked for the transfer of its functions to the Territorial government. There was no regional pattern in the voting; most of the legislators were Democrats and businessmen.[67] It was Riggs's program all over again, with the *bête brun* at the center of another attempt to gain local control of the Territory's natural resources (beginning with "the most important"), but triggered this time by the bear's alleged appetite for domesticated beef instead of its appetite for humans.

There was one other important difference. A month before the legislature's memorial, the first issue of the *Alaska Sportsman* magazine appeared. An attractive, illustrated, regional version of the popular outdoor periodicals, it met with astonishing success. Front pages of the first issue contained good wishes from Stewart Edward White, Frank Buck, and (of all people) Thomas Riggs. John Muir was quoted in the first editorial, though he would have frowned upon all the hunting articles.[68] The role of the *Sportsman* in Alaskan conservation during these years paralleled that of *Forest and Stream* in American conservation generally during the last quarter of the nineteenth century. In time, the *Alaska Sportsman* became the single most important private, institutional influence in the history of game animals and people in the Territory, as it spread the message that Alaskans could have their game and shoot it too.

The new magazine did not play any direct and influential part in the demise of the legislature's memorial and Dimond's bill. These were the years when wildlife protection, which had been the springboard of American conservation, was finally recognized formally as a significant part of Franklin Roosevelt's New Deal. The federal Duck Stamp Act to fund the acquisition of refuges for migratory birds had been enacted in

1934. The year before, Aldo Leopold's pioneering textbook on game management was published. Automobile companies and the manufacturers of sporting arms founded the American Wildlife Institute in 1935, and the president called the first North American Wildlife Conference the following year. A new lobby later named the National Wildlife Federation appeared. The outstanding wildlife law of these years was the Pittman-Robertson Act of 1937, which allocated funds to state wildlife research projects approved by scientists in the Bureau of Biological Survey. The Alaskan move against the bears was timed badly, transparent in intent, and easily shot down in a national atmosphere sympathetic to game conservation.[69]

Wardens Jack O'Connor and Clarence Rhode looked into stories of cattle-killing bears during the summer of 1937. The investigation satisfied them that some cattle were lost to the bears, but there had been no effort by Kodiak cattlemen to fence or herd stock, and some part of their loss was due to natural causes other than the brown bear. Cattlemen were promised an investigation by a commission scientist the following summer. L. J. Palmer, the field biologist, recommended the employment of professional hunters to control the bears.[70] The game commission adopted the suggestion. It was the Biological Survey's favorite technique to control predators, and political heat was again being generated over the brown bear question.

Delegate Dimond complained once more that bears were protected but not people. At Belkofski, on the Alaska Peninsula, "the bears wander through the village," Dimond said. "One of them approached some children playing on the beach. They even dig into newly made graves." The United States commissioner at Kodiak (whom Warden Sarber described as an old, feeble, though perhaps well meaning man who knew nothing about bears and had never been on the cattle ranges) wrote in December 1938 to the secretary of agriculture, recommending that Kodiak bears go the way of the buffalo. The commissioner enclosed a photograph of a steer or cow with a large segment of its hide ripped off the right rump and dangling pitiably.[71]

Hosea Sarber was chosen to lead the small party of hunter-investigators who roamed the Kodiak range during the spring and summer of 1939. They were permitted to destroy twenty-five cattle-killing bears. They killed only seven.[72] The party had traveled nearly 1,800 miles on foot, almost 1,700 miles by outboard motorboat, 700 miles on horseback, 200 miles by airplane, and 44 miles by automobile.

Sarber told Dufresne: "We had the cattlemen's confidence; shared their cabins and bunks, their hardships and troubles. We helped them lift weak cattle to their feet, doctor sick cows, and assisted them in general. They in turn gave us every assistance. . . . Their doors were open to us day and night whether they were home or not. We liked them and they were our friends and we have the deepest sympathy for the hard working men they are."

But they were wrong said Sarber. His conclusions about the neighborliness of bears and cattle were in direct contrast to those of the cattlemen. Sarber had rediscovered what the Russians learned more than one hundred years earlier, and what Americans relearned at the beginning of the twentieth century: Kodiak was not the stockman's Eden that it appeared to be, and federal agricultural scientists had implied that it was.

Of the 108 head of cattle lost during the previous winter and spring, only nine could be blamed on the bears. Though Kodiak ranchers were hard-working men, most of their stock losses were due to neglect. Cattle were left to wander in huge areas untended and unfenced. Many head were lost when they bogged down in the swamps or fell off cliffs. Some were trapped on the beach by winter tides. Others were killed by exposure to severe weather and by starvation.

Sarber continued: Kodiak in late June was "a riot of green," suggesting superb livestock country. Cattle did thrive then, but killing frosts in the fall rendered the long grass "so much dead straw" that cattle refused to eat the following spring, even if they were starving. Were it not for the presence of beaches with kelp and seaweed, it would be impossible to raise cattle on Kodiak, one rancher told Sarber. Several admitted that it was cheaper to feed their animals imported cottonseed cake at fifty-three dollars a ton than to try to put up native hay, since hay that was put up rotted in the damp climate. The weather did not permit ranchers to raise sufficient feed crops. Consequently, winter range requirements were huge. One cattleman occupied an island of 117 square miles. Another said that he needed at least 30,000 acres to succeed.

The brown bears were blamed for more damage than they caused because their numbers were exaggerated, and their reputation was maligned when they were caught feeding on the carcass of a cow killed by other natural agents, Sarber reported. More important, any loss was a heavy loss to these marginal ranchers, and the bear was the only cause of loss that might be controlled. As a result, "bitter hatred toward the bear . . . has grown into an obsession," and the Kodiak cattlemen "have shouted their hatred to the world."

One rancher's advice to anyone encountering a brown bear was, "Shoot them in the guts, in the foot, any place, but get a bullet into them."[73]

Sarber's conclusions were reinforced by numbers. Only nine cattle ranches had been involved. In March of 1939, when Sarber began his study, only one of the nine ranchers was grazing public land with legal authority, according to the secretary of the interior. The nine together had only 500 head of cattle and about 100 head of sheep. A scant 150 beef carcasses, valued at $100 per animal, were marketed locally each year. Sheep when sold averaged twenty dollars apiece. There were many more bears, and their value per animal when taken by a nonresident hunter was far in excess of the value of a beef. In numbers of dollars, the bears were a much more profitable industry. In their range they enjoyed a larger number of square miles on Kodiak Island than did the cattle, but the bears preferred rough country to the livestock-grazing areas, and the number of acres of public land that cattlemen required disturbed a number of ordinary Alaskans, as well as the policymakers. Alaska game commissioner Earl Ohmer's opinion in 1952 had probably been a familiar complaint in 1940. "Why the hell don't those two bit outfits demand all of Alaska and then insist that the caribou, reindeer, moose and every other d—— thing that feeds on grass, moss or brush, be killed off? And why the hell are they dishing out 50,000 to 73,000 acres of grazing land to one individual?"[74]

The problem of numbers of people became important to the Kodiak bear's future too, when navy and army personnel arrived on the island in force, just prior to America's entry into the Second World War. The population pressures convinced Washington that three-fourths of the island should be declared a wildlife refuge for the big bear; only controlled hunting was permitted. The bear's new status did not soften its reputation among Kodiak stockmen, but there the old controversy stalled in 1941, when General Buckner took the game commission to court.

In January 1939, even before Hosea Sarber began his investigation, the game commission had changed the name of one of its patrol boats from *Seal* to *Bear*, and the name of another vessel from *Marten* to *Black Bear*. By then, because of their insignia, commission agents were known as "brown bear men."[75]

4
The Science of Wildlife
and Technology
of Hunting

In a land where the world's largest land-based carnivore is at home a few miles from the pygmy shrew, the world's smallest mammal, Alaska's "brown bear men" had more wards than their colorful sobriquet implied. Some of the animals were exotic. Twenty-three bison were introduced from Montana to the Alaskan interior in 1928. By 1960 there were nearly four hundred of the animals in two herds. Eight wapiti, or Roosevelt elk, were planted on Afognak Island, also in 1928, and have thrived, despite their proximity to the big brown bears. Ring-necked pheasants, brought to the Matanuska Valley, did not survive.[1]

Perhaps the most publicized transplantation was the reintroduction of the gregarious musk-ox, a smaller relative of the bison. The shaggy ox was at one time an important element in the life of the Eskimo. The animal's defensive habit of forming a circle, side-by-side, rumps in and horns out, with the calves inside the circle, made it easy prey on the northern, Arctic coast; the last musk-ox native to Alaska was killed in 1865. In 1930, thirty-four of the animals were brought to Fairbanks from Greenland, and a few years later most of them were taken to Nunivak Island, off the southwestern coast in the Bering Sea. By 1970 their numbers had increased to 750 and there were serious doubts that the island could support the large population. Planned hunting was proposed to thin the herd, but opponents declared that such a hunt would be unsportsmanlike. During the next two winters, natural conditions trimmed the herd to 550 oxen.[2]

Native animals were also moved from one part of Alaska to another, with mixed results, at the direction of the Territorial legislature, which took responsibility for the transplantation program after the Alaska Game Commission was established. The early efforts, according to recent students of the activity, culminated in the 1920s and were "based on very little, if any, biological knowledge and scant consideration was given to its feasibility or desirability."[3] The truth is, even by 1950 the science end of scientific game management in Alaska was not much advanced beyond its status during Governor Riggs's bewildering scuffle with Washington over the brown bear.

A lack of Alaskan biological exploration characterized both the Russian and the early American periods of Alaskan history despite a good beginning. The country was discovered by Europeans in 1741 as one result of an elaborate scientific enterprise. The first white man to land on Alaskan soil was the biologist Georg Wilhelm Steller. Later maritime expeditions by the Russians, English, Spanish, and French paid some attention to biology but were chiefly concerned with oceanography, mineralogy, anthropology, and cartography. Biology—excluding an obvious interest in the distribution of fur-bearing animals—continued to be deemphasized by persons associated with the Russian American Company, a paragovernmental trading company that ruled Alaska. A notable exception was the work of Ilia Voznesenskii, of the Imperial Academy, undertaken more than fifty years after the company's founder had urged his men to "ask and note down where . . . beasts and birds and curious sea-shells . . . may be found."[4]

Exploration by Americans tended also to undervalue zoological studies and concentrate upon cartography, geology, and anthropology, excepting (again) the interest in marine fur-bearing animals. This was in keeping with the American preference for utilitarian sciences, but practical goals did not prevent individual investigators from researching Alaska's flora and fauna. William Healey Dall's work before and after the abandonment of the Western Union Overland Telegraph (1865–68) was an outstanding individual achievement. He continued to study the biology of Alaska, on the side, when he returned later as an employee of the Coast and Geodetic Survey and the Geological Survey. Lucien McShan Turner between 1874 and 1881, and Edward Nelson during the years 1877–1881, made important contributions to the natural history of western Alaska while serving as Army Signal Service weather observers. During the last quarter of the century, John Muir visited the Panhandle and the Bering Sea, Frederick Funston botanized for the Department of Agriculture on the southern coast and in the interior, and the luxurious Harriman Alaska Expedition cruised along the coasts in 1899. Organized by C. Hart Merriam, the Harriman group eventually produced a magnificent collection of volumes dealing with Alaskan coastal plants and animals. The millionaire sponsor, Edward H. Harriman, was credited with shooting the first Kodiak bear taken by a sportsman. It was a small female.[5]

In 1899, 1900, 1902, and 1903, the Biological Survey sent Wilfred H.

Osgood on summer biological surveys of the Yukon regions, the Cook Inlet, and the Alaska Peninsula, in response to the demand created by the gold rush for more scientific information about Alaska. Each trip was a reconnaissance only. Osgood was expected to cover too much territory and do too many things. Although his opinions were solicited during the preparation and passage of the earliest Alaskan game laws, his reports may not have been widely read.[6]

During the first sixty years or so of United States rule, most Americans got their knowledge of Alaskan botany and zoology from private adventurers, naturalists, and sportsmen such as C. E. S. Wood, John Muir, H. W. Seton-Karr, James H. Kidder, Dall De Weese, Andrew J. Stone, J. Alden Loring, Colonel Claude Cane, Charles Sheldon, and Belmore Browne. A surprisingly large number wrote travel and hunting books and articles for outdoor magazines, other popular periodicals, and newspapers.[7] They were enthusiastic if rarely systematic in reporting Alaska's biology. An exception is Charles Sheldon's study of mountain sheep in Mount McKinley National Park. Other sportsmen made contributions to the natural history of Alaska, usually in the form of specimens. When everything was put together there was still not enough coherent applied science available to manage game animals scientifically.

This was not an exclusively Alaskan condition. The foundations of American big game biology in general were shaky when Riggs invoked legalism to permit market hunting of brown bears. The discrepancy that he found appeared in a game law written in large part and administered by the natural historians. The legal weakness would surely not have existed and been ignored by the scientific bureaucrats for so long if large wild-animal mammalogy were theoretically, empirically, and institutionally a mature zoological specialty.

Although in fact very little was known about the big mammals during most of the nineteenth century, American mammalogy was considered too finished, or complete, a science to warrant productive empirical investigation. At the Smithsonian Institution, apparently, more solid work was done on the marine mammals than on their big terrestrial relatives.[8] The evidence available for generalizations about large land mammals was rarely acquired or assembled in a methodical, scientific way. The brown bears enjoyed their privacy in remote locales and were difficult to catch and ship. Information about their breeding habits in the wild was not acquired easily; as one biologist wrote recently, "Most animals coming under close observation are usually seen over the sights of a rifle, and rarely live long enough to carry on their normal activities."[9]

Most of the large-animal zoology that did exist was descriptive, and the theoretical basis for description and classification lacked precision. Slight variations in color, size, shape, internal characteristics, or geographical location of the habitat were frequently used to differentiate among animals. Often specimens were measured against the first one of the type described, whether the first was typical or not. As more specimens became available the variations increased, and what were once thought to be firm criteria for classification melted away. Biologists tended either to lump animals together under broad definitions or to split them by name into numerous subdivisions. Important parts of a new biological theory that could organize the data were at hand, but not until the 1930s were all the parts brought together into the synthetic theory of evolution.

Meanwhile, taxonomists solved the species problem by adopting one of three ideas of what a species was. The Aristotelian "essentialists" adopted a typological approach stressing external variations and later, more detailed, morphological differences which, in the case of the brown bear, took the form of variations in the skull's configuration. A second group of biologists, called "nominalists" by Ernst Mayr, considered the idea of species an idea only; they were aided by the meaning of the Latin word *species*, which can be translated as both "idea" and "species." A third and modern "biological species concept" had taken the first step of its development decades earlier with the proposition that a true species should be able to reproduce its kind, which in turn could reproduce the type. Animals that could not interbreed at all or that reproduced sterile offspring were not considered to be of the same species, but there was no unanimous agreement among mammalogists that cross-fertility was essential to the definition of a species.[10]

External to the scientific content of mammalogy, the discipline was inchoate institutionally as well, and this too helps to explain indirectly how loopholes in the Alaskan game law could exist. The American Society of Mammalogists was not founded until 1919. During most of the nineteenth century mammalogical studies were often undertaken by biologists who were considered specialists in other fields, and (if the five most prominent men associated with the brown bear episode are typical), as late as the early twentieth century such studies still tended to be dominated by men who were largely self-taught in the specialty and by gentlemen naturalists.[11] Although specialization, professionalization, and institutionalization in the life sciences discouraged the unsystematic collector in better organized zoological disciplines (such as entomology, ornithology, and ichthyology), the mammalogists still relied for much of their data about the large animals on the amateur naturalist and big game hunter.

There was still in this branch of mammalogy some of the "collectivitis" that was often a characteristic of pre–Civil War American biology. The scramble to find, describe, and name a new species of animal life was motivated by the celebrity a new discovery might bring to the finder, or by financial advantage in the form of wages or payment for future expeditions, or by the right to name the new animal after a friend, sponsor, or oneself. The last practice, according to the sociologist Robert Merton, is a form of reward for scientific achievement that heightened the prestige accompanying the priority of discovery.[12] One illustration from the Pacific Northwest is sufficient. Andrew Stone, an "explorer-naturalist," made several trips to western British Columbia, the Yukon Territory, and Alaska between 1896 and 1901 and reported a caribou he named after Madison Grant, of the New York Zoological Society, a "monster bear" he named after Merriam, and a black mountain sheep that was named after Stone himself.[13] None of the animals deserved specification as a new animal by the interbreeding criterion.

Also on the institutional side of the discipline's history, scientific administration of large animals was relatively new at the federal level. The central government came late into the management of game. Before the twentieth century the states had dominated policy for game animals. The symbolic starting gun for participation of the federal government in game policy was the Lacey Act of 1900, which protected animals that crossed state boundaries. In Alaska, with its territorial status, the responsible agency—the Bureau of Biological Survey—was an arm of the Department of Agriculture with more experience in the administration of birds and bugs than bears.

All these internal and external weaknesses in large animal mammalogy came together in the person of C. Hart Merriam, who put his by-line on a study of North American brown bears and grizzlies, on the monograph that Governor Riggs planned to use against the bears. Theory was not congenial to Merriam. He gathered his facts about the bears, labeled them, and made little effort to interpret them broadly. The first issue of the *Journal of Mammalogy*, in 1919, contained a paper in which Merriam pleaded for an emphasis by taxonomists on "degree of differentiation" and argued against the practice of demoting a species to a subspecies when "intergrades" (transitional forms) were found. He was a splitter, not a lumper, in the earthy colloquialisms of systematic biology. Of his classification scheme, George Gaylord Simpson said (after Merriam died): "On such a system twin bear cubs could be of different species." Merriam was trained formally in medicine and was largely self-taught in mammalogy. For his study of the bears, he relied heavily on specimens collected by amateur naturalist-hunters. He was a founder and the first president of the American Society of Mammalogists. In 1886 he headed the Division of Economic Ornithology and Mammalogy in the United States Department of Agriculture, and when he resigned as chief of the Biological Survey (the division's successor), he worked as an associate in the Smithsonian Institution. He lived a long life, until 1942. He was, as the author of one obituary—Wilfred Osgood—observed, "a power in the land with a reach into posterity that will long be felt."[14] Followers of the "great man" theory of history might blame Merriam alone for every deficiency in the science of mammalogy in the United States during the first two decades of this century.

That explanation is too neat for Alaska. Even with the best science possible, there were still too few representatives of the Bureau of Biological Survey in the Territory, the area they were expected to supervise was too vast, and the financial support they received was minimal. Under the circumstances, they could not be expected to raise the quality of game management dramatically. They worked also as fur wardens and game wardens at a time when enforcement was more important to the bureau than scientific research. Conditions in Alaska during the twenties support one scholar's conclusion that the bureau was mainly an economic agency,[15] but up north the emphasis upon enforcement rather than biology seems also in retrospect to have been the wisest policy, with limited funds.

The first resident agent of the bureau in Alaska was Alfred M. Bailey, a curator of birds and mammals for the Louisiana State Museum in New Orleans. Starting in southeastern Alaska in November 1919, he worked for seventeen months before resigning to spend a year collecting Arctic specimens for exhibition at the Denver Museum of Natural History, which he later headed. After his retirement Bailey remembered Governor Riggs as "a friend indeed" who had allowed the naturalist to use government boats on field trips.[16]

Bailey was replaced by Ernest P. Walker, who nursed along Alaskan support for Nelson's reform of wildlife management in the Territory. Walker later became the game commission's first executive secretary, a job he held until 1928, when he resigned to become assistant director of the National Zoological Park. From his sanctuary on Rock Creek in the capital, he wrote in 1939: "Alaskans are not a bad lot . . . [and] love the outdoors and its animal life and in the last analysis . . . have the fate of the big brown bear in their hands, for . . . they are the jurors who pass on prosecutions." Walker also became the principal author of a classic reference work on the mammals of the world.[17] Meanwhile, the Bureau of Biological Survey managed to field two biologists who became important figures in Alaskan natural history, Lawrence J. Palmer and Olaus Murie.

Palmer was a grazing expert trained at the University of Nebraska. He came north in 1920 with Edward Nelson and veterinarian Seymour Hadwen to begin studies of the domestic reindeer. Palmer's Alaskan career spanned more than two decades and included theoretical investigations of lichens—the mosslike, complex, and delicate northern plants, often resembling hoarfrost, that are a staple of caribou. He discovered that lichens needed about as much time to recover from destruction as a forest does. He knew that overgrazed ranges would trigger a disastrous crash in the reindeer population, but there was nothing he or anybody else could do about it.[18] His considerable achievements have failed to register on the collective memory of Alaskans. Palmer did not have the literary inclination of the Dufresnes or the Muries to recount his northern adventures in the popular style of the nature writers.

Olaus J. Murie arrived in Alaska the same year as Palmer. Murie was given the job of learning as much as he could about the caribou while serving as a fur warden in the interior. Certain people in Fairbanks were convinced that his caribou study was a cover story for a "secret mission" to enforce the liquor laws. In time they were persuaded otherwise. The full result of Murie's four-year investigation of the herds was not published until 1935. Both it and Palmer's work could be justified as utilitarian, with economic consequences. Over the years Murie made additional studies of Alaskan bird and mammalian life, and eventually served as president of the Wilderness Society, founded by Robert Marshall, a biologist who came to Alaska on his own in the 1930s for adventure and for geographical exploration.[19]

In 1922 Adolph Murie joined his older brother for a summer and a winter of studying the biology of Alaska. The younger Murie also became one of the few federal scientists to study Alaskan wildlife in the field before 1950. A controversy over the effects of wolf predation on the mountain sheep population in Mount McKinley Park resulted in Adolph's employment in 1939. His report was a model of the field naturalist's art.[20]

The Muries, Osgood, Bailey, Walker, Hadwen, and Palmer represented the new breed of wildlife specialist with at least some college training. Four of the seven earned doctorates, usually after their first exposure to Alaska.[21] Before about 1940, only Walker was a permanent employee; the others came and went. The federal commitment to scientific management was not set firmly until more than two decades after the establishment of the Alaska Game Commission.

The passage of the Pittman-Robertson Act of 1937 did not have any sudden, direct impact on the science of Alaskan game. Changes in the Alaskan game law approved in 1938 extended the game commission's authority to undertake wildlife studies, and a resident biologist—Lawrence Palmer—was assigned to the Territory. His research was limited by pressing political and economic needs to resolve disputes over predation. Not until the post–Second World War period did funds from the Federal Aid in Wildlife Restoration program become important in Alaska, and not until 1950 was an Alaskan Cooperative Wildlife Research Unit activated.[22]

After that date the game commission continued to rely for much of its knowledge of the hunted animals on casual informants, unsolicited letters, and wardens, who were expected to report their own observations about the health and happiness of the various species in their charge. The wardens did remarkably well, considering that their primary duty was to enforce the hunting regulations. Unfortunately, sometimes it became obvious to the public that regulations were not always grounded on solid information.

The everlasting quarrel over cattle and Kodiak bears is a case in point. The fish cannery interests had, for the most part, remained detached from early squabbles about the table manners of brown bears. But the situation changed in the forties, when the Alaska salmon pack declined alarmingly, and the fishing industry began to look around for something to blame other than its own greed. The brown bear was a handy, experienced, whipping boy who ate fish, so the cannery men joined the handful of Kodiak cattlemen in a renewal of the war against the bear. The big animal's fortunes were not enhanced by the coincidental acquisition of federal administrative authority over fish and bears by the same man, Ira Gabrielson, at the time when the salmon population began to diminish. Neither did the wildly fluctuating estimates by scientists of the number of salmon taken by Kodiak bears help the bruin's defenders.

A fishery biologist working out of the state of Washington reported in 1951 the results of a study he had made in 1947 of a creek at Karluk Lake, on Kodiak Island, where (he said) the bears killed over 30 percent of the spawning fish. Applied to all spawning streams, the figure represented a loss to the salmon canners of $117,649. The commercial fish lobby presented these conclusions to the Territorial legislature without prior inquiry at the game commission office. No mention was made of a relevant historical fact: the Karluk district was the oldest on Kodiak and the most heavily fished, sometimes illegally, in its seventy-year history (to 1950).[23]

Once again the legislature directed its righteous wrath at the evil bear, heeding the reflection of Representative Chester Carlson, a fisherman: "These bears can't vote and they don't pay taxes. I see no reason why we shouldn't get rid of them whenever they endanger our lives or our livelihood."[24]

Once again the Fish and Wildlife Service reminded Alaskans that bears were more profitable than cattle. Since 1937 (thirteen years), ninety-three head of cattle died from all causes; their market value was $357.70 per head. The income from a legal kill of a Kodiak bear was $200 to $250 per bear, and 150 bears were taken in that year.[25]

Once again the indefatigable friend of the tame bovine, Jack McCord—now called "Sourdough Jack" or the "Baron of Sitkalidak Island," instead of "Lightfoot Jack"—appeared on behalf of Kodiak cattlemen among the makers of high policy. His recommendation that the Alaska Peninsula, not Kodiak Island, be reserved for brown bears was reported to a breathless nation by radio newscaster Lowell Thomas in 1951.[26]

And once again the Territorial legislature passed a resolution condemning the bear. Memorial number 6 was sponsored by Representative Carlson and Jack Scavenius, the latter a bush pilot who had been in Alaska for a dozen years. It was signed by Speaker of the House (and Alaska's first state governor) William Egan, a storekeeper from Valdez, and, for the Territorial senate, by Gunnard Engebreth, the owner of the Maytag washing-machine franchise in Anchorage and formerly the proprietor of a hardware store with a large supply of hunting equipment. The memorial was critical of the bears for preying on domestic livestock but did not refer to their appetite for salmon.[27] Perhaps the local legislators decided that it was unwise to snuggle up to the fisheries lobby when the absentee cannery interests were, with federal bureaucrats, proclaimed to be the major enemies of home rule and statehood for Alaska.

It came out during the controversy that the bear's take of salmon, as reported in studies conducted in 1947, 1948, and each year from 1950 through 1952, varied from 0.10 percent to 31.4 percent. The game commission tried to explain away the discrepancies by claiming in 1952 that the effect of the bears' consumption of humpback (pink) salmon was negligible; the bear kill of salmon in large streams and lakes was also low; and only the kill of red (sockeye) salmon in small spawning streams tributary to lake systems was substantial, maybe 20 to 30 percent.[28] The margin of error did not create local respect for the science behind the hunting regulations.

Use by the game commission of a new and unusual technique to estimate bear populations generated additional distrust of the biologists. Frank Dufresne was sent to Admiralty Island in the 1930s to count grizzly bears, in the hope that a census might help to modulate contentious discussions over the island's future. It was not an easy assignment. The thick vegetation could (as Dufresne said) hide a bear the size of a horse within twenty feet. A resident of the island, Allen Hasselborg, told Dufresne that every bear paw imprint was as unique as a person's fingerprint, so Dufresne with a forest ranger and two helpers spent one month surveying the animals' tracks. They reported a population of about 1,600 grizzlies on the island, or one for every square mile. The novel census made newspaper headlines in Alaska.[29]

Jack Hellenthal was not impressed. "Men of science," he wrote, "have

fingerprinted the bears on one island, so that a prospector on that island can rest assured that if the bear knocks his block off, the guilty cul-
prit will be brought to justice." Hellenthal considered the bear census "a
fair sample of the 'scientific data' that the Alaska bureaus have on file in
Washington. The rest of it is just about as accurate and just about as reliable."[30] On one important issue there was always room for argument:
the abundance or scarcity of the animals.

Not until well after the Second World War did the game commission
have fairly reliable statistics on the number of game animals in Alaska.
The lack of firm data about wildlife populations had been embarrassing
to Bureau Chief Edward Nelson on one occasion. In 1918, when he
testified on the Sulzer bill, he was asked how many moose, caribou, and
mountain sheep were in Alaska. When forced to admit that his agency
had not sent anyone to the Territory to estimate the number of game animals, he was berated by congressmen who wanted to know how he could
set bag limits and the like when he did not even know how many animals
were there. His best defense was to point at states with large wildlife appropriations and no accurate game censuses.[31]

In defense of the Alaskan biologists and wardens, wildlife was
difficult to count and to study because it ran freely in a huge territory of
wildly differing topographical characteristics. Some animals are easier to
see than others. The gregarious caribou herd together in open tundra
country part of the year, and their numbers are somewhat easier to estimate than are the numbers of hermit bears or lonely moose. But the caribou's crowding and nomadic habits complicate any tally of its population. The fearless brown bear can sometimes be seen in open meadows
during the day, but its more timid relative, the black bear, prefers the
cover of a forest during the long hours of Alaskan summer daylight. In
the winter both animals retire to their private dens. The mountain goat
resists human encroachment because it likes the high and remote crags
and ravines of Alaska's complex, soaring mountains, where it is difficult
to find. Other animals too are camouflaged from the prying hunter's or
naturalist's view. The white mountain sheep is hard to spot on the snowy
peaks it inhabits. The snowshoe rabbit and tundra hare turn white in
winter. The spruce grouse and ptarmigan are so convinced of their
invisibility that a hungry wilderness traveler can sometimes pick one up
by hand and wring its neck.

Furthermore, scientific game management was a new profession with
imperfect investigative techniques. If mammalogy was immature in the
1920s, game management was fetal. Reliable statistical methods to estimate wildlife populations accurately were slow to appear. And although
wildlife protection was an important root of the whole conservation
movement, once the movement got under way wildlife became low-

priority research because, by the late 1930s, wild animals were thought to be economically insignificant and because they were already "largely exterminated," according to Theodore Roosevelt's National Conservation Commission.[32] Another reason for the low political priority given wildlife research was the notion that any citizen had a democratic right to shoot wild animals. The opinion was deeply imprinted on the frontier psyche, and politicians challenged it at the risk of losing their jobs. Any successful justification of game laws had to cite the democratic necessity of protecting wild game animals from the bloodthirsty and piggish.

One undemocratic privilege of which the Alaskans were rightly suspicious was a legal provision that took the issuance of permits to scientists out of the hands of locals. The secretary of agriculture, not the governor or the game commission, decided which scientists would be given permission to collect wildlife specimens. The privilege was abused, Governor Riggs alleged, and should be abolished, or applicants should be investigated more carefully. Museums that wanted specimens to stuff and exhibit were among the scientific institutions allowed to hunt animals under the special license. Riggs said that he himself was offered the chance to ship out trophies under a friendly museum curator's special permit.[33] The game commission in 1930 opposed the granting of permits for scientific collecting to "institutions not of recognized standing" (in this case, Kansas State Teachers College of Pittsburg, Kansas). The privilege became especially galling to the commission in 1938, when it vigorously protested the issuance of a "scientific" permit to Polish Count Potocki (or anybody else) to take bears from Afognak Island. Forty-two scientific permits were issued in 1940, and only 115 nonresident big game hunting licenses.[34] Obviously, Alaskan game animals had reason to fear their supposed friends, the scientists, as well as their obvious enemies, the hunters and politicians.

Even more ominous for the future of Alaskan wildlife than poor science, a few poaching collectors, unfriendly politicians, and hungry hunters was an assortment of technologies that would have dazzled earlier American frontiersmen, and that raised questions about just how frontierlike Alaska was after the middle of the twentieth century. The most important tool of the hunter had been perfected before the gold rushes. For two hundred years, to the early nineteenth century, the common firearm was a single-shot, muzzle-loading flintlock that fired a ball. Beginning around 1820 the technology changed rapidly. By the end of the American Civil War, breech-loading repeating rifles and revolvers used ammunition consisting of a fixed cartridge with percussion cap and conoid bullet. Long-range, choke-bored, breech-loading shotguns appeared in the 1870s, and reliable repeating shotguns in the 1890s. As their power and accuracy increased, rifles and guns became available at a price affordable by almost anyone,[35] and their widespread use called for a response from conservationists.

Remarks often heard in opposition to the conservation of natural resources are: "We can't halt progress," or "We can't turn the clock back," or "We can't abandon our machines." American conservationists have resisted the implication in these platitudes that people should become the tool of their tools (in Henry David Thoreau's phrase). In fact, technological obsolescence and technological reaction have been successful policies in the drive to preserve and conserve. National parks and wildlife refuges have been created to "halt progress," laws requiring the use of older technologies in order to give the wild animals a fighting chance have "turned the clock back," and regulations prohibiting altogether the use of certain weapons or hunting techniques have, in effect, represented the abandonment of specific machines that do their job too well. Such policies were formally adopted early in the history of Alaskan game management.

The first comprehensive Alaskan game law, of 1902, made it unlawful to hunt with hounds, to use a shotgun larger than ten gauge, "or any gun other than that which can be fired from the shoulder." Only boats propelled by oars and paddles could be used lawfully in the hunt; the use of steam launches was forbidden. The revision of the law in 1908 retained these prohibitions. The law of 1925 establishing the game commission altered the rules slightly. The use of poison was outlawed. The ten-gauge remained the largest permissible shotgun. Hunters, in taking game animals and birds, could not "use any airplane, steam or power launch," only boats driven by oars, paddles, and poles. The secretary of agriculture, after consultation with the commission, was authorized to determine by what other means game animals could be taken.[36] In 1931 the commission's secretary recommended that machine guns and submachine guns be prohibited, and that shooting from a moving automobile be declared illegal. Regulations approved in 1941 made it illegal to shoot game within one-half mile of a road or of the Alaska Railroad, and other game reserves were established.[37]

The history of wildlife in the old American West is overflowing with evidence of the destructive influence of railroads. Wild creatures were shot to feed railroad construction laborers and to supply dining cars, shot as meat and hide for rail transport to markets, and shot to amuse trainmen and passengers. The railroads brought hunters and settlers to the heart of game country, where they destroyed animals that could be eaten or sold or that were in the way. In Alaska during construction days the railroad bought wild sheep killed legally for one of its mess halls, surveyors locating the right-of-way occasionally killed game to eat, and a few professional hunters were employed by contractors. But market hunting in general was discouraged because the game laws were already on the books when the tracks arrived. In Alaska the adverse impact of the railroad on wildlife was direct.

The Alaska Railroad is the only railroad of any consequence in the state. It runs about 500 miles from Seward, on Resurrection Bay in southcentral Alaska, through an eastern portion of the Kenai Peninsula northward by Anchorage to Fairbanks in the interior. It was built by the federal government. President Warren Harding drove the golden spike in 1923. The line is Uncle Sam's only railroad and is unique also because of the mortal damage it inflicts on moose. The trains killed 100 to 300 moose each year, and as many as 500 in years of heavy snowfall. About 60,000 pounds of dressed moose meat were shipped to public and charitable institutions every year, because the railroad was required to salvage as much of the meat as possible.

Moose that find themselves in the path of a train choose to escape by remaining on the track, either because they cannot get over high banks of snow alongside of the tracks or because they can run faster on the cleared right-of-way. The heaviest kills are at night. Trainmen have tried several expedients to drive the large creatures safely off the tracks, including a hotfoot administered with flares when the animals sit down in front of a locomotive and refuse to move. On occasion the moose have had their revenge. Once, when the temperature was forty-five degrees below zero Fahrenheit, a pregnant moose suddenly appeared on the track from behind a railroad building just as a train approached. The hapless cow was thrown against a switch stand; two engines, two baggage cars, and several passenger coaches were derailed.[38] The Alaska Railroad is nicknamed "The Moose-Gooser," a witticism wasted on the moose that were killed by trains and on the trainmen who confronted this singular occupational hazard.

If the railroad was a threat to the moose of Alaska, the highway was the caribou's worst man-made enemy. Frank Dufresne recommended in 1928 that Twelvemile Summit and Eagle Summit, of the Steese Highway between Fairbanks and Circle, be declared off limits to hunting. Caribou that pass there, he said, were exposed to merciless shooting from motorists in cars parked along the road. Nine years later Territorial Senator John Powers told the game commission that hunters were slaughtering caribou by the hundreds near the road and leaving the carcasses on the ground the rot. The caribou's fortunes depended upon whether they crossed the road during hunting season. If they did not, only a handful might be killed; if they did (as they did in 1947), as many as five hundred might be killed by the motorized gunmen.[39]

Other man-made communication routes also disturbed the caribou. Charles Sheldon told congressmen in 1918 how one herd encountered a telegraph line, did not want to pass under it, and instead ran along the line into mining camps near Fairbanks, where "people went out with axes and killed them right there and got their meat. Some of the caribou got their horns fastened in doors and were killed in that position."[40] Unstrung telegraph lines could be just as lethal. Olaus Murie found bulls who had hanged themselves on the abandoned wire after their antlers became entangled in it.[41]

Fortunately for the animals, in Alaska there were few telegraph lines or roads as late as 1940. The Richardson Highway from Valdez to Fairbanks, and the Steese, were ready for automobile traffic in the 1920s. Both traversed rich game country. Shorter highways connected Seward with Hope, and Anchorage with Palmer in the Matanuska Valley. Additional roads were in the immediate vicinity of towns.

Rivers were more numerous, and game along the main waterways was drastically reduced in number during the gold rushes. A tragic illustration of the impact of new transportation and weapon technologies on wildlife was witnessed in 1894 by a clergyman traveling by riverboat on the Shagaluk Slough of the Yukon River. The pilot blew the boat's whistle to draw his passengers' attention to several moose swimming across the stream: "In a few moments the whole front of the steamer was ablaze with repeating rifles, so that the poor things had no chance for life."[42] Small watercourses that could float paddleboats or outboard-powered craft provided access in season to much of the Alaskan bush.

A later improvement in transportation technology was even more dangerous to wildlife than outboard and inboard motors, steamboats, highways, or railroads. The airplane tamed Alaska, beginning in the twenties. Wilderness trips by dogsled or summer trips by boat that once took days or weeks could be made in a few hours or less by air. Alaska's lakes, rivers, dry stream beds, frozen watercourses, and snow-covered meadows became landing fields for a new kind of romantic pioneer— the bush pilot. Areas so remote that no hunting regulations applied, where certain species could make their last stand, became subject to hunting pressures, thanks to the airplane. Yet aircraft posed only a minor threat to game before the Second World War. The human population of Alaska was still small when the air age dawned, and air travel was expensive. Furthermore, one Alaskan warden seized quickly on the idea of using the airplane as a tool of law enforcement.

Sam O. White, game warden from Fairbanks, learned to fly in the twenties and bought a Swallow biplane in which he patrolled his own sector and sometimes the neighboring warden's sector also. By airplane he could certify legal beaver catches on several rivers, instead of only one, by boat. In addition to the wider coverage, patrol by air increased the element of surprise in enforcement. White, however, got little encouragement from the game commission for his efforts. The commission sometimes did and sometimes did not pay for his fuel during the early years. Later the commissioners chartered his airplane but were still reluctant to buy their own, or to pay for the training of pilots. Although an airplane was about the same price as a patrol boat (White recalled later), the commission continued to buy "a couple of bad river boats when it could have bought a couple good airplanes." It considered air patrolling too easy. Dufresne told White, "Our most successful agents travel on snowshoes." Eventually, however, the necessity rather than the advantages of using airplanes came to be appreciated. Aircraft were purchased, a new pilot-agent category of employment was created in 1940, and by 1944 Dufresne was boasting in print of how the Alaska Game Commission had pioneered the worldwide use of airplanes in game management.[43]

The use of airplanes by the game commission became a necessity because their use by hunters spread. Gus Gelles, secretary of the Alaska Guides Incorporated of Anchorage, tried an airplane hunt in the summer of 1928. It was, he told Biological Survey Chief Paul Reddington, too successful, and he hoped that airplane hunts would be outlawed. That same year nineteen big game guides from the Anchorage area petitioned the game commission to prohibit the transportation of hunters, hunting equipment, and dead game by air.[44] The commission was informed by legal counsel in Washington that the use of airplanes in the hunt itself might be declared illegal (it was in the law of 1925) but that outlawing the transportation of hunters and equipment to camp and back probably was not justifiable. For a while, therefore, the commission promoted a voluntary program of compliance. Wardens asked pilots not to fly over game, drive game, or fly hunters to otherwise inaccessible areas near game refuges.[45]

Airborne hunters continued to threaten supplies of wildlife as the game commission's request for cooperation was ignored by many pilots. By 1941 there were still no effective regulations against driving game with an airplane (to exhaust the animals and make them easier to kill, or to herd them to a suitable landing place where the game could be shot and packed aboard without much exertion). In 1944 sixty-two small planes were used by hunting parties in the Anchorage region alone. The commission received complaints that some pilots would spot game and drive it into the gunsights of hunters waiting on the ground. There was probably shooting from the air also. Two hunters on the Susitna River flats were shot at from the air, perhaps to discourage their competition for game.

By the end of the Second World War such stories had aroused public opinion and resulted in demands to prohibit altogether the use of aircraft by hunting parties. One suspicious measure of the comparative success of hunters traveling by air and hunters traveling on foot was reported in 1956; the former were 77 percent successful in killing caribou from the Nelchina herd, and the latter only 20 percent successful. Although recent regulations permit transportation but forbid driving, spotting, and shooting from the air, and although the commission moved in 1951 to prohibit the use of helicopters in killing or transporting game, the misuse of aircraft in hunting remains one of those appalling examples of man's inability to manage his own technologies.[46] Jay Hammond, formerly a guide and later governor of Alaska, wrote in 1969 that hunting by airplane "is often less venturesome by far than lady's night at little league."[47]

Meanwhile, airplanes continued to serve the game commission well as patrol vehicles, despite an occasionally ingenious attempt to foil the airborne wardens. One market hunter who had killed five moose illegally arranged the dead animals to appear from the air as though they were lying comfortably in the snow. The flying warden knew they were not, landed, and arrested the poacher. The agent had observed from above that two magpies were perched quietly on the antlers of one of the dead bulls.[48]

After the population changes initiated by the Second World War, the new technologies, especially in transportation and communication, did more than anything else to mark mid-century as the beginning of the end of frontier Alaska. Prior to the war, most Alaskans traveled to and from the States by ship. There was no highway connection, and the only airline connecton was not established until 1940. Following the war regular airline service by Northwest Airlines began between Asia, Anchorage, Seattle, and Minneapolis. An international airport was completed in Anchorage by the end of 1951; the military air base had been used until then. During the war, army engineers built numerous emergency airstrips throughout Alaska. They were maintained by the Civil Aeronautics Authority after the war for private airplanes, the use of which increased dramatically in the late 1940s. The army built a short branch line of the Alaska Railroad to Whittier, on Prince William Sound. Also during the war, army engineers constructed the Alaska Highway through Canada to the States. Inside Alaska new roads connected most of the population centers north of the Panhandle, opening huge wildlife habitats to access by auto. The new roads were not superhighways, but the introduction of four-wheel drive vehicles, the most famous of which was the jeep, made the roads and roadless areas nearby accessible. Where a road ended at a river or lake or salt water, motorized watercraft could continue man's penetration of the wilderness. At the same time, close verbal contact was possible with two-way radios. In such a technological environment the man / land ratio as a measure of the frontier's existence was meaningless, as was the conception of the frontier as a line, or boundary, between humans and the wilderness. About the only frontier characteristic remaining in Alaska shortly after the Second World War was the existence of large wildlife populations, and some subsistence hunting.

5
The Hunted

Until recently, the academic historians paid even less attention to game animals than did the biologists, and they exhibited little recognition of the role of wild meat on the advancing frontier. Plenty of history has been written about the economically important fishes and too much about fur-bearing animals (except those in Alaska), but historians have been reluctant to credit wild creatures that did not become an "industry" with any influence on the course of American history. Although we remember the wild meat eaten by the Pilgrims on Thanksgiving Day and the bison slaughtered to feed railroad construction workers, we hear little about how much the first Euro-Americans relied upon edible animals running wild near early settlements in the New World. Meat was one vital contribution of wildlife to European colonization. Before farms and cattle and pig ranches were established and transportation lines perfected to distribute food, the availability of game may have made the difference between the success or failure of a settlement. Further, animal populations that were decimated by pioneers made additional white settlement easier in Indian country. The Alaskan experience differed chiefly in that for years there were not enough people in the huge country to exterminate the game, the Natives joined the white hunters to threaten the supply of wild meat, and when increased settlement finally occurred conservation was already an established national policy capable of erecting obstacles to the senseless destruction common on earlier frontiers, and to slow down the killing.

In Alaska as well as outside, the animals were in danger because nobody knew exactly how many were there. Two official estimates of the total number of big game animals in the United States in 1941 differ by 1,000,000—5,850,000 and 6,748,424. Both calculations agree that about 90 percent were white-tailed deer. Among the remaining 10 percent were 550,000 elk and pronghorn antelope; Alaska had no antelope and only 200 transplanted elk. Of the remaining 162,000 large game animals in the States that year, Alaska had perhaps five times as many moose but there were still 11,800 in the States, three or four times as many mountain sheep but there were still 10,000 bighorns in the Rockies, about the same number of black bears (perhaps 100,000), slightly fewer mountain goats (12,500 to 16,400), and only 300 transplanted bison compared with nearly 5,000 in the States. Southern Alaskans hunted the Sitka deer, numbering some 40,000 animals in 1941. The Territory's most spectacular game animal—the brown bear, or grizzly—outnumbered its stateside relatives 18,500 to 1,200. The caribou population of Alaska had dwindled from Murie's million to a few hundred thousand, but *Rangifer* was still Alaska's most numerous big game animal and was to northern Alaskans what the deer came to be south of the forty-ninth parallel. Even counting the caribou, Alaska in 1941 probably contained less large game than Pennsylvania or Michigan.[1] What, then, made the Territory a special place for game in the popular mind—a last chance to save the wild creatures who had played so large a part in the earliest history of the European settlement of North America?

Part of the answer can be found in the memory of past abundance. Some American game species had been extinguished forever. Large areas in the Lower Forty-eight that had once hosted game animals supported in 1941 only the small, noxious quadrupeds—such as rats, mice, squirrels, and skunks—that thrive wherever man dominates the landscape. Other regions had some big game but not as much and not the variety those areas had once supported. Most of the big game stateside consisted of restored populations of deer. Impressive types have existed only in Alaska: the white mountain sheep, the polar bear, and the caribou. Some Alaskan versions of familiar animals were far larger than their relatives outside, in particular the moose and the brown bear. Equally important, stateside game species were often kept animals, in refuges or parks. In Alaska most were wild. A grizzly in the wilderness touches the imagination and strikes a different note of excitement than a black bear begging for food in Yellowstone National Park. Finally, the Alaskan game animals were interesting in their own right. The reader has already met the brown bear.

Less reliable information was available about the brown bear's smaller, unromantic cousin, the black bear. Frank Dufresne reported 75,000 in 1942. A state biologist in 1965 said nobody knew how many black bears were in Alaska, but an "educated guess" would be fewer than 15,000. The widely discrepant estimates were probably the result not so much of increased hunting pressures as of careless approximations due to the black bear's lowly position in the hierarchy of Alaskan game. Apparently the wildlife experts did not try very hard to count the despised animals carefully. Unlike the brown bear, the black was small (though the Boone and Crockett Club recorded an Alaska black, bagged in 1939, that was seven feet from the tip of its nose to the tip of its tail, with a skull more than fourteen inches long and nearly eight inches across).[2] The black was considered more or less harmless, and cowardly. It posed no threat to the health, only to the happiness, of humans.

But black bears were everywhere. They seemed to care very little about the low estimate humans placed upon their worth. When hungry, they were forever sticking their noses into human society, digging up garbage dumps or tearing apart the usually flimsy constructions of the newly arrived prospector, miner, trapper, or fisherman. To those Alaskan pioneers, the black bear was an expensive nuisance. If found around a human habitation, the bear was routinely shot. The experience of Mr. J. E. Wilson, the lone resident of Lake Nancy, in south-central Alaska, was not uncommon. Wilson was a kindly gentleman who liked animals. But there were limits to his patience. He wrote to the game commission in late August of 1938: "I gather, from reading the laws, rules, and regulations . . . that anyone who kills a black bear during closed season . . . shall report the matter to the Commission. Well, I have killed two black bear this summer. Each a big, old 'residenter' male, and each killed . . . in defense of my grub pile, camp furnishings, and, in fact, the cabin itself. . . . You may hear from me again on this subject, for these were not the only bear in Alaska, and with bear, at the present writing, I am not in a very good humor."[3]

The black bear had one social advantage over his larger relative. In a bluish color phase the black became a rare, sought-after, glacier bear. In a brown color phase the black bear could pass as the lovable cinnamon bear of children's literature, or as a small grizzly, especially when browsing exaggerated the humped back. Most probably the brown bear was blamed for some of the black's pestiferous behavior when the latter was seen in a brownish phase, for Alaskans would rather tell brown bear stories than black bear stories.

The black bear's habits and life cycle do not differ substantially from the grizzly's. The black is two or three feet high at the shoulders when standing on all four paws and weighs 200 to 400 or more pounds. It follows approximately the same reproduction procedures, has about the same food preferences, and engages in similar social activities as the brown bear; the main difference is that its smaller size and thinner hide require more prudent hunting techniques. It is primarily nocturnal, prefers the woods to open country, and is not found on certain islands in southeastern Alaska, the Kodiak Islands, and that part of the Alaska Peninsula where the big brown bears are concentrated.

One thing that irked some Alaskans was the black bear's legal classification as a fur-bearing animal, though its pelt was worth little on the market and almost nobody bothered to hunt it commercially. It was killed as a pest or a predator, for bait, sometimes for human food when it was on a diet of berries, as feed for domestic foxes, and for recreation, but rarely for its hide. The classification placed the black as a furry creature under the Department of Commerce in 1903, and then in 1920 under the Department of Agriculture's Bureau of Biological Survey.

The bureaucratic confusion was something that local politicians could cite as an example of federal inefficiency. The criticism was meaningless insofar as the bear was concerned, for no management of the black existed until 1934—no closed season and no bag limit.[4] The animal was finally designated big game in 1938, for reasons consistent with its maligned personality. Big game guides in the Panhandle thought that lazy stateside hunters on yachts cruising the Inside Passage would be satisfied with a black bear trophy.[5]

Like the black bear, the moose ranges over most of Alaska but avoids Kodiak Island and the islands in the Panhandle. Moose do venture into the upper Alaska Peninsula, where the big brown bears also live. Unlike the black bear, the moose is highly prized by Alaskans as a source of meat and by sportsmen looking for trophies. The reason that hunters value the moose is certainly not the animal's beauty. A more ungainly beast than a long-nosed, humpbacked, bearded moose is hard to find in Mother Nature's cupboard. If the camel is a horse designed by a committee, the moose is a horse designed by Congress. The black bear is gorgeous by comparison.

The reason for the moose's popularity among sportsmen is its immense size. The largest member of the deer family, it stands five to seven feet tall at the shoulders, and weighs 600 to 1,200 pounds. Males carry an enormous, flat, palmate rack of antlers that can measure nearly eighty inches across. Although the moose is not built like a racehorse, it is fast. It can swim as swiftly as two canoeists can paddle, and on land it has been clocked at speeds as high as thirty-five miles per hour. Males shed their antlers at the beginning of the new year, and lose their velvet in the fall, in time to fight other bulls for the right to mate with a cow. One to three calves, usually two, are born in May or June; they may remain with their mother for two years. During that time the cow moose is considered by some Alaskans to be a more dangerous animal than the brown bear.

A moose, if it avoids human and animal predators, can live twenty years wandering in the forest, near streams and lakes, browsing on young willow bushes, birch, and aspen, or what biologists call subclimax vegetation. The name *moose* comes from an American Indian word referring to the animal's habit of stripping off the bark of such plants. During the summer moose like to submerge in a lake, sometimes entirely, to feed on the bottom plants. A 1,200-pound moose will eat approximately one-half ton of food each month. An individualist, the moose is rarely seen in a group.[6]

The most famous moose in the world are residents of the Kenai Peninsula, easily accessible in south-central Alaska on the eastern shores of Cook Inlet. The earliest sportsmen who came to Alaska wanted most of all a Kenai moose trophy, and were willing to pay dearly for one. Under the Alaska game law of 1908, a nonresident citizen of the United States paid $50 for a big game license and was required to hire a guide while hunting on the Kenai. Foreigners paid $100 for their license. To ship a moose out of Alaska, the successful hunter paid $150 per animal for a shipping license. By the end of 1941, after a large take by hunters of 1,700 animals, and other losses due to predation, the estimated number of Kenai moose had dropped to 4,000. In December President Franklin Roosevelt created by executive order the Kenai National Moose Range, encompassing two million acres.[7]

Elsewhere in Alaska the moose were plentiful until the late nineteenth century, when hungry prospectors and Natives almost wiped out the species along well-traveled routes and near villages and camps. Moose were scarce in the Susitna Valley of central Alaska from about 1910 to the middle thirties, when they began to thrive in the region. By the early fifties they were plentiful in the best winter browsing districts of both the Kenai and the Susitna.[8]

The moose was a major source of game meat in those regions. In the Panhandle its more graceful little cousin, the black-tailed deer, provided the bulk of the wild mammalian meat consumed by residents. For many years more deer were killed annually than any other Alaskan big game animal, though moose meat often exceeded by weight the amount of deer meat consumed because a deer when dressed averaged 100 pounds, and a moose perhaps 600. In 1938 and 1939, 1,750 to slightly more than 2,000 deer were shot, and from 1941 through 1943, 5,000 to 6,000 each year. The numbers do not reflect a kill by some fish cannery, lumber mill, mine, or boat operators—Native or white—seeking outside the law to reduce their grocery bills and vary their diets.[9]

Clearly, the deer's worst enemy (aside from the weather) was humanity. The swift, delicate animal coexisted more comfortably with grizzlies and shared with them the marine alps along the spectacular fjords of Alaska's famous Inside Passage. Part of the reason was the bear's habit of coming down the mountain in the summer, when the deer went up. The smaller animal was also fast and timid and took advantage of the opportunities for concealment in the thick vegetation of the rain forest. The deer made modest dietary demands on the cover of dogwood, grasses, huckleberry bushes, and the like, consuming perhaps 150 pounds of plant life each month. It mates at the end of the year and the male sheds his antlers soon thereafter. Following a gestation period of seven months, the doe gives birth to one, two, or three fawns. They will, if undisturbed, live ten to sixteen years.

Another member of the deer family indigenous to Alaska is the principal source of land-based game meat in the Far North, and is in many ways the most attractive of the Cervidae (hoofed mammals with antlers that are shed, who chew their cud). The caribou exists nowhere else in the United States and is Alaska's most numerous big game animal. It is hardy and the male is polygamous. Both male and female have antlers, which made it difficult for hunters to distinguish the sex of their target, if they cared. And the caribou is exceedingly gregarious, migrating in herds that can number in the thousands.

The barren-ground caribou's problems and to a degree its history parallel the troubles of the buffalo, a conclusion that Olaus Murie drew very early in his study of the former animal. Both the bison and the caribou migrated in large numbers, both were easy to see in the short vegetation they liked, and both were prized by settlers and Natives. Alaskan Natives ate the flesh, made warm clothing from the caribou's heavy coat, leather from the skin, and bone implements from the antlers and skeleton. The leather shrinks when it dries and is therefore valuable as snowshoe lacing.

The gold rushes threatened the caribou as they threatened every other wild creature in Alaska that was edible, salable, or underfoot, but there was still room in the Arctic and subarctic for the caribou to hide, and neither white nor Native knew much about the animal's habits. Unlike the bison, the caribou's main enemies were not human hunting and human technology, or even natural predation. Range fires, plus the animal's own fertility, appetite, and closest relative—the reindeer—explain the sudden and tragic decline in the caribou population beginning in the mid-thirties.

In 1921 Murie estimated the number of caribou in the Yukon Territory and Alaska at hundreds of thousands. The animal was thriving, all too well, as Lawrence Palmer quickly learned from his study of caribou foods. Every month a 250-pound caribou ate about 300 pounds of willows, sedges, grasses, blueberry and cranberry bushes, and—most of all—lichen.[10] In the fall a male caribou (which could weigh as much as 400 pounds, be seven feet long, and stand more than four feet tall at the shoulders) fights ferociously for a harem of five to forty females, each of which gives birth to one or two young during the next summer. Life expectancy is about fifteen years if the food supply is sufficient. It was not sufficient in the forties. Too many animals relied upon a fragile forage, and not all of them were caribou.

Domesticated reindeer from Siberia invaded part of the caribou's range beginning in the late nineteenth century, thanks to the well-meaning but uninformed political influence of Sheldon Jackson, a Presbyterian missionary and federal education chief of Alaska. The missionary's determination to save the Eskimos from what he thought were degraded living conditions and starvation caused by the commercial depletion of marine mammals helped significantly to stimulate an ecological disaster. Jackson knew next to nothing about Eskimo culture, the indigenous economics of northern Alaska, or its biology. His lack of expertise did not prevent him from trying to civilize and feed coastal Eskimos by importing reindeer from Siberia and Laplanders from Scandinavia to teach Alaskan Natives the arts and rewards of herding.[11]

During a ten-year period, to 1902, 1,280 reindeer were transported from Siberia to Alaska. Under Native and white ownership, the smaller, docile reindeer multiplied because food was plentiful. By 1926 there were perhaps 350,000 of them. Eventually the number may have topped one-half million. A small local market offered twenty cents a pound for reindeer meat, and 938 tons were shipped to the States between 1918 and 1925. Approximately 30,000 reindeer were shipped out from 1928 through 1930. At the same time the caribou increased to the one million or so animals estimated by Murie. Where the range was overgrazed by reindeer or caribou or destroyed by fire, reindeer and caribou began to starve by the thousands. By 1950 there were about 25,000 reindeer left, and Murie's million caribou had shrunk to an estimated 160,000 head.

There were other ecological ramifications, in addition to the dramatic crash in population. Not even the most experienced herdsman could always prevent his reindeer from answering a call from the wild caribou and running off. Perhaps the most talented white herder of Eskimo-owned caribou, Ben Mozee, when driving between 1,000 and 2,000 reindeer to Broad Pass in the interior during the early twenties, made a habit of lassoing caribou bulls and tying them to a tree by their antlers until his reindeer passed safely by. Such expedients could not prevent an intermingling of the animals that produced a hybrid offspring less resistant to the harsh natural conditions of Alaska. Some biologists are now reluctant to distinguish between the two creatures where the crosses do exist,[12] and what we now call caribou might, in some places, be more accurately designated carideer or reinbou.

The experiment was socially as well as biologically disruptive. Caribou were killed and their flesh peddled as reindeer meat. Very soon Jackson began to encourage white ownership of reindeer,[13] perhaps because he became dimly aware of the difficulty of making shepherds out of whale hunters overnight, even a long, Arctic night. The policy made human rivalries as inevitable on the open lichen ranges of Alaska as they had been among cattlemen, or between shepherds and cattlemen on the unfenced

Great Plains; except in one way they were more so: hot branding of reindeer was not feasible and earmarking was no solution.[14] Nobody knew exactly who owned what. Prospectors and trappers—white and Native—who ate or fed their dogs caribou quarreled with Eskimos and whites who claimed private ownership of reindeer that could not be identified, that could not always be distinguished from caribou, and that drove caribou away. In 1938, after the government eased white entrepreneurs out of the reindeer business, a resident of Kotzebue, north of the Arctic Circle, claimed that federal teachers and employees of the Reindeer Service were urging Eskimos to kill caribou to save the reindeer.[15] Finally—although competition from the reindeer was not the sole reason for the caribou's fate—the Natives and whites who subsisted on the wild animal would surely have suffered more seriously from its sharp decline and would have lost far more than they ever gained from the imported reindeer if an upswing in the economy resulting from the Second World War had not intervened.

The white, streamlined member of the bear family that touched Alaska near where the caribou roamed was more precious on the sportsman's scale of values than caribou, even though it was classified as a fur-bearing animal, not as big game. A polar bear can weigh 1,000 pounds, stand four feet tall, and measure seven feet from end to end. It behaves more like a seal than a bear, spending most of its time at sea on the ice floes hunting fish and marine mammals. When it does came ashore, it rarely travels very far inland. The polar bear mates biennially and has a life span of approximately thirty years.

During the early part of this century nobody seemed to have a clear idea of how many polar bears visited Alaska. Apparently, until well after the Second World War, when aerial hunting began, the number of Alaskan white bears taken each year was much lower than the number killed in Canada and Norway. In 1925, 190 polar bear pelts were shipped out of Alaska. Between 1925 and 1937, in only three years were 100 bears taken and in only five years were more than 50 killed. Most were shot by Eskimos who liked the meat. Dufresne estimated the total population of polar bears in Alaska to be 3,000 in 1937. Since the late 1950s, increased hunting for the expensive hide has added Nanook's name to the list of endangered species.[16]

The two remaining big game animals in Alaska were almost as scarce and almost as difficult to find as the polar bear. One—the white Dall sheep—was a favorite trophy of many sportsmen because of the skill and stamina required to capture the animal in its mountainous retreats, and because of the sheep's majestic head, crowned on the mature male by two thick horns sweeping around the ears in a nearly complete circle. The length of the horn's curve could measure as much as forty-seven inches. The Dall sheep was killed for meat as well as for sport and trophy, on its vast habitat stretching along the rugged mountain ranges of continental Alaska.

The sheep's attractiveness as a trophy animal never seriously threatened its existence, but its utility as cheap food for immigrants during the gold stampedes into the Alaska Range did cause its population to decrease alarmingly. In the thirties the annual reported kill was small, usually around 200. Dufresne's estimate in 1937 for the National Resources Committee was 40,000 sheep throughout the Territory. Three years later the number of sheep taken by hunters doubled. Bad weather, the increased hunting, and predation reduced the population sharply in the 1940s. Biologists (in what was probably the first reliable census for both sheep and caribou) reported fewer than 12,000 of the magnificent animals still around in 1950.[17]

A ram weighing two hundred pounds will eat about six pounds of willows, sedges, grasses, lichens, blueberries, and similar plants each day.[18] The ewe is small, with smaller horns. Mountain sheep travel in small groups. In early winter they gather on some relatively flat portion of their highland homes, and the rams duel for possession of a harem. Loud thwacks echo off the slopes as they slam into each other headfirst with such force that occasionally one of the combatants is killed. Mating follows, and in the spring from one to three young are born. Frank Dufresne believed that Dall sheep were intelligent as well as farsighted and surefooted.

The sheep's south-central territory overlaps that of the shaggy, white, short-horned, bearded mountain goat. Horizontally, the goat's range in Alaska extends from the Kenai Peninsula through the southern coastal mountains and mainland of southeastern Alaska. Vertically, the goat prefers the highest crags and slopes above timberline. For decades the isolated habitat and the animal's agility protected it from hunters and the intruding eyes of scientists. Very little was known about its population, private habits, and temperament. Modern descriptions of it still contain a few "probablies." It was "probably" monogamous. Snowslides were "probably" its worst enemy. It is not a true goat but a goat-antelope. It is larger than the mountain sheep by one hundred pounds but lacks the latter's beauty, grace, and daring. Goats prefer the company of their own kind, in small bands. Dufresne once saw a goat, using its short, pointed horns, calmly toss a wolf off the side of a mountain and then quietly continue grazing. The kids learn fast: they can stand, nurse, and jump all within thirty minutes of birth.

The domesticated goat's wild progenitor is the ibex of Asia, North Africa, and Europe. The ibex looks more or less like the evil-eyed backyard goat, except that its horns rise dramatically from its head, on a slight curve, as much as three feet. Although its presence wild in the Western Hemisphere is not acknowledged by zoologists, sightings of the ibex in Alaska threatened in the early twentieth century to become as frequent as reports of the Abominable Snowman have become more recently. In response to one ibex report dated 1925, Edward Nelson replied: "It is interesting and amusing to know that the legendary ibex has again appeared in the mountains of Alaska. . . . The great difficulty in dealing with this wonderful game animal in America is the fact that . . . no one has ever yet actually taken one alive or found one dead."[19]

Among Alaskan small game animals, the welfare of migrating waterfowl stimulated an early interest in Alaskan game generally. After the "duck egg fake," continental populations of waterfowl plummeted in the mid-thirties to 27 million. By the end of the war the number had risen to more than 100 million. Dufresne's rough Alaskan estimate, in 1937, of 30 million migratory ducks, geese, brants, swans, and cranes included some waterfowl that did not leave the Territory during the winter. According to a game commission estimate in 1949, 300,000 ducks and geese wintered in southern Alaska.[20]

Grouse and ptarmigan are also residents. Their populations, and the population of rabbits too, are cyclical, peaking about every eight or nine years. Between the years 1938–39 and 1941–42 the number of hunters reporting their small game catch doubled (from 6,000 to 11,500), and the number of grouse and ptarmigan killed increased about seven times (from 11,000 to 80,000). The number of rabbits taken increased three and one-half times during the same period (from about 7,000 to 24,500).[21] The figures, though imperfect, make clear how important small game as well as big game was to the burgeoning wartime population of *Homo sapiens*, and how much the new immigrants might affect older attitudes toward Alaska's game.

In size, another class of Alaskan wildlife fell between the small and the big game. They were among the hunted and were hunters too. Called predators, they were obnoxious to every other hunter, to the sportsman and the subsistence hunter, to other wildlife, to settlers, and to real estate speculators. Yet, in a sense, the use of the term *predator* is unfair to these animals because predation (as Ortega y Gasset averred) occurs along the entire zoological scale that includes man. Human predators may have hunted certain species to extinction in late Paleolithic times,[22] and most Alaskans who hunted before the Second World War hunted for food. Here the term *predator* is used to mean those animals and birds that prey on other animals and birds considered by man to be more desirable for economic reasons.

Predator control was not a new idea in the early twentieth century, when the Bureau of Biological Survey began to spend a large portion of its time and budget on the destruction of animals noxious to man. From almost the beginning of the English colonization of North America, rewards, or bounties, were offered for the lives of predators. Bounty laws date back to 1630.[23] Interest in predator control by the Bureau of Biological Survey quickened in the latter part of the nineteenth century as farmers in the West began to complain about wolves, coyotes, rodents, and predatory birds. In 1899 the American National Live Stock Association in Denver advocated a uniform and universal bounty system. The bureau cooperated with state agencies but came to favor the employment of professional hunters rather than a catch-as-catch-can bounty system.[24]

The bounty system was criticized for both economic and ecological reasons. A study by Theodore Palmer, of the Biological Survey, published in 1896, emphasized the economic inefficiency of bounties; at the same time, he admitted that general costs and effects were unknown. C. Hart Merriam did a clever cost-benefit analysis of Pennsylvania's system. He claimed the state had spent $90,000 over a period to destroy hawks and owls that killed rodents and other pests and were therefore worth $3,857,130 to the farmers, all in order to save $1,875 worth of poultry.[25]

Merriam's analysis introduced ecological (at this date, read "balance of nature") considerations, which came to dominate the criticism of predator control by some scientists. Should time and nature, without man's intervention, be allowed to keep in check all animal populations, or should certain animals be exterminated or severely reduced in number as dangerous in a habitat where natural balance could no longer be reestablished? The issues split the mammalogists, alienated civil scientists from government scientists, farmers from bureaucrats and biologists, easterners from westerners, sportsmen from sportsmen, utilitarian conservationists from preservationists, and sentimental nature lovers from everybody else. There was gory evidence of the destructiveness of the predators, and evidence also of the danger of exterminating them, as in the Kaibab National Forest of Arizona, where protected deer overpopulated their range and nearly destroyed it.[26]

Conflicting evidence helped to generate the controversies, but underlying influences of this period (roughly the late twenties to the early thirties) were more important. The rationalization of game management was under way. Modern ecological theories were emerging. Evolutionary theory and genetics were being synthesized. Mammalogy was struggling for legitimacy as a scientific discipline. Farmers were hurting financially. The national economy was wobbling. The sportsmen's fields were shrinking. Conservation as a federal program was a generation old and up for reappraisal. Predation was an emotional issue that reflected these changes and uncertainties. Also at this time—more precisely, the summer of 1927—the Bureau of Biological Survey began a predator control program in cooperation with the Territory of Alaska.

The Territorial legislature had authorized a ten-dollar bounty on wolves in 1915; two years later the reward was raised by five dollars and it remained fifteen dollars until 1929, when it was lowered to ten dollars, and a five-dollar bounty was approved for coyotes. In addition, the Seattle Fur Exchange offered hunters a total of $1,000 in prizes for the most predators taken in 1929. The Territorial bounty was fifteen dollars a head for either wolf or coyote in 1931 and twenty dollars in 1935. In the latter year the legislature appropriated $40,000 for two years, but the amount was quickly exhausted and a $45,000 supplementary appropriation was necessary. In January 1937, $80,000 in Territorial funds were allotted for two years, and $15,000 for cooperative work with the Bureau of Biological Survey; again a large—$50,000—deficiency appropriation was needed to finish the biennium.[27]

The dates and the sums are important. In this period of national depression, bounty hunting was an occupation. Income from trapping fur-bearing animals was down, and trappers begrudged every pelt and every moose steak lost to a predator. To certain Natives the income from bounties was especially important during these years.

That is not to say that wolf and coyote predation was negligible and bounty hunting purely a phenomenon of the depression. Game commission wardens thought the problem was serious and taught Alaskans how to capture predators more efficiently. Complaints against the wolves were commonplace in the commission's mail. The commissioners were told that deep snows around Lake Minchumina made moose, caribou, and sheep easy prey for wolf packs. From Nenana, also in the interior: "If I don't get permission to trap . . . [wolves] after the season closes on other fur I will trap without it, or do you think its best for all of us to turn outlaws and try and kill off the last furbearer and game animal there is, and then quit the country and let the Indians and wolves have it?"[28]

Feelings were running high in the Territorial legislature early in 1939, when the wolf and coyote bounties were continued at twenty dollars each. The senate enacted another memorial to give the Territory full authority over fur and game. The memorial was justified by an alleged need to deal more adequately with predators. Altogether, between 1915 and 1950, the Territory paid $500,000 in bounties for wolves and coyotes.[29]

Meanwhile, pressures on the National Park Service moved that agency to hire Adolph Murie in 1939. As always, Mount McKinley National Park was said to be a breeding ground for wolves, which were blamed for a sudden decline in the number of Dall sheep in the park. Murie's study began in April 1939 and was completed in August 1941. The results were published in 1944. They did not terminate the controversy. They prolonged it.

Caribou and mountain sheep were the principal food of the wolf, Murie reported. The wolf preyed on lambs and calves, as well as on the older and diseased sheep and caribou. Wolves took a "heavy toll" of caribou calves. Nevertheless, the caribou was "maintaining its numbers." Predation on lambs was "the most important limiting factor" on the population of sheep in the park. Those populations had been reduced markedly during the winters of 1929 and 1932, after thriving for several years of relatively mild weather. But the reduction in the number of sheep resulted from deep, encrusted snow and starvation more than from wolf predation. Such predation, Murie concluded, was beneficial to the sheep as a species. The two animals, he contended, had a normal predator-prey relationship over the long haul.[30]

Murie's investigation did not resolve the controversy over wolf predation control. It emphasized the ecological function of the predator, not the economic and dietary preferences that humans had for sheep. The study widened the distance between the average Alaskan hunter and the scientific ecologist. Another study, undertaken during the summer of 1952 by A. Starker Leopold and F. Fraser Darling, separated the two camps still more. This time predation was blamed for a great crash in the populations of Alaskan caribou and reindeer that began in the thirties, but Leopold and Darling concluded that range conditions, not predators, explained the crash, and once again general ecological conditions rather than hunting (the explanation favored by preservationists) or predators (the guilty parties according to hunters) fueled the debate over predator control.[31]

The chief villain in the piece was *Canis lupis*, the gray, or timber, wolf. The animal ranges in color from almost white to nearly black, is about four feet long (not counting a bushy tail), stands more than two feet high at the shoulders, and weighs from seventy to more than one hundred pounds. Wolves hunt in packs, and range widely. Each spring the female gives birth to about one-half dozen pups after a short, nine-week gestation. Very few wolves are left in the contiguous United States.

A lesser villain in the story of four-footed hunting in Alaska was the coyote, a late immigrant from Canada and the States that arrived soon after the gold rushes, following trails of carrion and garbage left by the miners. The coyote was reported on the Stikine River, in southeastern Alaska, in 1899 and was seen in Alaska near the border farther north between 1915 and 1917. It soon spread over most of the Territory, even into the Arctic. Coyotes are energetic scavengers and will eat almost anything, but they subsist mainly on squirrels, mice, and rabbits. In 1941

Frank Dufresne reported the results of an examination of twenty-six coyote stomachs: 31 percent of the contents were rabbit, 29.6 percent carrion (chiefly moose meat), 25.4 percent rodents, 9.8 percent birds, 3.6 percent livestock (sheep wool), and 0.6 percent miscellaneous animal matter. Of eighty-four coyote scats analyzed in 1952, 57 percent contained hare remains, 20 percent sheep remains, and 19 percent moose remains.[32]

Coyotes are smaller than wolves, perhaps three feet in length, weighing twenty to fifty pounds (according to William Henry Burt's most recent *Field Guide to Mammals*). Five to ten pups are born in the spring after a two-month gestation. Coyotes have lived as long as eighteen years in captivity. The animal has a pointed face. Unlike the wolf, which hunts in a group, with its tail high as it runs, the coyote prefers solitude and holds its bushy tail down between its legs when running, which may explain in part the sneaky, cowardly reputation of this unloved canine.

Other animals too were the objects of scorn as predators. The bears have already been discussed in detail. A warden in the Yukon-Kuskokwim region asserted in 1931 that gulls were "one of the worst enemies ducks and geese have," along with foxes, minks, and otters.[33] In 1952 it was estimated that approximately 10 percent of the waterfowl were lost in the nesting stage to gulls and jaegers (the latter resembling a dark gull). Glaucous gulls were considered the worst predators. The gullets and stomachs of 149 glaucous gulls were examined and revealed that 68 percent had eaten ducks, geese, and other birds.[34]

Two more predatory Alaskan animals deserve special attention because of their ties to human institutions—one to the family and one to the nation. The latter received a great deal of publicity. Predation by the former was rarely mentioned in public because of its honored place as a friend of man.

Bears, wolves, and coyotes were often blamed for predatory activities committed by domestic dogs. Ironically, the despised wolf and the beloved dog are close relatives. A sociobiologist writes: "The intensely social nature of wolves, their eagerness to express submission by groveling and ritual licking, their readiness to follow the leadership of a dominant animal, and their habit of hunting in packs preadapted them to become symbiotic companions of man."[35] In short, the same characteristics that brought the wolf as predator into disrepute endeared the dog to man and protected the dog's predation from criticism, though not entirely.

Most people were aware of the dog's propensity to hunt. Dogs took their toll of domestic livestock on Kodiak during the Russian period. An American rancher on the island admitted that his dog, not brown bears, had killed several of his sheep. In 1916 two residents of Kenai, where one hundred dogs made their headquarters, observed five moose carcasses partly chewed on by dogs and saw the dogs giving chase. In 1928 a guide complained about twice that number of dogs running loose at Kenai.[36] Similar stories were not unfamiliar to Alaskans, but no campaign to eradicate killer dogs was mounted, not even a program to restrain dogs that might kill economically desirable wildlife. The situation was complicated in a country where dogs were an important form of transportation. Sled dogs were often fed big game meat when fish was not available—and sometimes when it was.

The conflict over control of predation by the eagle was another matter. For more than thirty years, debate about the national bird's behavior in Alaska, and about the behavior of Alaskan officials toward the eagle, was public and loudly acrimonious. The bald eagle and the golden eagle (the two are often confused in the historical documents) are among the largest birds of North America. Alaskan eagles are larger than southern eagles, have wingspans more than eighty inches across, weigh about twelve or thirteen pounds, and may live for fifteen years. Their principal food is fish, mostly salmon, probably only 10 percent of which is alive when captured. The remainder is carrion. The bird supplements its diet by consuming other birds that are unable to defend themselves, young deer, and miscellaneous small animals.[37]

Many Alaskans were convinced that eagles preyed on valuable fur-bearing animals in the wild, and on domesticated foxes. Edward Nelson, in an article published in 1914, said they destroyed fox pups; he changed his mind later.[38] Alaskan fishermen often accused the national bird of depleting the salmon and were disinclined to believe that eagles ate primarily carrion, usually salmon dying on the creek banks after spawning. One sighting of an eagle seizing a salmon in the air as it jumped out of salt water could be dramatic enough to throw doubt on the scientists' opinions, and catching an eagle in the act of robbing a set net for salmon might invite the use of a rifle.

The legislative reaction between 1917 and 1940 was a bounty program that paid out almost $100,000 for evidence of the deaths of 103,459 eagles. A federal law approved in 1940 protected bald eagles under the jurisdiction of the United States everywhere except in Alaska. Killing eagles in the Territory, Governor Ernest Gruening said later, "had become more or less of an established custom." In 1941, perhaps as a patriotic gesture, the Territorial appropriation for bounties was rescinded, and no money was allotted in 1943; in 1945 the bounty law was repealed.

William Egan, a businessmen who would soon become the first elected governor of Alaska, introduced a new, two-dollar bounty law in the Territorial legislature and it passed overwhelmingly in 1949. Governor Gruening let the bill become law without his signature, because he shared the sentiment associated with the eagle as a national symbol, because he thought the two-dollar fee would be a drain on the budget, and because he believed those biologists who said that the eagle was not a serious predator.[39]

Throughout most of the history of the eagle bounty law the Bureau of Biological Survey and other naturalists had tried to encourage Alaskan politicians to abandon the system as uneconomical and unnecessary. Alfred Bailey, the agency's first resident naturalist, inquired around Alaska in 1920 and concluded that eagles were mainly scavengers. After Bailey, wardens and naturalists began to doubt out loud the need for an eagle bounty. Olaus Murie and two investigators studied the Aleutian Island eagles in 1936 and 1937. Hosea Sarber collected bald eagle stomachs for the game commission in 1940, 1942, and 1943. From this evidence laboratory scientists were able to determine the bird's diet, and the evidence did not support the fears of Alaskans that eagles were economically significant predators.[40]

Although the evidence did not persuade Alaskan legislators, over the years the eagle's case was heard sympathetically by a variety of outsiders. In the twenties Mr. Flying Eagle Strong, of the American Indian Association, told Alaska's governor that his organization condemned the bounty on eagles. A boy whose letterhead identified him as "America's Youngest Author" wrote to protest the bounty in the name (he said) of the twenty million children of America.[41] Governor Gruening was informed in 1941 that the Fraternal Order of Eagles objected to the bounty.[42] After Egan's renewal of the bounty, a lady in Denver introduced an argument that was embarrassing to the local politicians: "The Alaska legislature, hoping to become the 49th state under the wings of the eagle, nevertheless voted Wednesday to place a bounty on eagles." She called attention to the sentiments of one Territorial legislator, Frank Barr, who defended the bird: "For the privilege of seeing them impressively in flight, I'm willing to throw them a few fish."[43]

Barr's aesthetic appreciation of the avian wild was not shared by most of his colleagues in the statehouse in 1949. Of the Territorial senators who voted for the bounty (the tally was twelve to three in favor, with one member absent), one was a Native in the fishing business, one was Alaska's first woman senator, who was also a member of the Alaska Sportsmen's Association, and one was a wildlife photographer and sometime outdoors writer. Although no regional pattern is detectable in the vote, almost all the senators were townsmen.[44]

6
The Motives

At no time during the controversies over the game laws was there any loud expression of sympathy for the large and small animals as "worthy of respect in their own right as fellow members of the world community of living things" (in the words of Fraser Darling). The reasons advanced to justify preservation of game in Alaska were usually practical and Aristotelian. There was no nonsense about "the rights of rocks." As an ethical question conservation was supported by reference to its value for mankind. Ethics was assumed to be a human invention to solve human problems, and man's ideas of right and wrong could not be applied to animals. The animals should be managed in the interest of man. That was the central message, the core philosophy of the pioneers in Alaskan game protection.[1]

The utilitarian argument for game management was chiefly economic. Game species should be protected to yield an annual surplus that could be cropped by Alaskans, white and Native. Unlike American sportsmen hunting below Canada's southern border, Alaskans hunted more for food than for recreation. Even townspeople, who did not need game for survival, often counted on wild meat during the Great Depression or when supplies of imported meat were interrupted by, for example, shipping strikes. A moose could dress out at six hundred pounds of choice meat. At the high price of beef in Alaskan stores the monetary value of the animal represented a substantial supplement to the family income at any time.

In 1938, 10,900 licensed resident hunters killed 4,260 big game animals, not including bears, and 33,340 ducks, geese, ptarmigan, and grouse. Allowing 500 pounds for a moose, 200 for a caribou, 100 for a dressed deer, goat, or sheep, and 2 pounds for each bird, white Alaskans consumed 986,000 pounds of big game and wildlife meat, or 25 pounds for every non-Native man, woman, and child in the Territory, or a month's supply of meat. Given the price of imported meat, the dollar value of the game was significant too; it may have been 10 percent of the annual per capita personal income of many Alaskans. The figures represent only the reported, legal catches, at a time when about 30 percent of the trappers and about 60 percent of the licensed resident hunters failed to report.[2]

Frank Dufresne (following the lead of conservationists outside) regularly estimated the value of Alaskan game taken during the Second World War to illustrate one contribution of game management to the war effort. In 1941, 10,000 big game animals (not including bears), 176,000 game birds, and 25,000 rabbits were killed by hunters for food. The game when dressed weighed about 2,400,000 pounds and was valued at $1,000,000. In 1943, 1,244 tons of dressed wild meat were logged, for an estimated value of $1,370,000.[3] Clarence Rhode, one of Dufresne's successors, estimated conservatively the dollar value of big Alaskan game used as meat to be $2,500,000 in 1948. Eighty-four families homesteading on the Kenai Peninsula reported as late as 1955 that moose meat was worth nearly $400 per family, or 10 percent of the family income.[4]

The dollar estimates of kill figures do not include game taken by Natives. By the Second World War, some of the Tlingit Indians of the Panhandle, Tanaina Athapaskans of Cook Inlet, Koniags of Kodiak, and coastal Eskimos had become commercial fishermen. Other Natives held wage-paying jobs, at least part of the year. Still others sold the products of Native art and craftsmanship. But most Natives still relied heavily on wildlife, on hunting and gathering. Wildlife protection was construed during the New Deal period as part of the central government's responsibility for the Natives' welfare. Many could not have survived without game animals, especially in the interior.[5]

A second economic argument for game preservation on a sustained yield basis was the value to Alaska of nonresident big game hunting. To determine the economic impact of hunting by stateside sportsmen, the Bureau of Biological Survey mailed questionnaires to sportsmen who had hunted in the Territory between 1914 and 1922. Forty-four responded. They had made, collectively, fifty-two trips to Alaska, spending an average of nearly $2,000 per trip and taking 312 animals. The total spent was about $108,000, which broke down to approximately $5,000 for hunting and export licenses and $102,500 for guides, outfits, and miscellaneous expedition-related costs. The average expenditure to the hunter for each animal was more than $325. Expenditures by scientific and exploring parties were not counted. Seven of the forty-four hunters had become financially interested in some Territorial industry since their hunt. One editor of the Juneau *Daily Empire* thought that this was, altogether, a good thing.[6] The poll was the beginning, mathematical discrepancies and all, of official attempts to weigh the dollar value of game animals to Alaskans.

Similar economic pleading was introduced during political scuffles between Kodiak cattlemen and the game commission. A more sophisticated study of the dollar value of wildlife in general, undertaken in the 1950s as one of the early projects of the Cooperative Wildlife Research Unit, affirmed that recreational hunting and fishing by residents and nonresidents was an important industry indeed. Nonresidents paid perhaps $880,000 during 1957 to sport hunt and fish. The food value of wildlife in remote areas was approximately $3,250,000 in that year, and residents and nonresidents may have spent $17,000,000 in 1957 as sportsmen and sportswomen.[7]

A third economic justification for preserving the animals was their attractiveness to tourists, who spent cash to view the Alaskan wild. More than 25,000, for $100 each, traveled the Inside Passage of southeastern Alaska between 1884 and 1890, urged northward by publicists such as Sheldon Jackson and John Muir.[8] Tourism beyond the Panhandle was restricted by high prices during the gold rushes, by distances, and by the absence of roads and railroads until the 1920s. In 1940, 35,000 people visited various parts of Alaska, many expecting to see big game.[9]

The existence of wild animals enhances the recreational value of natural landscapes. True, the animals may hide from view. But knowledge alone of their presence increases enjoyment of the land and certifies its classification as wilderness. Aldo Leopold could not "by logical deduction, prove that a thicket without the potential roar of a quail covey is only a thorny place. Yet every outdoorsman knows that this is true." Part of the explanation lies in the importance of contrasting environments, or change, to recreation.[10] Wildlife increases the wildness of wilderness and points up the contrast between wilderness and the man-made, artificial societies from which many people seek to escape on their vacations. Another part of the explanation is the fear and therefore the excitement of possible exposure to certain big game animals, even at a distance. Still another reason why wildlife is important to outdoor recreation is the aesthetic reaction stimulated by the animals. This is eloquently demonstrated by the large place that wild creatures occupy in the art of Alaska. Perhaps the anticipation of a social benefit also helps to explain why wildlife is important to the landscape. Wildlife stories are trophies. To return with a bear story is as rewarding socially as to bring back a bear skin; in fact, the physical trophy only documents the story, which is more important. The pages of the *Alaska Sportsman* (now *Alaska*) contain ample evidence of the urge to tell and the desire to hear outdoor adventure stories of life among the wild animals.

Noneconomic arguments for game protection called upon justice, patriotism, and Darwin to support the cause, and on usufruct, nationalism, and evolution. Usufruct—the right to enjoy and use something without harming it—was invoked indirectly, not by its ugly name. Alaskan conservationists apparently did not quote Thomas Jefferson's epigram "The earth belongs in usufruct to the living" (that is, to have and to use but to pass along unharmed and unencumbered to later generations), but the idea was there.[11] Ernest Walker reminded all his fur wardens in 1921: "No people or generation should forget that it is their duty to pass on to posterity all that can be saved of our wildlife, for future generations likewise have a claim on it"; and Frank Dufresne thought in 1937 that Alaska's wildlife "should continue to be utilized to the greatest possible degree consistent with maintaining a safe breeding supply for those who follow in our footsteps."[12] Dufresne put the following words into the mouth of a hypothetical Alaskan sourdough: "Help us keep this kind of fishing. Your own boy might want to come up here some day." It was a northern echo of Aldo Leopold, writing about the same time: "I am glad I shall never be young without wild country to be young in. Of what avail are forty freedoms without a blank spot on the map?"[13]

Most of the few blank spaces left were in Alaska. If the animal life that inhabited wilderness areas were to be preserved under the American flag, wrote Dufresne, "it must be done in Alaska where not only are there suitable climatic and geographic conditions but where the all-important factor of space is favorable. Kodiak bears and Dall rams may not be propagated in backyard bush patches like cottontail rabbits." He went on to say that unique animals must be preserved as a reminder of our national heritage: "We still have our hundreds of thousands of caribou, as the West once had its buffalo. Our willow ptarmigan of the northern tundras still darken the skies as their passenger pigeons once did. The lordly white dall ram strides Alaska's peaks like their bighorns once did the Rockies. Our moose are as widespread as their wapiti used to be. Our bears are more varied and plentiful than anything the West ever knew." Again, the sentiment expressed by Dufresne may be compared with the writing of Aldo Leopold about the cultural advantages of wilderness generally: "There is value in any experience that reminds us of our distinctive national origins and evolution, i.e., that stimulates awareness of history. Such awareness is 'nationalism' in its best sense." Alaska was a last chance to preserve a part of American history; and, said Leopold, it was not necessary for everyone to experience Alaska firsthand: "To those devoid of imagination, a blank place on the map is a useless waste; to others, the most valuable part. Is my share in Alaska worthless to me because I shall never go there? Do I need a road to show me the arctic prairies, the goose pastures of the Yukon, the Kodiak bear, the sheep meadows behind McKinley?"[14] Knowing that wilderness and wildlife were there was enough for many Americans.

Nationalism was a two-edged blade in the argument over preservation of wildlife. It was flourished by opponents of wildlife conservation as well as by defenders of wilderness. Patriotic support of unlimited hunting privileges for soldiers might threaten the game supply. Appeals to nationalism were also used by proponents of economic development who considered large game animals impediments to progress and who rallied support with the patriotic demand that Alaska be allowed to recapitulate the stages of change enacted earlier in American history. Placing limitations on the use of natural resources was not loyalty to the American past, in this view. It was a subversion of economic freedom that short-circuited fulfillment of the American dream of a clearly stepped, upward movement to material happiness. Alaskan entrepreneurs wanted the freedom of their forefathers to get rich or go broke on the frontier. If they did the latter it was the fault of bureaucrats and conservationists and absentee monopolists. If wealth came to them it signaled a state of patriotic grace. The agricultural scientist C. C. Georgeson had honestly believed that Alaska should pass through an agrarian phase, and to nudge the general processes of American history along he recommended the extermination of the Kodiak bear.

Prewar Alaskan newspapers almost invariably favored economic development over wildlife preservation, and the more complicated arguments for wildlife protection were rarely aired or printed in the northland. Madison Grant, in New York City, could assert the interest of all Americans in preserving Alaskan forms of "animal life that have come down through years of slow evolution." Dufresne talked around the point in referring vaguely to the protection of "unique mammal forms."[15] His "unique forms" were the genotypes which, if lost, were lost forever, thus reducing (in Carl Sauer's phrase) "the possible future range of utility of organic evolution." Sauer, a geographer in California, coined that phrase in the late thirties. He could "check off" the big predators and grazing wildlife because they failed to survive in environments altered by economic needs.[16] Not so Aldo Leopold, who saw nature as too complex for judgments about where utility begins or ends: "If the biota, in the course of aeons, has built something we like but do not understand, then who but a fool would discard seemingly useless parts?" More directly, "Who knows for what purpose cranes and condors, otters and grizzlies may some day be used?"[17] Later ecologists would state flatly that genotypes are "irretrievable treasures," genetic resources that might be used to improve domestic animals, to understand biological processes in general, or to meet problems arising from changes in the environment.[18] But the point that must be made here is this: outright public reference to Darwinian evolution was still indelicate or unfamiliar in the Alaska of those years.

Religious arguments were not much more likely to be advanced in defense of the animals; appeals to respect them as the handiwork of God are muted in the local communication media. Some Alaskans read Stewart Edward White's plea in the *Saturday Evening Post* of 1930 to contemplate God's planet before deciding to junk the whole scheme. Rarely in prewar Alaska, however, can one find any powerful, religious, antihunting sentiment of the kind expressed by Joseph Wood Krutch in 1957: "When a man wantonly destroys one of the works of man we call him Vandal. When he wantonly destroys one of the works of God we call him Sportsman."[19] John Muir came to Alaska several times in the nineteenth century, did some exploring, wrote about a grand "design" in nature, and (according to Grant McConnell) respected the "divinity in all the wild things of Creation." Muir did not kill or eat game animals. The Tlingit Indians, he said, made "a good deal of sport of my pity for the deer and [my] refusing to eat any of it and nicknaming me . . . the deer and duck's *tillicum*," or friend, in Chinook jargon.[20] Such theistic and pantheistic opposition to the exploitation of wildlife was exceptional in the vocabulary of Alaskan conservation.

So were scientific arguments about the interdependency of all life. An article by Dufresne describing the balance of nature on the tundra first brought him to Edward Nelson's attention. Officially, the subject of natural equilibrium was rarely broached in the Bureau of Biological Survey's Alaskan literature advocating conservation. To stress the need for a self-regulating "balance of nature" was to invite emotional responses in the debates over wildlife management, especially when the conversation turned to predation.[21] Adolph Murie's famous study published in 1944, *The Wolves of Mount McKinley*, created as much controversy as it resolved. Also unusual were appeals to preserve undisturbed natural systems for use as controls for the scientific investigation of partially exploited and disrupted ecosystems. That argument for wilderness preservation is commonly heard nowadays;[22] in Alaska before 1950, it would have had a hollow ring because few theoretically sophisticated biological studies had been undertaken by that date.

Totally absent from the Alaskan public record was the Freudian interpretation of wildlife preservation, which is exemplified in a recent essay by A. D. Graham, an African game warden. "In the simplest sense," Graham writes, "game saving is nothing more than the outcome of repressed aggression redirected on to animals by humans paralysed in their relations with their fellow men. The preservation of the wilderness, of the image of Mother Nature, is the cultivation of a fantasy, a desperate regression into the idealistic memory of childhood's mother-love."[23]

The convenient to-hell-if-you-do, to-hell-if-you-don't flexibility of Freudian psychology, which accepts identical reasons for opposite forms of behavior, could explain why people hunted as well as why they preserved wildlife. Hunters could be accused of satisfying their repressed aggression toward society by killing animals, and hunting could be characterized as a regression into the sexual fantasies of childhood. A less tortuous and better-documented psychological interpretation of hunting saw the activity as an affirmation and demonstration of manhood, of the qualities of "manliness" and "self-reliance," in the words of Theodore Roosevelt and George Bird Grinnell. William Kent, a congressman from California and a conservationist of sorts, said that after a kill "you are a barbarian, and you're glad of it. It's good to be a barbarian . . . and you know that if you are a barbarian, you are at any rate a man."[24]

Kent's reference to the barbarian in modern man anticipated a more complex rationale of hunting as instinctive. José Ortega y Gasset, in his classic *Meditations on Hunting*, written in 1942, said hunting was "a renunciation by man of the supremacy of his humanity," a "confrontation between two systems of instinct," the animal's and the hunter's, and a survival of the predatory instinct, which Ortega noted "throughout almost the entire zoological scale."[25] Very similar views were expressed by Aldo Leopold at about the same time: "The instinct that finds delight in the sight and pursuit of game is bred into the very fiber of the race"; it was "almost a physiological characteristic," "something that lies very deep." Leopold would "not like to own the boy whose hair does not lift his hat when he sees his first deer." Even one of the most uncompromising, dedicated preservationists of modern times, Joseph Wood Krutch, wrote in 1957, "The blank assumption that the universe has no conceivable use or meaning except in relation to man may be instinctive."[26]

The conclusion that hunting is instinctive was elaborated and refined in the seventies by semiscientific social scientists in anthropology, quasiscientific natural scientists in ethology, and semi-social-scientific natural scientists in sociobiology, all of whom contributed to the development of the proposition that social behavior was genetically determined. According to this group, man has been around for 600,000 years, but his civilized agricultural and urbanized ways of life have existed for only a few thousand years, for perhaps one percent of human history—too short a period for the genetic modification of behavior that was acquired during the extended dawn of man as hunter and gatherer. Two anthropologists put it this way: "In a very real sense our intellect, interests, emotions, and basic social life—all are evolutionary products of the success of the hunting adaption."[27] Even the kindly René Dubos believes "the tendency to kill, the tendency to waste and to foul the nest seems to be inscribed in the genetic code of the human species." Aggression is instinctive, and quarreling over territory by humans is as inevitable as it is among geese. Hunting by people in this genetically deterministic scheme is natural and unavoidable and more in tune with man's true character than is wildlife preservation.[28]

Freudians, evolutionists, and genetic determinists were far away in space and time from territorial Alaska, or their ideas were unfamiliar. Thomas Riggs, in 1935, nodded toward the notion that hunting was instinctive: "I have covered a lot of the old territory with a rifle in my hand and have shot a lot of game. Lord, how it gets in your blood!"[29] Unfortunately, we do not know whether "the old territory" or shooting game animals, or both, got into Riggs's blood.

Another heritage—cultural, not instinctive—is more helpful in explaining why Alaskans hunted. White Alaskans called their territory "the last frontier" and considered themselves to be frontiersmen, the last exponents of a way of life that in American thought had molded the character of Americans and the history of the nation. And American frontiersmen hunted. Alaskans could not understand why, if hunting was a character-building activity for their ancestors, it was not a desirable exercise for them. When they hunted they were simply reenacting a part of the American historical experience.

Doubtless many Alaskans fancied themselves to be latter-day Daniel Boones and Kit Carsons, but the daydreams cannot stand inspection as central motives for hunting, and it therefore becomes necessary to return to the first point emphasized in this analysis: the most important reason for hunting was economic. Alaskan fur trappers relied heavily on game animals for food, as did individual prospectors. Resident fishermen often supplied themselves with game meat during the winter, and townsmen could reduce their grocery bills by shooting game for the table. There was no Alaskan beef available at low prices, and there was little need for it in some places. An aspiring cattle king tried to raise beef on the hoof near Fairbanks but failed because caribou and moose were too readily available.[30] In addition to the natural disadvantages (not including the brown bear), the Kodiak cattle business probably never amounted to much for similar reasons. As for the Eskimos, Aleuts, Athapaskans, and Tlingits, most were still hunters and gatherers, much of the time.

In short, reference to the complex and abstract psychological, sociological, anthropological, biological, theological, and historical motives for hunting is intellectually entertaining, but Alaskans hunted for food. Outside conservationists had difficulty appreciating that fact because subsistence hunting had for all practical purposes disappeared in the States. American game law in the twentieth century was designed to control recreational hunting. There was, of course, a recreational side to Alaskan hunting—the excitement of pitting the hunter's skill and wilderness wisdom against the animal's—but the recreational benefits were incidental, and bringing out the meat could be physically exhausting work. When General Buckner brought his case against the game commission to court, the people of Alaska still hunted to eat. There was little or no room in their attitude for academic abstractions. The abstractions would come later, with the other effects of modernization set in motion by events in the 1940s.

1. George Folta with one of his smaller bears

ONE DAYS SPORT.

A RECORD MOOSEHEAD
OF THE WORLD 69 INCH SPREAD
KILLED IN ALASKA

2. Big game hunter Dall De Weese with record Kenai moose horn

3. Thomas C. Riggs, Jr., on the Boundary Survey, 1907

4. Edward W. Nelson, architect of Alaskan game management

5. Sam O. White, *left*, who pioneered the use of the airplane in wildlife management

6. Some Alaska Game Commission Staff Members Photographed in Fairbanks, 1939. *Left to right*: Sam O. White, Jack Benson, Pete McMullen, Frank Dufresne, Clarence Rhode, Jack O'Connor, Grenold Collins, Frank Glazer.

7. Hosea Sarber with bear skull

8. Andrew Simons, famous big game hunter's guide

9. Naturalist Olaus Murie

10. Game Warden Jack O'Connor

11. Lieutenant General Simon Bolivar Buckner, Jr., by Edwin Chapman

12. U.S. District Court Judge Simon Hellenthal

13. **Dr. Romig's Wild Game Feast, 1941.** *Rear, left to right*: **Dr. Romig, un-identified woman,** *Anchorage Daily Times* **publisher Robert Atwood, Mrs. Adele Buckner, General Buckner, Judge Hellenthal, Ira Gabrielson.**

7

The Native Hunters

The Aleuts, Eskimos, Athapaskans, and Tlingits had a variety of hunting technologies and dietary preferences before the arrival of the Europeans. The Aleuts of the Aleutian Islands were skilled in hunting sea otter with harpoons thrown by hand from their fast skin kayaks. They relied mainly on birds, fish, and sea mammals for food. Coastal Eskimos hunted sea mammals, fish, and birds too. They also traveled inland to hunt terrestrial wildlife, especially caribou. Arctic inland Eskimos frightened the caribou toward snares, shooting them with bows and arrows, or toward lakes, where the caribou could be speared while swimming. Sheep were snared, shot with arrows, or chased over cliffs by dogs. Musk-oxen, moose, and black bears were also hunted and eaten. The anthropologist Robert Spencer describes an ingenious technique used by Eskimos of northern Alaska to catch wolves. Small pieces of frozen whalebone were sharpened, bent, and secured in suet; the wolf took the bait, and when everything thawed the bone snapped back and punctured the animal's stomach.[1]

Interior Athapaskan Indians adopted what might be described in modern jargon as a hunting *system* for caribou. Long fences were erected with an opening that contained a large rawhide noose. Caribou searching for a gap followed the fence or were driven along it until they were caught in the snare when they tried to cross. Or the barrier might end in a corral, into which the caribou would migrate only to find the single exit blocked by some Indians, while others killed the animals with arrows, spears, and rocks. Caribou meat was frequently cached for future use, since most Athapaskans did not occupy Alaska's most bountiful habitat. One division of this linguistic group, the Tanaina Athapaskans, lived on the shores of Cook Inlet and had a wider choice of land and sea animals on which to prey. They combined the technologies of their land-bound relatives and the maritime hunting techniques of southern Eskimos, with whom they shared part of south-central Alaska.[2]

Still farther east and south, the Northwest Coast Tlingit Indians lived in a land of relative abundance. The streams overflowed with fish, deer were plentiful, as were bears, and mountain goats were not out of reach. Tlingits killed game animals with spears, bows and arrows, traps, snares, and clubs. As elsewhere in Alaska, they also used deadfalls, devices that dropped rocks or logs on animals taking the bait. In the rain forest, where a foot or two or three of moss covered bedrock, no pitfalls were used. According to a German ethnographer who studied the Tlingits late in the nineteenth century, caribou skins traded into southeastern Alaska from the Canadian interior were the measure of value before the manufactured blanket appeared. A slave was worth fifteen or twenty caribou skins.[3]

The sale of firearms to Natives was forbidden by the Russians and later by the Americans. Guns found their way into the hands of Native hunters despite the ban. The single-shot muzzle-loader was no great improvement over many Native hunting tools in a damp, frigid climate. By the 1880s the Natives had better rifles, but American officials said the restriction against firearms was still proving a hardship on them. Even if they did possess breechloaders at that time, ammunition was difficult to obtain, and they needed better weapons to pursue their principal occupation.[4] From the American purchase of Alaska to the gold rushes, fur hunting and trapping was almost exclusively a Native vocation.

Between 1868 and 1890, 845,000 pelts of sea otter, land otter, fox, beaver, and marten, valued at nearly $13,500,000, were shipped from Alaska. The trade perpetuated the hunting activities of many Alaskan aborigines but was transitional, because total subsistence hunting was abandoned for commercial hunting and partial subsistence hunting. Natives traded their catch for credits with which to buy manufactured goods, thereby altering their economic life, their relationship to nature, and increasing their dependence upon outsiders. The pattern was a familiar one in early American history and was noted by the historian Frederick Jackson Turner in his dissertation, written before similar influences had disappeared from Alaska.[5]

Alaskan Natives were subject to a number of other, special, legal conditions. The Cession Treaty of 1867 with Russia left laws and regulations governing "the uncivilized tribes" to future determination. A customs law in 1868 reserved for the president of the United States the power to regulate or prohibit the use of firearms. In 1873 Alaska was designated "Indian Country" by the attorney general. The first Organic Act, of 1884, again reserved for future action the issue of Native rights but legalized the mineral claims of whites, and that (according to an official publication of the Alaska Native Foundation) in effect dispossessed certain Natives.[6] At this early date, the growth of the salmon canning industry probably did more to threaten Native life-styles along the coasts. The gold rushes, however, were especially disruptive, and their effect finally moved Congress to consider Alaskan legislation more seriously.

According to the Native Allotment Act of 1906, Alaskan indigenes were permitted to file on 160-acre homesteads; an 80-acre homestead act for whites had been approved in 1898. Natives who homesteaded did not get mineral rights with their land, but unlike white settlers they were not required to pay taxes, construct a dwelling, or clear and cultivate the land. After sixty years had passed, fewer than one hundred such land allotments had been made, partly because no money to survey the claims was appropriated for years, but chiefly because the Natives did not hear the news or were not interested. Also in 1906, white Alaskans were allowed to send a delegate to Congress; Natives, who were not considered citizens, could not vote for the delegate. The enabling act of 1912, which gave the Territory a legislature (without control over wildlife), did not alter the Native's status. However, the new legislature did pass a law in 1915 permitting a Native to become a citizen if he had "adopted the habits of a civilized life," had passed an examination, had five white sponsors, and had survived a hearing before a judge. In 1924 a law granted citizenship to all Natives born under the American flag.[7]

The territorial law of 1915 was not motivated by unalloyed altruism. The land question was nagging. Whites committed to economic development were expecting some of the migrants who came north early in the twentieth century to remain. More specifically, the white settlement expected to occur after the construction of the Alaska Railroad posed a threat to the claims and practices of the Athapaskans. A conference in Fairbanks between several Tanana chiefs, Delegate James Wickersham, railroad commissioner Thomas Riggs, Land Office officials, and Reverend Guy Madara was held in 1915. Riggs warned the chiefs that "after the railroad which we are building comes into this country, it will be overrun with white people. They will kill off your game, your moose, your caribou and your sheep. They will run all of them out of the country and they will have so many fish wheels on the river that the Indian will not get as many fish." The whites recommended that Indians either claim homesteads or opt for reservations, but the chiefs preferred to retain their freedom and customs.

Chief Alexander, of Tolovana, replied, "I tell you that we are people that are always on the go, and I believe if we were put in one place we should die off like rabbits." Paul Williams, of Fort Gibbon, believed, "As soon as we are made to leave our customs and wild life, we will all get sick and soon die." And Chief Joe, of Salchaket, made the point more bluntly: "We are suggesting to you just one thing, that we want to be left alone."[8]

In wildlife matters, the Natives could not be left alone or ignored.

They were still hunters and gatherers dependent on wildlife, and they constituted 40 percent or more of the permanent population, through 1940. Because of their habits and numbers they were a significant factor in wildlife management. Yet, when compared with whites, the Natives were left alone in their hunting, and had legal advantages not enjoyed by other Alaskans.

The game law of 1902 contained an exemption that allowed Natives to kill game animals and birds for food and clothing, and permitted miners, explorers, and travelers to kill game when in need of food; however, the game animals or birds so killed could not be shipped or sold. The exemptions were kept in the law of 1908, and affirmed by the solicitor of the Department of Agriculture.

The solicitor's opinion was requested in 1921 after Alfred Bailey, an agent of the Biological Survey, arrested an Indian for selling deer meat from his boat, which was moored at the Juneau city wharf. The commissioner (a local magistrate) agreed with the solicitor that Natives were exempt from the law if they killed for food and not for sale or shipment, but Bailey had not seen the Indian selling the deer meat on his boat, and there was no way of telling whether the meat would be used by the Indian as food. Despite that opinion the jury found the Tlingit guilty, and he was fined fifty dollars for illegally killing four deer. The jury was later told by the commissioner that "it was the craziest verdict he had ever heard."[9]

This incident and additional complaints by whites that Natives were abusing their hunting privileges motivated Edward Nelson, of the Bureau of Biological Survey, to lobby for changes in the law.[10] The game commission legislation of 1925 modified the exemption. Under the new law Natives were classed with prospectors and travelers, and were permitted to take game during closed seasons only when "in absolute need of food and other food is not available"; such animals could not be sold (except for the hides, within Alaska), and the secretary of agriculture could revoke the exemption if he decided that wildlife in a certain region was in danger of extermination. No exemption that contravened the Migratory Bird Treaty of 1916, with Great Britain, was permitted.[11] Heavy hunting by whites and Natives in Alaska during the gold rushes was probably one reason for the decline in migratory game birds that stimulated negotiation of the treaty in the first place.

The treaty was a landmark in wildlife conservation. It, and enabling legislation, established a closed season on migratory birds during the spring and summer, from March 10 to September 1, and limited open seasons to three and one-half months. Eskimos and Indians could take certain sea birds and their eggs for food and clothing, and Indians could take scoters at any time, but the prohibition of spring and summer shooting made it illegal for any Alaskan to kill certain game birds at the only time when they were readily available in parts of the Territory. For some Eskimos in the Yukon-Kuskokwim Delta region, migratory birds were the first fresh meat to arrive after a long, hard winter. The Natives there did not forgo the pleasure of consuming a raw goose in the spring or capturing a duckling in August, when the bird could not yet fly, merely because of a paper law. They ran no risk in continuing their old ways because the law was not enforced among the aborigines before the Second World War.[12]

Alaskan Natives had other privileges as well. Rephrasing the legal exemption did not alter its interpretation, said the lawyers within six months after passage of the game commission bill. Agents in the Panhandle wanted to charge an Indian who had killed a doe, but the Department of Agriculture in Washington said no. The intent of the law, according to the solicitor, was to permit Natives to take game for food whenever they wished; the Tlingit in question did not need to prove that there were no buck deer around before he killed a female. Warden Sam White, and probably other wardens as well, did not (he said later) arrest Indians engaged in subsistence hunting that did not seem wasteful, even if it appeared to violate the law, but he did enforce the regulations against market hunting by Natives for money to buy whiskey.[13]

The law of 1925 did not require the purchase of hunting, trapping, or fur-trading licenses by "native-born Indians, Eskimos, or half-breeds who have not severed their tribal relations by adopting a civilized mode of living or by exercising the right of franchise."[14] The problem came when game commission agents tried to determine whether Natives had adopted "a civilized mode of living." In effect, Washington told the commission to stop trying to define that phrase. Whether an Indian had money or not was not a proper test, and the commission could not require Natives who held normal jobs to buy licenses. Neither, said the solicitor emphatically, should Natives who frequented card rooms and poolrooms be singled out for licenses, because the Alaska game law "is not intended to be used for the purpose of making a good Indian out of a bad one." An attempt in 1939 to have the aborigines carry a free hunting certificate in order to encourage them to report their kills for management purposes apparently floundered.[15]

To summarize: Alaskan Natives before the Second World War, unlike other residents, could by law and interpretation kill most game animals whenever they wished. Though forbidden to hunt migratory game birds during the spring and summer, they did so with impunity. Other wildlife laws applicable to the indigenes were enforced unevenly. Natives were not required to buy a license or to report their take in the interest of wild animal management. Given such privileges, it should be appropriate to ask how well the Alaskan Natives behaved, especially in light of the popular notion that indigenous hunters were conservationists—the first ecologists. The documentary record, at first glance, does not support that conclusion.

Since 1867, white observers had remarked about the wasteful manner in which the aborigines treated the wildlife on which they relied, their use of wildlife in trade, and their participation in market hunting. In southeastern Alaska the Tlingit Indians near Sitka supplied the first American settlers with wild meat, for a price. Up north, toward the end of 1867, two Native boys killed two caribou and brought to William Healey Dall the tongues and kidneys only. The naturalist "rated them well for the folly of destroying game which they could not use or bring home."[16] On a visit to Glacier Bay in 1880, John Muir's traveling companion, a Presbyterian minister, asked a young Indian to shoot a goat with the preacher's breech-loading rifle. To Muir's dismay, the youngster returned with a fine buck deer, explaining that it was the fattest of eleven deer he had killed.[17] On another occasion a Tlingit needlessly killed a sea gull; Muir "asked him why he had killed the bird, and followed the question by a severe reprimand for his stupid cruelty, to which he could offer no other excuse than that he had learned from the whites to be careless about taking life."[18]

Governor John Brady testified in 1902 that Tlingits had brought to town the hides of 150 deer clubbed by hand after the animals became exhausted in deep snows. The carcasses had been left in the woods or on the beach. In the winter of 1901, at least 15,000 deer hides were shipped out of southeastern Alaska, according to a grand jury estimate. The Indians received forty cents per pelt.[19] William Paul—Indian, attorney, secretary of the Alaska Native Brotherhood, and Territorial legislator—must have forgotten that gory episode by 1939, when he pleaded the Indians' right to shoot deer: "Conservation of deer which necessitated present restrictions . . . [was] induced by white people, not by Indians who have ever been mindful of their grandchildren."[20] In fact, news of the deer slaughter in 1901 had helped to pass Alaska's first game law, which effectively halted the hide trade and saved the deer from decimation at the hands of Indians hunting for the market.

Other horror stories about wanton waste of wildlife during the gold rushes also help to explain the passage of the earliest game legislation. Natives were not exempt from criticism. Naturalists and big game hunters such as J. Alden Loring, Wilfred Osgood, Andrew J. Stone, and James Kidder all reported heavy and wasteful hunting by Natives.[21] Dall De Weese in 1897 saw Natives of the Kenai Peninsula fail to retrieve wounded sheep that had run or fallen off a cliff some distance away, saying, "too much work; shoot more." Eskimos of Unangashik, on the north shore of the Alaska Peninsula, killed 500 caribou between October 1, 1902, and May of the following year, and sold the skins for approximately one dollar each to a trader who had established himself there for the sole purpose of dealing in caribou skins.[22] As the years went by and mining camps disappeared, fish canneries, logging camps, construction camps, and wilderness roadhouses carried on the market tradition, as outlets for game killed by Natives and whites.[23]

The mountain of testimonial evidence that Alaskan Natives wasted game animals does not prove that Natives were any more prodigal than immigrant whites, but it does throw a shadow over the fashionable idea that all aboriginal hunters were practicing ecologists, or natural conservationists, with a body of social, magical, and religious beliefs that prevented waste and ensured a continuous supply of wildlife needed for food, clothing, and the implements of everyday life.[24] If that were the case in Alaska, why did the old customs collapse so quickly? Why, if these magical-religious beliefs were deeply rooted, did they seem to disappear suddenly, well before the Natives abandoned their dependence upon wildlife? Only a few of the possible answers need to be assayed here.

It has been charged that the testimony of whites about Native misbehavior is untrustworthy and the product of competition for game, or racism. There is evidence that white-Native competition explains some reports of overkill by Natives during the period between 1908 and 1925, when appointed governors of Alaska supervised the staff of game wardens. Racism was not absent from Native-white relations, although it was rare in towns where there were few Natives and was probably mild in the bush, where racial cooperation was often important to the survival of everybody. One example of racism was that Natives might be paid less for game meat than competing white market hunters.[25] Overall, however, there is no reason to distrust the bulk of the testimony on racial or economic grounds. Some of the evidence came from Natives themselves. Much of the documentation is from reliable sources. Naturalists with excellent credentials, such as Wilfred Osgood and Olaus Murie, and later, A. Starker Leopold and F. Fraser Darling, recorded waste by Natives but did not think the aborigines were a threat to the fauna. More often than not, in fact, the scientists considered Native hunting, by itself, a beneficial weight on the ecological balance.[26] There is, in sum, too much evidence of waste on the record to dismiss it with a generalized impeachment of the many witnesses.

If the evidence is reliable, what then explains the disappearance of the Natives' alleged conservationist inclinations? A favorite answer is that modern weapons encouraged the wasteful behavior. Ernest Walker thought his race should take most of the blame for Indian waste because whites supplied the Natives with better guns. An old Koyukon

Athapaskan was quoted in 1942 as saying: "After the guns came some men would go out and kill caribou just for the tongue or for sinew and leave the rest there."[27] Anthropologist Rolf Knight, studying the Algonkians of the northeastern United States, concluded that modern rifles encouraged the division of that society into smaller groups, because moose hunting (which became easier) did not require large, cooperative activity as did caribou hunting, and the change may have resulted in cultural readjustments.[28] In Alaska, improvements in the hunter's tools can be only a partial explanation, for hunting was still difficult, a new method might be taboo, the new technologies were expensive, and some of the older methods were better, or at least as satisfactory. A repeating rifle that permitted the hunter to kill solitary animals more easily also allowed more discrimination and less waste in taking gregarious animals. In the 1920s Olaus Murie still found Natives using the old techniques to capture caribou, and the reader will recall that hundreds of deer were killed wastefully in southeastern Alaska by Indians using no firearms at all.[29] It becomes necessary, therefore, to look beyond technology and ask, Has the evidence of ecological consciousness among Natives been exaggerated or misinterpreted?

The opportunity for misinterpretation is great because so many of the beliefs and behavior patterns in question were related to Native reliance on game mammals, birds, and fish. Distinctions between men and animals were blurred. Athapaskans believed that animals could be men reincarnated. Northern Eskimos believed that animals thought and talked like men. Northwest Coast Indians had numerous rules to ensure good relations between themselves and the "salmon-people."[30] Such attitudes do not prove automatically that Natives were ecologically wise. Mickey Mouse was not created as a conservation measure to protect mice, and although some writers have concluded that the popular practice in America of assigning human qualities to animals helps to explain conservation and anticonservation sentiment among whites, the point is difficult to prove.[31]

Indigenous beliefs may only illustrate the wish of the aboriginal hunter not to offend the animals in order to encourage their availability for dinner, a characteristic anthropologists have noticed among all Alaskan groups. But listen to how ecologist F. Fraser Darling interprets one Indian practice: "When an Athabascan Indian asks the forgiveness of the bear he is about to hunt and kill because of his need, he is philosophically conscious and understanding of his own ecological situation which demands what the bear has to offer to his continued survival. His prayer is a beautiful example of restraint."[32] It need not be anything of the kind. It may be only a request that the hunter not be injured and that bears remain in the vicinity to be killed in the future. The bear cere-

monialism pervading North American Indian cultures may be no more
than an elaborate safety measure. The bear stories told by whites may
have the same unconscious function: to warn fellow humans that bears
are dangerous.

According to anthropologist Robert Spencer, northern Eskimos set
only five traps at a time for wolves, which appears at face value to be a
hunting restriction for the purpose of conservation (though Spencer
does not say as much), yet almost in the same breath an Eskimo tale is recorded the moral of which is that any hunter who does not protect caribou from wolves will not be successful. When firearms first became
available the Eskimos believed that brown bears should not be shot with
arrows or with guns. This taboo also appears to be an animal conservation measure, but hunting brown bears with bow and arrow or with
muzzle-loading and single-shot rifles is extremely dangerous. The belief
protected the Eskimo more than the bear. Among the same people, caribou hunting was restricted in the period just prior to the birth of calves,
and this rule too sounds very much like an example of conservation consciousness; unfortunately, its effect is not weighed against the popularity
of unborn caribou calf meat among Alaskan Natives.[33]

Another illogical route to the conclusion that hunters and gatherers
were conservationists is to note the presence of large numbers of wild
animals in America at the time of European contact despite their regular
prior use by aborigines. The difficulty with this approach is in what remains hidden from view. An influential policy committee for Alaska
told the president of the United States in 1964: "Migratory birds—a staple item of diet each spring for the western Alaskan were denied him by
international treaty fostered by outside sportsmen. That the Native had
long been a practicing conservationist is attested to by the fact the birds
had returned annually for centuries."[34] The annual return of the birds
proves no such thing. It proves only that the Natives *did not* take enough
birds and eggs to affect the migration. It may be that they *cared not* to kill
or *could not* kill enough birds to interrupt the annual flights. Juxta-
posing those two statements in the quotation also illustrates the danger
of ignoring history, for the Migratory Bird Treaty Act of 1918 was not in
any real sense enforced among the Natives until 1961, when the reaction
of Alaskan indigenes was so dramatic that the federal government soon
returned to its historic policy of nonenforcement.[35]

These observations collectively do not mean that all taboos, rituals,
and magical and religious practices of the Alaskan Natives were not conservationist in intent or effect. Many obviously were. Spencer describes
how the Eskimos trapped only five foxes at once, because only five
skins were needed for a parka. A group of Tanaina Indians on Kenai
Peninsula trapped only one of their seven beaver lakes each year to allow

natural restocking, according to a journalist writing in 1875.[36] Additional customs seemingly incapable of misinterpretation can be found readily in the literature; most seem to exemplify the Natives' attitude toward fur-bearing animals, which were valuable in trade, and there is evidence that Alaskan aborigines were more respectful of wildlife laws affecting these animals than of laws protecting game animals.[37] The two classes of wildlife should probably be separated when the question of Native attitudes toward conservation is analyzed.

Historians are not innocent of misinterpreting the evidence. Wilcomb Washburn compares the northern Alaskan Eskimos' respectful attitude toward a big game animal about to be killed (as reported by Spencer) with the wanton slaughter of pigeons by white characters in a Fenimore Cooper novel. "The act of killing an animal in the two societies," Washburn suggests, represents "almost diametrically opposed human facts." Like the ecologist Darling, Washburn leaps (though Spencer does not) from the fact that Natives appear respectful toward their animal victim to the implication that they may be natural conservationists. He equates the treatment of large mammals and wild birds without mentioning Spencer's comments (in the pages cited by Washburn) that birds "appear to have played no part in the system of ritual prohibitions," and that "no hunting taboos relating to birds and no special treatment of them or their eggs existed."[38]

Washburn's small illustration is one of several introduced to support a plea for the employment of ethnohistorical methods to produce what he calls "history in the round," a cause worth pursuing. In his survey of American Indian history, he is careful when approaching the issue of aboriginal environmentalism, but he thinks enough evidence exists "to support the assertion that the Indian was the first ecologist." He admits that relevant "ceremonial gestures" toward wildlife disappeared quickly after European contact.[39]

Historian Wilbur Jacobs is less cautious. The American Indian, he states flatly, "was basically a conservator, whose religious and totemic beliefs and tribal customs prevented him from following a policy of soil exhaustion or animal extermination." Jacobs calls for a full-scale revision of American frontier history. "We can no longer write about a peaceful occupation by English peoples of a fertile Appalachian frontier. Rather, we have to deal with the displacement of millions of people, an invasion of Europeans into densely populated lands. And we must understand that the process decimated many Indians who had developed life styles to support millions of people without obliteration of the land and its resources."[40]

Obviously, the size of the population is a crucial factor. If the land held "millions of people," those people must have known how to support themselves without upsetting the balance of nature; otherwise, the natural abundance that greeted Europeans could not have existed. Jacobs draws upon new estimates of the pre-Columbian population—especially those of Henry Dobyns—to sustain his thesis. The early population was much larger than formerly believed, but when the sources are examined closely, a different picture from the one painted by Jacobs emerges. In one note he mentions that Harold Driver halves Dobyns's calculations for North America. A glance at Dobyns's classic article and Driver's book reveals that Dobyns's estimate was heavily weighted for Mesoamerica, where the population was dense, and his estimates are not too reliable for prehistoric northern Natives, who were hunters and gatherers. Driver places the precontact Indian population of the United States at about 2,500,000 (and that of Canada, Alaska, and Greenland at 1,000,000). The refined figures suggest that those parts of the continent with which Professor Jacobs is mainly concerned were sparsely occupied after all, even before imported epidemic diseases killed the Natives in large numbers.[41]

Modern scholars have emphasized the significance of epidemic disease, to which the Natives were not immune, in the conquest of the New World, and disease is important to this examination of Native ecological practices for three reasons. First, disease-induced mortality may have distorted our perceptions of pre-Columbian adaptation by confusing the population statistics; second, disease-ridden aboriginal groups may have undergone general cultural changes that undermined sound ecological beliefs; and third, epidemics may have been directly responsible for the widespread slaughter of wildlife by Natives.

The first connection is obvious in the work of Wilbur Jacobs, who recognizes the role of disease on indigenous populations. The second effect of disease has been noticed by many "anthropomedical" scholars.[42] Death or incapacitation from the new diseases might have called traditional beliefs into question, and may have killed or disabled members of the group with specific social functions, thereby requiring difficult cultural readjustments. Leadership, followership, and spiritual guidance might have disappeared overnight, resulting in a general and sudden collapse of the community's social values and practices, including ecologically wise hunting traditions.

The third connection, which is more direct, has been made recently by Calvin Martin. Martin (in a book that is invaluable to any understanding of the whole problem) concludes that before the wholesale immigration of whites, European diseases wiped out a great part of the indigenous populations. The Natives then blamed the wildlife for violating the spiritual contract as embodied in ritual hunting practices, and began vengefully to kill and waste the animals.[43] The hypothesis is ingenious but empirically weak and structurally too complicated. More important to this analysis, Martin's interpretation does not fit the Alaskan evidence available to date.

Foreign disease was only one part of the sudden change that came with the gold rushes. Large numbers of strangers in the land with exotic technologies, values, material possessions, and behavioral traits could have triggered (with disease) traumatic reactions resulting in social disorganization and the renouncement of older eco-religious beliefs. The sociologist William Burch asks the question: "Might it be that extreme exploitation occurs when the social order is in a high state of flux—that is, when traditional frames of reference no longer seem operable?"[44] The difficulty with this explanation is its circularity.

Historical continuity rather than discontinuity is at the center of an older interpretation known to scholars since 1891, when Frederick Jackson Turner described the significance of the fur trade in easing the transition from Indian to white rule.[45] The Alaskan Natives were also lively traders. They traded within tribes, interethnically within Alaska, with the Siberians, with the Russians when the Russians came, and with the Americans before and after the purchase of Alaska. When contact occurred, conflict between the races was probably muted in some measure by economic similarities in the different cultures. Both Natives and whites were petty capitalists.[46] Alaskan Natives had monopolized the inland fur collection business until the gold rushes at the end of the nineteenth century. Trading game animals in the white man's market may have been a natural transition from the fur trade, which fell off during the stampedes and was increasingly infiltrated by unlucky prospectors. Or the shift from fur to food animals may have represented a shrewd trader's adjustment to changing market conditions. The possibility is enhanced by the suddenness of the gold rushes. A psychological as well as economic premium may have been placed on the trading experience, erasing more superficially held customs and values.

Marxist scholars, who prefer not to see in Native cultures a hint of any innate acquisitive impulse, will reject the Turnerian explanation. The "substantivist" school of anthropology will reject any attempt to understand basic Native behavior in Western economic terms.[47] Unreformed quantifiers will dismiss the evidence of Native waste as anecdotal. Proponents of a theory that emphasizes the humanness of hypocrisy will claim that gaps always exist between the expressed attitudes and the actual practices of people.[48]

Whatever viewpoint prevails, the documentary evidence is overwhelming that Alaskan Natives, at the turn of the century, overexploited the game animals on which they still depended. They were eagerly joined in that wasteful endeavor by white hunters. Perhaps the two races are more alike than some theoretical scholars care to admit. Certainly by mid-century, contact between Native and white was complete, accelerating rapidly during and immediately after the Second World War. The races soon shared the same economy, technology, and most of the same institutions.

8

The Euro-American Hunters

To understand the role played by whites in Alaska's history, a distinction must be made between resident and nonresident hunters. Nonresidents included sportsmen, military personnel, and seasonal workers in fishing, mining, and construction. Just how many residents hunted is difficult to determine for the early years because resident hunting licenses were not required until 1936. The delay was a deliberate tactical decision to gain local favor for the game laws.[1]

During the first year of licensing, 2,000 locals applied. The following year, 4,500 resident licenses were issued; this figure is probably closer to the number of actual hunters than is the figure for the first year. Trappers were also licensed; their numbers fluctuated between about 2,000 and about 5,000 each year from 1926 to 1936. The total number of residents licensed between 1937 and 1941 was 10,000 or more each year. The total white population in 1930 was just under 30,000, and it was just under 40,000 in 1939; therefore, from one-fourth to one-third of all non-Native Alaskans were licensed to hunt during those years.

Subtracting all white females (though some did hunt), and white males under fifteen years of age (of whom no licenses were required though many also hunted), there were approximately 23,800 potential white male hunters and about 11,600 licensed resident hunters in 1939. Thus, 49 percent of the non-Native resident males over fifteen were licensed to hunt. Although not every licensee did hunt, the proportion is astounding. Residents killed and consumed annually enough wild animals to provide twenty-five pounds of meat and fowl for every white person in the Territory, and this figure is calculated from the reported, legal kills made by whites only![2] No species was endangered because the kill statistics did not represent a significantly visible fraction of any animal's total estimated population. Natives probably used more wildlife, but between the gold rushes and the Second World War whites and Natives together did not threaten big game with extinction except near settlements.

That happy condition contributed in part to the proposition, widely embraced by residents, that Alaskans did not waste the edible big game animals. The contention, an ingredient of Alaskan pioneer ethnocentrism, is as difficult to prove as the idea that Natives were the first ecologists. The notion that pioneers were practical conservationists was at the foundation of arguments for local control of game soon after the earliest laws were passed.

Governor Walter Clark informed the secretary of the interior in 1911 that residents in general did not disobey the game laws though newcomers and itinerants did. In 1921 Alfred Bailey thought "old-timers" were conservationists but not all "drifters" were. Naturalist Olaus Murie wrote that same year: "The Alaskan is prone to harp on the point that no meat is wasted. This I have found is really true, in general." One official of the Fish and Wildlife Service repeated the contention in 1952: "The resident sportsman is interested in a permanent sheep population in his favorite sheep hills and grayling for all time to come in the nearest stream. Your transient hunter is motivated by the souvenir instinct."[3]

Unfortunately, there is also plenty of testimonial evidence that residents and old timers violated game laws. In the same letter of Murie's complimenting Alaskans for not wasting wild meat, he reported widespread violation of the game laws in the Circle and Fairbanks regions, and until the thirties the disinclination of local juries to convict white residents for poaching was a standing joke in Alaska.[4] The number of arrests nearly tripled between 1936 and 1937; this statistic may help to explain the sharply higher number of licensees in 1937—about double, suggesting that maybe one-half of the residents had not exhibited their conservationism by hurrying to buy the new licenses.[5]

One problem in trying to determine how devoted the white Alaskans were to conservation is related to length and place of residence. How long a period on the ground was required to make the immigrant an "old-timer," or "sourdough"? And was residence in town equal to life in the bush? Wardens in general tended to consider ruralists more conservation minded than townsmen. Edward Nelson, of the Biological Survey, had experience in the Alaskan wilderness. Nevertheless, Governor Riggs told him that his residence in Alaska forty years ago and a recent summer trip had not fitted him to understand the territorial needs. "You have got to live with the country and absorb its problems day by day." Riggs's lecture came a mere one-half dozen years after he (and Delegate Wickersham) had been told by Chief Thomas, of Nenana: "You people don't go around enough to learn the way the Indians are living."[6]

The residence issue was complicated by the highly mobile character of the Alaskan population. Do ten years in Alaska make a sourdough out of a cheechako? Official, printed, decennial census figures show that at least 90 percent of the non-Native population in 1890 had not been there in 1880; some 26,000 of the 30,000 white people in Alaska in 1900 had not been there in 1890; according to the census figures, 17 percent of the population in 1910 had not been there in 1900, but it is more than likely that in actuality a far higher turnover in white population occurred between 1900 and 1910. The population of whites dropped 22 percent between 1910 and 1920; and between the end of 1929 and the end of 1939 it increased by more than one-quarter.[7]

Population instability continued thereafter. A sizable percentage of those who remained more than a decade did not plan to stay permanently, which weakens their claim to the game animals on the basis of being old-timers. The miners, the very group that locals often felt deserved priority as true Alaskans, were singled out by General Buckner as especially fickle in their regional allegiance. "Most prospectors came to Alaska," he is quoted as saying, "with the idea of taking away a fortune and leaving only a hole in the ground and a couple of halfbreeds. Even those who remained twenty or forty years still cherished the hope of going home with a fortune." It was strong talk. In 1939, 17 percent of the Alaskan labor force was in mining.[8]

On one thing almost all Alaskans with a single winter behind them could agree: transients did not deserve to hunt. There was nothing historically unique about this opinion. Before 1783 the American colonies had discriminated against nonresidents. For example, North Carolina in 1745 did not allow people without "settled habitation" to kill deer.[9]

In Alaska the stateside sportsmen were accused of framing the game laws solely to obtain a monopoly of "hunting privileges, to the exclusion of prospectors and 'poor people'," according to one prospector. Such class and regional animosities were heard again and again. Thomas Riggs, as railroad commissioner, justified his use of big game meat to feed railroad construction men as "an occasional luxury" to which laboring men as much as rich sportsmen were entitled. There were two types of hunters in the Territory, according to "Alaska's Viewpoint," an article that appeared in a 1919 issue of *Outdoor Life*. One type wanted to satisfy his hunger. The other

belongs to the class of those who come from wealthy and aesthetic homes gained from hard labor in fleecing lambs on the stock exchange or thru war profits or some kindred activity and, who seeking horns and skins to decorate their dens and smoking room, embark for Alaska, and with the assistance of a twenty-dollar-a-day guide and a half dozen cooks, packers and bottle washers and fifteen or twenty pack and saddle horses, go into the wilds and kill as much game in two months as would keep all the inhabitants of the . . . [Chisana] for six months, and then from their wide experience presume to criticize.[10]

The "viewpoint" was probably Riggs's, but the sportsmen annoyed other Alaskans too during the early years of the century.[11]

Sportsmen occasionally did waste game, but the nonresident hunter's impact on animal populations was insignificant. There were too few visiting big game hunters. The number hunting in any year before the First World War probably did not reach 30, and the number hunting each year from 1926 through 1940 never rose above 120; during eight of those last fifteen years 90 or fewer sportsmen were in the field annually.[12] Of the big game killed from June 1, 1938, to July 1, 1939 (a heavy year when measured by the number of nonresidents who were licensed), sportsmen reported 57 brown bears shot, 32 caribou, 21 mountain sheep, 18 moose, 9 goats, and 1 deer, or 138 big game animals, far less than one percent of the game killed and reported by all hunters during the period. Proportionately, the brown bear suffered more than the edible species of game; hunters from outside shot about 25 percent of the big carnivores that were killed that year. But the outside sportsmen took fewer than 200 of the nearly 35,000 game birds killed and reported that same year.[13] Clearly, the visiting hunter's impact was infinitesimal, a point broadcasted by game commission officials. By the thirties, if Alaskans listened and did their homework, they should have disagreed with Riggs's earlier contention that sportsmen from the States were the worst enemies of Alaskan wildlife. One small group of Alaskans—the big game guides—never believed it.

Nonresident hunters were required by the law of 1908 to hire a registered guide if they hunted on the Kenai Peninsula. The governor was empowered to make regulations for the registration of guides and to fix their fees. Any American citizen or Native of Alaska, "of good character," who complied with the laws and rules could obtain a guide's license. The authority to enact regulations affecting guides and the authority to determine where sportsmen would be required to employ a guide was transferred to the game commission by the law of 1925.[14] When the governors were in charge of local enforcement, guides were not supervised closely. Visiting hunters in 1911 alleged that the licensed guides lacked local knowledge of the country and were generally inefficient. Complaints were inevitable if for no other reason than the high cost of hiring a guide. The maximum fee in 1924 was $12.50 per day; it soon rose to $20. Between 1927 and 1941, fifty-seven to eighty-nine guides were registered each year.[15]

The commission tried harder than the governors to make the Alaskan big game guides a respectable corps of reliable men in an honorable profession. A written examination consisting of thirty-three questions about the regulations was one requirement. Another was an oral examination on practical questions, for example, on the skinning and care of trophies and meat, on the correct use of firearms, on river boat operations. Character and sobriety were important. In 1931 the commissioners asserted that character, ability, and reputation were 50 percent of the requirement for a guide's license. "No fear need be felt by an applicant," the commission's pamphlet announced, "by reason of a lack of education, ability to write a perfectly worded answer or a flourishing display of penmanship. It is not the desire of the Commission to make of their guides a bunch of molly coddlers." Guides were strictly enjoined not to "make rash promises of what game they can help a hunter to obtain."[16]

The commission also expanded the guide's clientele. Eventually, nonresident hunters were required to hire a guide throughout Alaska. In 1931 visiting photographers were obliged to employ a guide (and if the cameramen killed a bear and claimed self-defense the animal would be seized). In 1937 sportsmen from the States hunting black bears and polar bears were ordered to use a guide. A guide could accompany only one hunter at a time in 1931.[17]

Despite official solicitude for the big game guide's profession the game commission, during its early years, was kept busy overseeing performance. In 1928 one guide, according to a warden, "wantonly killed a 12 ft. brown bear near Kukak Bay giving the pads to a New York man, and permitting the skin to rot." Another man is described in the record as "a fairly good hunter, although it is questionable if he possesses the courage required of a guide hunting Kodiak bear." Another had "a violent temper" and was an "extremely dirty person, both in his personal and camp life." Still another did "not possess sufficient mental capacity to plan and conduct a successful trip." During that year others were refused licenses because of low examination scores, deafness, an inability to handle boats, and an improper "attitude toward conservation." In 1933 a guide in southeastern Alaska shot his client in the arm when the hunter reached out to point at a bear. On another occasion the same guide, while cleaning his gun, discharged it in the pilothouse of a client's yacht.[18] As the years passed, criticism for the most part diminished and such incidents became rare. The commission had achieved its goal of making Alaskan big game guiding respectable.

The guides, visiting sportsmen, resident whites, and Native hunters were probably unanimous in their dislike of hunting by a fifth group —the seasonal workers. Every summer approximately 20,000 people came to labor in the fishery. Nonresident fishermen sometimes shot deer from the decks of their moving boats for recreation. Ashore, cannery workers—often Chinese during the early years of the salmon fishery, then Filipino—were accused of wanton and illegal destruction of wildlife. In 1918 the dried carcasses of unborn fawns were seized from Chinese cannery employees in southeastern Alaska. The U.S. commissioner at Yakutat wrote in 1924: "The cannery crew shipped in every season is a fearful enemy of all game . . . , each one trying to excel in killing birds."[19] Seasonal workers in the mines, lumber mills, and in construction (judging impressionistically from the documentary sources) were a problem chiefly because their employers wanted to economize by feeding them the meat of wild animals.

The nonresident license requirement was intended in part to protect the game from seasonal workers, as was Nelson's effort to restrict the use of firearms by aliens. The game commission law of 1925 stated that no alien could take any animals or birds or own or possess a shotgun, rifle, or other firearm, unless he held an alien special license.[20] The wardens spent a great deal of time at the canneries dispossessing aliens of firearms held illegally.

After Frank Dufresne was told by the U.S. attorney in Fairbanks that Filipinos were not aliens, he was disappointed: "There is nothing I can add to this," he told the game commission, "except to state that I think it highly important that we have full power to disarm this race at any and all times in Alaska." But in 1933 the attorney general ruled that Filipinos should not be classified as aliens under the Alaska game law, and in 1935 the solicitor of the Department of Agriculture ruled that the establishment of the Philippine Commonwealth had not changed the status of Filipinos to that of aliens. Five years later the Department of the Interior's head counsel ruled that Filipinos who had become residents of Alaska were as eligible for resident hunting licenses as anyone else. The same law that eventually gave General Buckner the statutory rights he wanted by implication also permitted Filipino residents the same privileges given to soldiers. By 1943 the lawyers had decided that any statute to prevent aliens from killing wild game by prohibiting them from owning or possessing firearms was invalid. Through it all, the Alaska Game Commission continued to issue its "Alien Special" licenses; in 1941 a mere thirty-nine were granted.[21]

The hostility to aliens was not exclusively Alaskan. It was a phase of the general American reaction to heavy immigration from southern and eastern Europe and Asia, which reached one million newcomers in six separate years during the first two decades of the twentieth century, and which culminated in anti-immigration laws passed one year before the Alaska Game Commission bill. In 1898 William Hornaday referred in the *New York Times* to "hordes of ignorant Italians and some other foreigners [who] throng the woods [on Sunday] with cheap guns and kill everything that wears feathers except women." Railroads hired the new immigrants as unskilled laborers; their weekend hunting forays enraged citizens. Many were from Italy, where wildfowl protection was weak or nonexistent, and they brought with them from the land of St. Francis "a taste for songbird stew." Four wardens were killed in Pennsylvania in 1906 when they attempted to arrest alien hunters. In 1907, 113 Italian laborers were arrested in Iowa for game violations. New York State by that year prohibited aliens from carrying firearms in public, nine states required aliens to hold nonresident hunting licenses, and two states charged higher fees for alien licenses than for nonresident licenses.[22]

One infamous response to the new immigration was a book published in 1916 and entitled *The Passing of the Great Race*. It was written by Madison Grant—wildlife conservationist, gentleman zoologist, one of the most influential figures in the passage of Alaska's big game laws, and pacifier of the disputatious Thomas Christmas Riggs. In the book Grant worried about "the conservation of race." He was afraid that immigration from the wrong part of the world was "sweeping the nation toward a racial abyss" into which the superior Nordic race on which democracy depended would disappear. To support his opinions, he played inexpertly with anthropology, history, and philology, but the physical "science" on which he relied was somatology, the study of bodily characteristics, especially skull types. He staked his racial theories on the same kind of evidence that C. Hart Merriam was using at that time to differentiate among brown bears, and with equally unscientific results. Grant believed "the finest and purest type of a Nordic community outside of Europe will develop in northwest Canada and on the Pacific coast of the United States." Perhaps unconsciously he wanted to preserve Alaska for his superior race of people as well as for the biggest game animals. At any rate (in another one of those ironies that lace the history of wildlife and people in Alaska), Grant considered the Frisians "a very pure Nordic type" and "the handsomest and in many respects the finest of the continental Nordics." Judge Hellenthal's father was a Frisian immigrant.[23]

In those years Alaska was a poor place to entertain nativist or racist attitudes. The white population was too new, too small, too mixed, and too mobile. In 1920, of the 28,500 whites in a territory of 586,000 square miles, 43 percent, or 12,270, were foreign born. Half of the foreign born had immigrated to the United States since 1901. Recent Scandinavian immigrants had made early gold discoveries on the Seward Peninsula. Felix Pedro (Felice Pedroni), an Italian immigrant, made the first gold strike in the Fairbanks region. Andy Simons, a Finn who became Alaska's most famous big game guide, was still an alien in 1923, fifteen years after his arrival on the Kenai Peninsula. Most ironic of all: for several years Alaska's chief executive, charged with enforcing the game laws, was a Canadian who never bothered to become a citizen of the United States, or to mention that he had not—Governor J. F. A. Strong.[24]

Military personnel, considering their small numbers, were a particularly troublesome group of white hunters well before the game commissioners worried about General Buckner's troops. The first American soldiers and sailors to reach Alaska in 1867 inflated the price that Tlingit Indians received for the wild meat they brought to Sitka. John Muir, disgusted, described how in 1881, when he was traveling aboard the Coast Guard cutter *Corwin*, the ship steamed in pursuit of swimming polar bears, and five "fun-, fur-, and fame-seekers" on the ship fired forty times at the helpless animals: "It was prolonged, bloody agony, as clumsily and heartlessly inflicted as it could well be." It was not the last complaint against the Coast Guard, whose officers were ordered by the game laws of 1902 and 1908 to act as wardens.[25]

The navy was the object of criticism too. In July of 1920—during the closed season—the governor of Alaska boarded the battleship *Idaho* anchored in Kachemak Bay, an arm of Cook Inlet, just in time to witness the return of a hunting party with the carcass of a cow moose. Two years later the deputy U.S. marshall at Sitka arrested twelve crewmen from the minesweeper *Swallow* for killing deer illegally; they received light fines and their government rifles were returned. In 1924 personnel from a naval vessel cruising among the Aleutian Islands allegedly killed some foxes and smoked others out of their holes, taking the pups aboard ship.[26]

When the army returned to Alaska during the gold rushes, to preserve the peace and construct communication lines, soldiers were again censured for the misuse of wildlife. In 1915 Governor Strong complained to the War Department after receiving numerous complaints of violations by officers and men of Fort Gibbon in the interior, and after allegations were made that officers contracted with market hunters to buy game meat. Strong ordered his warden in the area to get some convictions at Fort Gibbon, which "has at all times shown a disposition to disregard the game law. . . . If they do not have fresh meat enough to last them throughout the winter, it is nobody's fault but their own commissary department's, and, therefore, no leniency should be shown them." Fort Gibbon and all other posts except Chilkoot Barracks (Fort Seward), located in southeastern Alaska, were abandoned a few years later.[27]

The decrease in the number of servicemen did not erase tensions between soldier and warden. Personnel at Chilkoot Barracks—two hundred or so of them—managed to upset the local residents, especially neighboring Indians, who were the army's worst critics in the Panhandle. In 1918 Tlingits reported seeing a government launch drop off soldiers who shot deer, leaving "many" carcasses in the woods. The Grand Camp of the Alaska Native Brotherhood resolved formally in 1934 that "hunting by soldiers who are not family men and who hunt for sport only be stopped if possible."[28]

But the commander at the barracks, R. W. Dusenbury, petitioned the game commission for more freedom to hunt. The regulations, he complained, discriminated against army personnel. Soldiers, he contended, should be classified as residents on arrival. Coast Guard Captain H. R. Searles, commander of the Bering Sea Petrol, requested the same treatment for his men, emphasizing (as did Dusenbury) the limited recreational opportunities in Alaska. The commission argued that existing law prevented such changes, and "in view of the public feeling in the Territory" the commission could not recommend special legislation.[29] These points should be remembered: there was a history of friction between the military and the wardens before 1940, but the minor hunting pressure of a handful of servicemen caused the commission, deliberately or inadvertently, to license soldiers as residents after they had been in Alaska one year. The arrival of thousands more was certain to worry the commission.

Frank Dufresne raised the issue in Anchorage in August 1940, during a visit by his boss, Ira Gabrielson, of the Fish and Wildlife Service. In early November Dufresne forwarded the opinion of George Folta, counsel in Alaska for the Department of the Interior, that soldiers should be considered nonresidents if they wished to hunt, even after one year, depending upon their intentions to remain or leave the Territory. "In this connection I respectfully suggest," wrote Dufresne, "that Alaska's game herds simply will not bear up under the hunting of several thousand additional hunters. At the present time, the big game animals are an important economic asset . . . and regulations are so geared as to permit the fullest possible utilization consistent with maintaining an adequate breeding supply."[30]

The head of the Washington agency's Division of Game Management told the commission's distraught executive officer that counsel for the Fish and Wildlife Service agreed with Folta. Dufresne was asked to supply all the arguments and evidence that might help to block modifications in the law. He obliged in December. The regulations, he reported, were "keyed to the economic needs of a small number of frontier people," and the "inequality of permitting these soldiers and sailors to shoot game which forms a vital part of the Alaska resident's scheme of living should be apparent." The Kenai moose furnished a specific example. A total of 1,000 bull moose was the very maximum which could be spared, but if soldiers were allowed to purchase resident hunting licenses, no fewer than ten thousand additional hunters would seek moose in the area. There were only 10,000 big game hunters licensed in all of Alaska in 1940, but Dufresne did not mention that. He repeated: "We simply do not have enough game to furnish shooting to many more people unless our game laws are rigidly revised." Dufresne reminded

Gabrielson that some of the new military personnel would have been in Alaska one full year in July 1941, after which the issue of military hunting would come to a head.

"Fortunately," he continued, "General Buckner, in charge of all Army activities in Alaska, appears to be a real wildlife conservationist and this may help us."[31]

9

Buckner versus
Dufresne and O'Connor

General Buckner also wanted clarification before July. At a conference in Juneau he was told how the game commission's interpretation would apply to soldiers and sailors. One year in Alaska did not automatically make the soldier a resident legally domiciled in the Territory. The law of 1925 had stated flatly: "For the purposes of this Act a citizen of the United States who has been domiciled in the Territory not less than one year for the purpose of making his permanent home therein . . . shall be considered a resident." Determination of the intent to remain was important, and Counsel Folta believed that residence on a military reservation did not signify intent to stay in Alaska.[1] Nonresident licenses were therefore required of recent arrivals living on the new bases. Soldiers who were domiciled in Alaska when they entered the service were still residents. So were the few Signal Corpsmen scattered around the Territory manning Alaska's electronic communications; they lived in town, raised families, and often extended their enlistments.

Apparently Buckner accepted the new rulings in June and agreed (in Dufresne's words) to "cooperate in the protection of wildlife in the Territory" if the requirement that nonresidents hire a guide were waived temporarily for military personnel and if the game commission tried to get the law changed to allow servicemen, after one year in Alaska, to obtain resident hunting licenses regardless of the location of their living quarters. Later that month the general wrote a long letter advising Dufresne how to manage Alaska's wild animals. It was amicable if gratuitous, and reflected opinions held in the commission.[2]

It was in Fairbanks, not Anchorage, that the controversy first took an ugly turn. In late 1939 the 3,500 people in Fairbanks were supported by the Alaska Railroad, the Fairbanks Exploration Company and its extensive gold-dredging operations, the tiny University of Alaska, and service industries that made the town a supply and urban recreation center for the interior. It was the "big city" to one-half of all of Alaska. It became the site of Ladd Field, an Army Air Corps base, when the military buildup began just prior to the Second World War. The first commanding officer, Lieutenant Colonel L. V. Gaffney, told his superior: "It has been an old custom in Fairbanks for the local population to enjoy spring shooting of migratory wildfowl."[3] The wardens then in Fairbanks were Sam O. White, who pioneered the use of airplanes in wildlife management, and Clarence Rhode, later executive officer of the game commission.

Trouble soon erupted between Rhode and the army officers. Rhode's plan, Gaffney asserted, was to control military hunting because the commission could not control white residents or the Indians. Sam White maintained friendlier relations until early July, when he discussed with Gaffney the commission's decision to waive the guide requirement for soldiers. White, in confidence, reported Gaffney's response to Dufresne: "I was plainly informed that this is 'only an opening wedge' and that they fully expect to gain sweeping concessions before this thing is settled. He also made the remark that they would 'blow the Game Commission wide open.' "[4]

Without White's permission, Dufresne reported the conversation to Buckner in another "confidential" communication. White was told about the exchange, and about Dufresne's faith in Buckner's concern for the welfare of Alaskan game animals. Buckner said that he regretted Gaffney's remarks but thought they might have been misunderstood. In a few days Gaffney flew to Anchorage to express his indignation. Then, in two long letters, he defended himself mainly by attacking Rhode, and then White, when he learned which warden had talked. Buckner accepted Gaffney's claim that White was guilty of pure fabrication, and he passed along to Dufresne Colonel Gaffney's thinly disguised suggestion that all the wardens in Fairbanks be discharged.[5]

Dufresne planned to fire nobody. He believed White. He also seemed to suggest that General Buckner should reread Gaffney's second letter: "One paragraph of his report is devoted to an explanation of this incident, whereas fifteen paragraphs are devoted to attacking his former friend."[6]

Meanwhile Lieutenant M. E. Walseth, of Ladd Field, had bought land in Fairbanks and started construction of a house. He had been in Alaska one year when he applied for a resident license. When it was refused he began a vigorous campaign against the game commission's ruling. A festering sore in the controversy was the resident status of Army Signal Corpsmen. Walseth mentioned two by name. The commission pointed out politely that one had lived in Alaska six years before his latest enlistment, and the other ten years.[7]

At the same time, Gaffney also pressed the commission for a resident license, criticizing the licensing of new civilians and regulations permitting the licensing of aliens but not soldiers.[8] The commission could defend its policies toward aliens and the Signal Corps, but loose licensing procedures for civilians probably allowed some nonresidents to hunt cheaply.

The institutional reasons for General Buckner's decision to apply for a resident big game hunting license are clear. The individual motives behind his legal action are not. He may have been miffed by the refusal of a lowly bureaucrat to grant him a resident license, or he may have been anxious to hunt that season without prejudicing the army's demand for resident privileges. The recollection of Mrs. Adele Buckner is that her husband went to court only to obtain for his men treatment as fair and equal as the new civilians received.[9] Whatever his personal motivation, by the end of August it was too late for reconciliation with the game commission. Everyone's patience was exhausted. The chief antagonists were by then committed to defend what each considered his rights and duties. Subordinates had to be defended too.

Promises by Dufresne, dated September 2, to continue working on recommendations for changes in the law did not satisfy the general. His appearance at the commission office on September 5 with two lawyers formalized his application. The *Anchorage Daily Times* announced on September 6 that servicemen with a fifty-dollar nonresident big game hunting license (a sum about twice the amount of a private's monthly salary) could take to the field without a registered guide. On September 9 the opinion of George Folta was forwarded to Buckner from Juneau, with an official rejection of the general's application. Among other "irreconcilable discrepancies" in the document, said Folta, was residency at both Fort Richardson and Anchorage, which did not satisfy domiciliary requirements.[10] The following weekend, Mary Buckner, the general's daughter, left for Fairbanks to attend her sophomore year of college, and her brother William departed for San Raphael, California, to begin his second year of high school at a military academy. The general accompanied Governor Ernest Gruening to Mount McKinley National Park to locate recreational facilities for military personnel. Three days later, on September 18, the editor of *Alaska Life* magazine lauded the cities of Ketchikan, Juneau, and Seward for their recreational programs aimed to build the morale of servicemen; he urged other cities that had suddenly prospered from huge expenditures for national defense "to take their eyes off the cash register for a few minutes" and develop similar programs.[11]

On September 19 the *Anchorage Daily Times* reported that the completion of a service men's club on Elmendorf Air Base would be celebrated with a barbecue, "probably one of the largest ever held in Alaska. There will be reindeer, moose and caribou, probably a taste of goat, sheep and even a wild bull," the latter a donation from "Sourdough" Jack McCord. The game meat would be provided by legal Air Corps hunters and big game trophy hunters on the Kenai Peninsula. "Trophy meat is often not used because it is in difficult terrain, but the Air Corps boys are going in and [will] bring it out, wherever it falls." Trophies taken by military hunters would be used to adorn the walls of the new club as these decorations became available. On the day the forthcoming gala was announced, Federal District Judge Simon Hellenthal mandated the Alaska Game Commission to give General Buckner a resident license or appear in court.

Headlines in the *Anchorage Daily Times* called the action a test case that could set a precedent.[12] Residents who had come to the country because of its natural beauty, wilderness, and wildlife wondered what would happen to their Alaska if a legal precedent allowed several thousand more hunters into the bush. The game commission's policy was grounded firmly on the interests of those Alaskans, Native and white, who used game animals for food, but that constituency was silent. Instead, vocal townsmen talked of military morale and patriotism.

The court hearings opened on September 22. It was a one-sided assembly. Neither O'Connor nor Dufresne had been served with an order to appear. The court heard General Buckner anyway.[13] His civilian attorney, Warren Cuddy, asked the questions.

Q: Where do you reside?

A: I have resided at Anchorage, Alaska, since July 23, 1940. I have at various times been in different parts of Alaska, including a period in which I lived in a tent at Fort Richardson. My orders directing me to come to Alaska gave my station as Anchorage, Alaska, in command of Federal troops where stationed in Alaska.

Q: Have you made an application for a game license?

A: I have.

Q: Have you been granted that license?

A: It has been denied.

Q: I believe, General Buckner, you might tell the court when you first planned to come to Alaska, what steps you took and what declarations you made as to establishing your domicile in Anchorage, Alaska.

A: This matter goes back for a number of years. My first mention of coming to Alaska and desire to live in Alaska was expressed more than forty years ago when I attempted to get my father to let me come to Alaska gold rushes. After I graduated from West Point in 1908, I placed Alaska high on my preference card, where an officer is requested to state where he would prefer to go on overseas service. That remained on my preference card until I was promoted to . . . [a rank] for which there was not a vacancy in Alaska. . . . However, in May, 1940, when I was relieved as chief of staff, the Sixth Division was directed to proceed to Fort Lewis, Washington, and I remarked to . . . the division commander, I thought it was desirable that enough troops be sent to Alaska to warrant a general, an officer in command, and that it would be more favorable to secure it from Fort Lewis. After my arrival in Alaska, I immediately began to look around with an idea of becoming domiciled here, because for many years I have been looking around for that purpose and stated often that if I found a place where there was good climate, beautiful scenery, access to salt water, access to fishing and hunting and there were manly and congenial men, that is where I was going to settle when I retired. I made inquiries in regard to homesteading within reach of my duties, but was unable to find a place conveniently located. I also made inquiries regarding the purchase of land in the vicinity of Anchorage. . . . I was unable to rent proper quarters for myself and family in town, although I made many attempts to do so—for a short while my wife was living here in the Anchorage Hotel. We made attempts to secure a suitable house which was finally rented on November 15 of this year, and I have been occupying that ever since.

Hellenthal: You mean 1940?

A: November 15, 1940, a year ago. I have actually, according to a diary which I have kept, lived off the Fort Richardson Reservation for one year and eleven days, exclusive of fifteen days I was on a . . . [warship] visiting the Aleutians. I have purchased three city lots in the town of Anchorage and have consulted two architects with a view to constructing a permanent home for myself on the lots in spite of the fact that suitable quarters are being built for me on the Fort Richardson Reservation. . . . Also, I have removed my daughter from the University of California and she is now a student of the University of Alaska. It is my desire and intention to become an Alaskan citizen, barring the unforeseen, after my retirement.

Q: You had that intention since you first came to Anchorage?

A: I had that intention since I arrived at Anchorage.

Q: At the time you left the Fort Richardson area to live in town you had that intention?

A: That was in my mind, I announced to the governor of Alaska and to the officer of the game commission—they were both aware of it.

. . . . .

A: I intend to become a citizen of Alaska, even though temporarily ordered out of Alaska, I wish to vote here and ——

Q: When did you vote last?

A: In 1912, in Kentucky.

Q: And you wish to establish your voting rights in the Territory of Alaska?

A: I do.

Q: And pay the local taxes incident to your domicile here?

A: To fulfill all the requirements of a citizen of Alaska and avail myself of all the privileges of a citizen of Alaska.

Hellenthal: And you had such intention for more than a year prior to the time you filed your application with the Alaska Game Commission?

A: I did.

Aside from Cuddy's request that a temporary resident license be issued to Buckner by Judge Hellenthal because (the *Anchorage Daily Times* reported) "the hunting season was growing short and that further delay in the issuance of a license might limit the general's hunting activities," nothing more happened on this first day of the case. The matter was postponed until Wednesday, September 24, with the expectation that game commission defendants might be persuaded to appear.

That evening Judge Hellenthal was diverted by Dr. J. H. Romig's annual wildlife feast, a major social event in Anchorage each year. General Buckner was there too, and so was Ira Gabrielson, of the Fish and Wildlife Service, up from Washington, D.C., to study the salmon fishery.

In that Alaskan fall of 1941 Dr. Romig enjoyed a dab of celebrity. He first came to southwestern Alaska at the end of the nineteenth century as a medical missionary for the Moravian Church, and stayed for a half-dozen years. After the San Francisco earthquake of 1906 he returned to Alaska as the company physician at a fish cannery, and later worked as a physician for the Alaska Railroad, from which he retired in 1937. In between he held several government jobs and traveled widely in the lower half of the Territory. Romig's biography was published in 1940 under the title *Dog-Team Doctor*. It romanticized the doctor's career and secured his reputation as a courageous frontier physician.[14] From his country house on Spenard Road, atop a bluff looking north over the mouth of Chester Creek, he lived comfortably as one of the town's sourdough "characters." In 1939 he presented a bear cub to army officers who were in the region surveying future military reservations. They crated the animal and shipped it to the States as a mascot.[15]

It was Romig's habit each Wednesday noon to dine informally with friends whom he called "the board of directors." In the fall, when hunting season opened, "board" members collected game meats for a large banquet to entertain themselves and friends. On September 22, 1941, the annual feast was held for 150 people at the Idle Hour Club, on the shore of Lake Spenard. Twelve kinds of game meat were served, all labeled: sheep, moose, deer, goat, caribou, duck, reindeer, bear, goose, grouse, ptarmigan, and porcupine. There was much joviality. A set of "rare" candlesticks was scheduled for presentation to Dr. Romig; General Buckner made the presentation speech, but the candlesticks were "accidentally" broken on their way to the podium. One air corps major, a physician, patrolled the health of the diners with a box of baking soda. Another army major confused the diners by replacing labels on their plates with labels reading "cat," "dog," and "horse." There was community singing. The menu stated: "The wild game dinner is as much a testimonial of respect and esteem for Dr. Romig as it is a feast of thanksgiving for those who know and love this great Northland." A photograph of the event shows Buckner, Hellenthal, and Gabrielson standing with their heads together in conversation—perhaps about the future of the "great Northland" and about whether there would be many opportunities for wildlife banquets in the future.[16]

The next day Interior Counsel Folta, then three hundred miles away in Fairbanks, telephoned Judge Hellenthal. The U.S. attorney for Anchorage had informed Folta that no authorization to represent the game commission had been given to the district attorney by the attorney general of the United States. Folta said he could appear on behalf of the commission but that he would like to have until September 29 to prepare. According to Folta, the judge was eager to resume on Friday, September 26, because, in Hellenthal's words, "the general wants to go hunting and the season is getting short." Folta said he would appear on Friday and ask for a continuance, which Hellenthal agreed to grant. The judge delayed until that time, but from then on he grew impatient.[17]

On September 26, after a request by Folta for a continuance was denied, the hearing was resumed. Buckner took the stand again, this time to describe his attempts to obtain a resident license at the Anchorage office of the game commission. During cross-examination, Folta made a technical point that O'Connor had not been present when the general submitted his written application. Folta himself was then called to the stand to identify a letter containing his interpretation, for the commission, of Buckner's application. Then Warden O'Connor was called. He admitted uncertainty about the general's domicile when Buckner applied orally for a license. Folta again tried to make the argument that O'Connor had not been present when the written application was submitted by Buckner, implying that the warden was improperly named as a defendant.

The tactic was quickly checkmated by Judge Hellenthal in a move that surprised everyone. He ordered Buckner to hand O'Connor the application during a thirty-minute recess, swear to it, offer O'Connor one dollar, and then "come back and tell me what happened." Folta immediately objected, and the judge replied, "Oh, I think General Buckner will do it anyway."[18]

He did, and O'Connor refused. When the warden was asked why, he testified, "Dufresne turned it down and I couldn't over-ride my superior officer." A series of motions by Folta to dismiss the case or delay the writ were denied by Hellenthal. The judge said later of the day's activities: "I don't like the way the case proceeded. . . . It was all horseplay."

One tactic introduced on Saturday morning was even more unusual, so much so that the *Anchorage Daily Times* printed the entire defense

motion. It was to vacate judgment favoring Buckner because Folta was
not authorized by the attorney general to defend O'Connor and
O'Connor was dissatisfied with Folta's conduct and had discharged him.
The motion was introduced by the assistant U.S. attorney, Noel
Wennblom, who also asked for a continuance because Dufresne had still
not been formally ordered to appear and would not be in Anchorage for
several days. Cuddy called the first motion "frivolous and contemptuous." The judge said, "It was a new one on me," and decided to rule on
the matter Monday morning.[19]

He denied the first motion. Folta would remain in the case. As for the
continuance, the judge thought that he should be told when Frank
Dufresne could be there. Wennblom's understanding had been that
Dufresne would be in Seward on next Saturday's boat and could be in
Anchorage that night.

Hellenthal: I think that Mr. Dufresne had better fly by way of Fairbanks. See
when you can get Mr. Dufresne here. The point is when he can get here rather
than when he will be here at his convenience. [Wennblom was asked to instruct
O'Connor to stay in town.]

Hellenthal: I do not wish to have Mr. O'Connor leave the city, so that we could
not reach him within an hour. I might take further action in regard to Mr.
O'Connor if the real representative is not forthcoming.

Wennblom: I can appreciate the position of Mr. Cuddy and General Buckner in
this matter to some extent and heartily agree that no unreasonable delay
should be made in any form of litigation. But the delay in this case has not
been unreasonable.

Hellenthal: Don't you think that after ten days after the case started and you
don't even know where the defendant is is unreasonable?

Wennblom: Only last Friday evening I knew we had a defendant. . . . A writ of
mandamus is a remedy where time is the essential element. The general would
not be deprived of [his] right to go hunting. The general is one of the highest
paid in the army.

Hellenthal: I don't see your view.

Wennblom: Would you say that irreparable damage was being done because he
was deprived of ——

Hellenthal: The right to go hunting is hard to estimate in damages.

Wennblom: He could hunt by paying $49 more.

Hellenthal: I think he is being deprived of his rights.

To hunt under a nonresident license would require the general to sign
a false affidavit stating that his domicile was not Alaska, the judge asserted, recessing until the next morning.

On Tuesday Hellenthal allowed Wennblom until Thursday to prepare
O'Connor's side of the case, to introduce further evidence, and to cross-
examine the general. Before then, George Folta surfaced again, this

time with an affidavit to support a new motion for a change of venue, because, according to him, the court was prejudiced in favor of the general. Folta listed fourteen items to establish his contention that Hellenthal was partial to Buckner. O'Connor submitted another affidavit stating that Folta's services had been "reluctantly" terminated earlier because of the judge's obviously hostile attitude toward Folta. The motion to move the trial to another court was ignored when the hearings were resumed on October 2.

That momentous day began with the reappearance in court of Folta, who was told by Hellenthal, "You have had your hearing as far as O'Connor is concerned." To Wennblom's request that Folta cross-examine Buckner, His Honor replied, "Mr. Folta has had his day in court." Wennblom declined to cross-examine Buckner and moved for a jury trial. Hellenthal replied, "Motion denied. Exception granted. Motion denied for two reasons, it is too late and the law don't give you such a right. Quit stalling."

Wennblom tried other procedures. He referred frequently to the fact that Dufresne, a codefendant and O'Connor's superior, was not even there. The judge held that Folta's appearance was sufficient and Dufresne's side of it could be dealt with later. The plaintiff's lawyer, Warren Cuddy, then put Dr. Romig on the stand. After Romig established that he was an old-timer—he did not need to establish his wildlife expertise, for too many people had recently tasted it—he testified that he had met the general in late July of 1940.

Q: Where did you meet him?
A: At the air base.
Q: I will ask you whether during July and August you had any conversation with General Buckner in reference to his making his domicile in Anchorage, Alaska, or in Alaska.
A: Yes.
Q: What was the nature of that conversation?
A: Well, there was quite a bit of it. He said he must have pioneer blood in his veins, that he wanted to come to Alaska for a long time and now that he was here he intended making this his home, that he was going to buy or build and make Alaska his permanent home.

After Romig's testimony, the judge announced that he would render judgment in the afternoon. To nobody's surprise he ordered O'Connor to issue Buckner a resident big game hunting license.[20] Wennblom objected to the opinion, and Hellenthal observed, "That is childish to take exception to the opinion and the Court will not note it even if you ask it."

The most dramatic moment in this symbolic enactment of the beginning of the end of Old Alaska was still a few hours away.

When Cuddy confronted O'Connor with the court order, the stubborn warden still refused to issue the general a resident license. Cuddy asked whether the warden would be in court for a three o'clock hearing, and sign the license. O'Connor (according to the *Anchorage Daily Times*) said he had work to do and if the court needed him it could send the marshal for him. All this was reported to Hellenthal, who then ordered that O'Connor be notified to appear at four o'clock and show cause why he should not be held in contempt of court. The warden did not appear. Cuddy said his whereabouts were unknown. The judge responded, "I expected that."

Buckner's counsel was given the choice of one of two courses of action: O'Connor could be brought in by a marshal and jailed until he signed a license, or the clerk of the court could sign it in O'Connor's name. Cuddy wisely chose the second alternative. It might have been a courtesy to the dedicated and honest warden, or Buckner and his lawyers may have known or sensed that O'Connor had many silent Alaskan supporters who feared for the loss of their way of life and who privately applauded their neighbor's defiance of titled authority.

For the general public, the climax came in the afternoon of October 2, when the *Anchorage Daily Times* published an "extra" in large, thick, black headlines, announcing that O'Connor had thumbed his nose at the court and had probably flown off with another wildlife agent to search for an overdue party of hunters. The implication seemed to be that participation in a rescue mission was less important than compliance with the court's order.

It was not true that O'Connor had left town, he said on Friday. He had merely been investigating a serious game law violation locally; he was never served with papers ordering him to appear at four o'clock, and he had spent most of the time on Fourth Avenue, the main street of Anchorage. The *Times* learned that someone else had flown away in the game commission airplane to search for the lost hunters.

That same week, District Attorney Kehoe (who was as visible by his absence as Dufresne was by his), announced that the game commission would appeal Hellenthal's decision. During the next five days Judge Hellenthal reported the tardy arrival of a reindeer carcass, his contribution to Romig's feast, and voiced his hope that a special dinner of the "board of directors" would be held. Dufresne flew to Anchorage (on October 6) and promised that commission personnel would continue to enforce the law, even if it meant they would have to go to jail. As Dufresne boarded an airplane for Fairbanks, he announced that the Alaska Game Commission would not honor General Buckner's license because it had not been signed by an officer of the commission.[21]

An editorial in the *Anchorage Daily Times* appreciated the need for

modern game regulations: "Unless Alaska is to remain a frontier country, it is to be expected that new regulations will be found necessary." A
later editorial saw Secretary of the Interior Harold Ickes as the Grand
Pooh Bah who sought to place his bureaus and commissions above the
law, subject to review only by Ickes himself, "probably to the exclusion of
the Omnipotent Power." During the same week, at Sixth Avenue and
E Street, O'Connor's young son slipped and fell on a broken whiskey
bottle, severely cutting his right hand; Dr. Romig's son stitched it back
together.[22]

A few other events also occurred about that time. For one, Emperor
Hirohito commanded General Tojo to form a new government, replacing Prince Konoye's cabinet, which had tried to resolve differences
between the United States and Japan. The ascendancy of the Japanese
military was accompanied, reported the *Anchorage Daily Times*, by a Japanese press article that declared: "There is fundamental disagreement between the United States and Japan. We are now facing our rise or fall in
a crisis never before paralleled in our history."[23]

10

The Biggest Shoot-out
and the End of an Era

The issues raised by General Buckner's suit were not settled by the court. The mandamus action did not set a precedent for anyone except a soldier who maintained his own residence off a military base. Few Alaskans appreciated that point. The Territory's alert governor did. Ernest Gruening wrote in his diary on October 20: "Buckner had alleged right along that this was a test case for the whole Army; but of course it can't be since his situation is entirely different from that of men living on reservations."[1] Even that small legal victory for the army evaporated after the Second World War began, in early December 1941, with a Japanese air attack on the Hawaiian Islands. During the war, military personnel from outside lived on base and their dependents were transported to the States. Buckner had no time for big game hunts, he told a journalist; he was interested now only in hunting the Japanese. Neither could his soldiers or civilian defense personnel spare much time to hunt.[2]

The Alaska Game Commission did not push its appeal of Hellenthal's judgment vigorously. The case was eventually dropped. The commissioners, meeting in Washington, D.C., in January of 1942, decided unanimously after consultation with Army, Navy, and Interior Department officials to recommend a change in the law that would give servicemen resident hunting privileges after one year in the Territory, regardless of where they were quartered. The recreation of soldiers at war had become more important than concern over the long-range supply of wildlife. Alaska's delegate, Anthony Dimond, introduced the amendment in the House of Representatives, and the matter was left in the lap of Congress. Meanwhile, new regulations taking into account the added hunting pressure could be written.[3]

Relations between the wardens and the military remained ruffled. The delay in Congress chafed. Buckner seemed to imply that a certain commissioner, while pledging support for the one-year amendment, was lobbying against it. In three letters to *Field and Stream* Buckner mentioned several game law violations that he had observed personally. Dufresne asked him for the particulars, so wildlife agents could investigate. Dufresne also told the general that foxes were killed on the Aleutian Islands despite the fact that post commanders had been informed about the protected status of the foxes there. Buckner replied, "I have no doubt that soldiers are destroying these foxes in large numbers, but the soldiers concerned are Japs!"[4]

Drew Pearson, the syndicated newspaper columnist, rubbed the old wound publicly in September of 1942. Pearson claimed that Ira Gabrielson was "very irate" at General Buckner for traveling in amphibian aircraft to Alaskan lakes and shooting big game. Buckner, according to Pearson's column, "Washington Merry-Go-Round," was overdoing it, as were other officers. Pearson then reported briefly the old flap over military hunting in Alaska.

The charges elicited an open letter to Ira Gabrielson from Captain Roy Craft, editor of the army weekly, *Kodiak Bear*. Gabrielson was told to "lay off our General Buckner" and "play fair with the boys in uniform." Buckner had never killed a single big game animal. His total game bag was a couple dozen ducks, one ptarmigan, and assorted fish. "Does that sound like a game hog, Mr. Gabrielson?" asked the angry editor, who went on: "Stories grow pretty big in Alaska, as perhaps you know. Somebody must have fed you that juicy one about Army fliers machine-gunning moose out of P-38's. You know, perhaps, that they would be court martialed for that." As for the biggest game: "General Buckner has NEVER shot a Kodiak bear. He'd give his eye tooth to shoot one, as all of us would, but he hasn't been able to take the time."[5]

Dufresne answered for Gabrielson, who denied any guilt. (In a private letter to Major Kermit Roosevelt, Theodore Roosevelt's son then on duty in Anchorage, Gabrielson said of Pearson: "Not only do I not know him but I make it a practice never to talk with people of that type. I do know . . . Buckner and consider him a high class person.") Dufresne said the entire matter was in the hands of Congress, but the indignant captain was not pacified. He claimed that closure of the Alaska Peninsula west of Katmai to bear hunting was obvious discrimination against the military. Craft would not be surprised if—after soldiers were allowed to hunt with the resident license—both Kodiak and Afognak islands were closed to all hunting.[6]

The government had behaved suspiciously in its game reservation policies. Executive orders of the president had created the Kodiak National Wildlife Refuge in August of 1941, and the Kenai National Moose Range in December. Controlled hunting was permitted in both areas, which aggregated almost two million acres. But from the game commis-

sion's point of view, it was essential that regulations be changed to protect the animals. Captain Craft's charge was probably true but irrelevant.
New rules were necessary to protect the game from more people hunting, and soldiers were people.

Captain Craft's "tall tale" of military aircraft strafing helpless game
animals was more than a sourdough's story. Gabrielson had heard the
rumors. A personal friend of his, a major stationed in Anchorage, believed such things happened but could get no hard evidence of it. Investigation might reveal the bloody result but could not assign specific
guilt. Archival records of Alaskan wildlife management so far have revealed, with one exception, only unconfirmed reports that machine-
gunning of game animals occurred. The exception was an obvious
slaughter with automatic weapons of five buffalo, in the interior.[7] To
suggest, however, as the editor of *Kodiak Bear* did, that a threat of court-
martial would have prevented such tragedies is naive. It was a crime easily committed with impunity in Alaska's wilderness, and behavior easily
justified as being in the national interest because it provided fighter pilots with target practice. And the allegation of strafing was not a charge
the army would be anxious to investigate closely, while relations with the
game commission were still cool.

The publicity attending Pearson's report stimulated Congress to
amend Dimond's bill to give soldiers resident privileges immediately
upon their arrival in Alaska, but the new proposal was scrapped, and the
bill was finally passed. It was signed on July 1, 1943,[8] two full hunting
seasons after the rumblings of military discontent were first heard from
Fairbanks.

Announcement of the new rules permitting soldiers to buy licenses
after one year in the Territory was accompanied by General Buckner's
remarkable General Order 118, dated July 19, one day after his birth-
day.[9] He began by crediting the good conduct of Alaskan military
personnel with dispelling any "misgivings" about their conservation-
mindedness. Members of his command were enjoined to observe the letter and spirit of the game laws and to conduct themselves in a
sportsmanlike manner and avoid any greedy act that might brand them
as game hogs or unworthy citizens. Specific unsportsmanlike practices
were prohibited: taking too many fish or small fish; shooting at big
game from too far away, or with small-bore rifles or hard-point ammunition, all practices that might wound but not kill the animal; killing female bears with dependent cubs; killing any game where the meat and
trophy could not be carried in; firing at animals without first deter-
mining whether they were of legal size and sex; depleting the breeding
stock of animals anywhere; and "wanton destruction or waste of animals,

birds or fish, even though permitted by game regulations." The last must have been a dig at the game commission. Wanton waste was always prohibited.

Under the order, no army aircraft was permitted to land any hunters in a location not habitually used for landings, for example, on isolated lakes. The use of government firearms and ammunition in the hunt was prohibited. Hands should be wet when releasing fish that were hooked but unwanted. When a bear approached, the soldier was admonished to stand perfectly still and talk in a conversational tone, a method (said Buckner) used safely by photographers. When bears were killed illegally, under the pretext of self-defense, commanders were ordered to investigate fully and report to headquarters. Each post should have a game officer. "The foregoing regulations, if properly carried out," the order closed, "will not hamper legitimate sport but will set a high standard of sportsmanship and aid in preserving Alaska as a happy hunting ground for other good sportsmen of the future."

General Order 118, if obeyed, was the kind of cooperation with which the game commission could live happily. Acting Secretary of the Interior Abe Fortas complimented General Buckner in a letter to the secretary of war and reported his understanding that the regulations were proving effective. On the other hand, Fortas continued, if the same rules had been issued to Gaffney's men (he was now a brigadier general) and to the men under another general in Alaska, much unnecessary destruction of game and fish might have been prevented.[10]

The Buckners added a farm near Homer, on the Kenai Peninsula, to their Alaskan real estate. An enthusiastic cover story in *Time* magazine described the place and the intention of the Buckners to return after the war: "Wild game, including black and grizzly bears, abounds at the farm. A vein of coal lies offshore, and the tide washes up more than enough lumps for heating. . . . Said the General: 'I expect it will take me a solid year to catch up with my hunting and fishing. And I'll be so far away from things I won't be able to exercise a retired general's prerogative of cussing and swearing that the new Army has gone to hell since he got out of it.' "[11] Meanwhile the general had a war on his doorstep. A tiny part of Alaska was the only American territory in the Western Hemisphere to be occupied by Japan during the Second World War.

In late 1939 General George Marshall had considered it "highly improbable" that any major operation by an enemy would be initiated in Alaska. The House of Representatives did not even endorse an appropriation for fiscal year 1941 to build Elmendorf Air Corps Base at Anchorage until (as one postwar army historian writes) the "German blitzkrieg startled Congress into hasty approval." By October 1941 there were nearly 23,000 military people in Alaska, and by the end of 1943, nearly 154,500. On June 3, 1942, a Japanese task force consisting of two small aircraft carriers, two heavy cruisers, and three destroyers approached the Aleutian Islands and mounted an air attack on Dutch Harbor. The warplanes attacked again on June 4, and Japanese troops occupied two westerly Aleutian Islands, Attu and Kiska.

One-half of the Japanese airplanes on one carrier were lost during the operation because the attacking force did not know about an American airstrip on Umnak Island, just west of Dutch Harbor. Buckner is credited with proposing the secret landing field. It gave his undersized air arm a surprise advantage. At the time, Alaskans thought that Umnak saved the Aleutians and maybe the mainland. Actually, the Japanese assault was a diversion from the Battle of Midway.[12]

Alaska was a war zone, a theater of operations. Although Buckner commanded army troops and the Eleventh Air Force, technically all his men were under Rear Admiral Robert A. Theobald. The general's Alaska-trained Fourth Infantry was not even given the duty of evicting the Japanese from the Aleutians. The job went instead to a stateside division under the command of another general. In May 1943 about 11,000 Americans assaulted Attu, supported by 200 aircraft. It was a violent battle. Then American airplanes began to bombard Kiska, and in mid-August 39,000 American troops landed on the island.[13]

Nobody was there. The troops were greeted by tame foxes. Two weeks earlier Japanese warships had secretly evacuated 5,000 to 7,000 men. The *Anchorage Daily Times* editorialized bravely: "We know now that the Japs are not only rats. They are scared rats, ready to run if and when they can run." And Buckner's superior, General DeWitt, up from the States and doubtless embarrassed, wanted to attack Japan from Alaska. "We must carry the war to the Jap empire," he was quoted in the *Times* as saying. "We must wade in and tear Japan apart, dynamite and gut her with incendiaries, and kill."

Buckner received a distinguished service medal and called on President Franklin Roosevelt in Washington. "The President just wanted to see what an old sourdough who had been in Alaska three years looks like," said the general.[14]

The requirements of war diverted many potential poachers, but wildlife habitat disruptions occurred throughout Alaska as military roads, landing fields, and outposts were constructed. And the central human problem—an old Alaskan concern—remained: a large proportion of the population was transient. In 1943 the game commission fretted: "If we were dealing with people who intended to make their future homes here, it might be easier to convince them of the need for careful use of the limited wildlife resource. Instead, we are for the most part confronted with thousands of temporary inhabitants, eager to bag a big game animal as a momento of their visit to the northern war zone. This applies equally to men in uniform, and construction workers. Pleas that these game and fur animals will be needed more than ever in post war development of Alaska too often go unheeded. Get, and get out is more likely to be the attitude."[15] Temporary residents had destroyed wild animals carelessly in 1867, and along the gold rush trails at the turn of the century. Seasonal fishermen, miners, cannery workers, and railroad construction workers were often similarly irresponsible. Large segments of the population that appeared to be in Alaska to stay were in fact highly mobile.

Until the end of 1944 the danger remained suspended. Once the conclusion of the war was clearly in sight, however, duties and inhibitions too often vanished, and the commission's worst fears became realities. Transients, both military and civilian, wanting one last crack at the Territory's famous game animals, and Alaskans with more time to hunt for the dinner table, together with a severe winter in 1945–46, combined to inflict heavy losses on the wildlife population. The game commission's new executive officer, Frank W. Hynes, said that 1945 was the worst year for game on record. With the end of the war in August, thousands of hunters hiked into the wilderness to kill big game animals. The result was a slaughter of almost anything that could be shot, and much waste. Many animals were killed so far from roads or trails that the meat spoiled before it could be used. In one small area twelve cow moose were found shot, and rotting whole. According to the commission, some of the hunters slaughtered for the joy of killing, judging from the dead animals found in the hills. Cases prosecuted in the courts were of the most flagrant kind.[16] It was a dark and grisly time in the history of Alaska.

In the years following this bloody ending of the war, there was some friction between the commission and the military establishment,[17] but in general service-civilian relations improved. Although a study conducted in the States contended that military training and experience did not make ex-servicemen safe hunters, a postwar study in Alaska concluded that fewer game regulations were violated by servicemen than by a comparable number of licensed civilians.[18] More and more, game commission officials praised Alaskan military commanders for their positive conservation behavior. Clarence Rhode took General William Kepner on airplane patrols into the bush. Beginning in 1953, a military conservation officer's course was taught at the University of Alaska, to train officers assigned to serve as wildlife agents, a job Buckner invented in his General Order 118. Toward the end of the commission's life, one-fourth of all hunting and fishing licenses sold in Alaska each year were sold to military personnel.[19]

Managing a steady—in some cases, increasing—supply of big game animals, while the number of hunters multiplied, was the central task of the commission after the war. The number of trapping licenses issued remained around 5,000 to 6,000 during the fifties. The number of resident hunting licenses ranged from about 9,000 in 1946 to 31,500 in 1955 and 1956. The number of nonresident big game licenses rose to 1,400. Alaska was still a sportsman's paradise.[20] At the end of the fifties the Alaska Game Commission passed along to the new state of Alaska a fairly healthy population of big game. Part of the commission's success was due to improved scientific knowledge of the animals. After statehood was achieved, charges were made that wildlife management suffered from too much local politics, irrelevant biology, and not enough enforcement.

Frank Dufresne left Alaska during the war to work in public relations for the Fish and Wildlife Service, and thereafter devoted his time to writing outdoor books and articles. He died recently. Jack O'Connor was promoted to wildlife supervisor, operating out of Juneau, a job from which he retired to live in Southern California. Sam White, miffed at both Gaffney and Dufresne (the latter for revealing a confidential communication), quit the game commission in September of 1941 to fly for a bush airline at double the salary. He retired in Fairbanks. Other wardens were not so lucky. Horsea Sarber disappeared. His outboard-powered boat was found adrift in 1952, "the motor in 'start' position, his rifle and binoculars still aboard, his lunch untouched." Clarence Rhode, with his son and a second agent, in a Fish and Wildlife Service airplane, vanished in the Brooks Range in 1958; the wreckage was not found until twenty years later.[21]

Simon Bolivar Buckner, Jr., never got the chance to catch up on his hunting from his farm on Kachemak Bay. After his Alaskan service he was finally given his first major combat command, to invade and take Okinawa. Near the conclusion of that awful battle, and two months before the end of the war, while seated on a hill overlooking a mop-up operation, a shell burst nearby and one fragment tore a hole in his chest. He died within ten minutes, the highest ranking army officer to be killed in action during the Pacific war.[22]

The judge in the case fared poorly as a result of his participation. When Simon Hellenthal came up for reappointment in 1943, the attorney general balked. Apparently his role in the Buckner case was a pivotal consideration in the failure of Washington to reappoint him, in spite of endorsements from the Anchorage Bar Association, the *Anchorage Daily Times*, and local Democratic Party organizations.[23] Direct evidence of the Fish and Wildlife Service's role was not found in the archival records, and two minor objections came from other sources, but Hellenthal himself, his partisans, and Congressional Delegate Anthony Dimond all believed that opposition to the reappointment came out of the Department of the Interior. The overwhelming local support for Hellenthal, including a last-minute letter from Delegate Dimond to President Roosevelt citing the objection of the secretary of the interior, failed to get the judge retained.[24] He retired to Juneau, where he died in 1955. He appears to have been the only casualty of the Buckner case. Everyone else was promoted, including his courtroom antagonist, George Folta.

Folta left his job as Alaskan solicitor for the Department of the Interior to become federal judge of the First Judicial Division at Juneau, the job that Hellenthal had wanted most. The secretary of the interior had recommended Folta. He often traveled north to help reduce the workload of Anthony Dimond, who occupied Hellenthal's old position. By 1951, when Folta came up for reappointment, he had managed to make a handful of enemies in Anchorage's legal community, but the few complaints were directed at his performance on the bench. There is no mention in his Washington appointment file of the Buckner case or its ramifications. Folta was also criticized in the Island Lantern, a newspaper published by convicts at McNeil Island Federal Penitentiary, to which Alaskan criminals were sent. The Daily Alaska Empire of Juneau observed sarcastically that Judge Folta had been "censured severely by his critics at Anchorage, Fairbanks, and McNeil Island."[25]

Unlike Hellenthal, Folta survived the protest of a minority. He was reappointed judge of the First Division, a position he held until he was again scheduled for reappointment in 1955. He died that year, two months after Simon Hellenthal. Folta suffered a heart attack while sitting in the bow of a boat, off on another hunting trip.[26] Alaska's champion bear hunter was dead. The Kodiak bear–cattle problem was not, however, and neither were many other old problems facing the wildlife of Alaska.

Despite inadequate data from Kodiak, certain conditions probably still obtained after statehood: there were still more Kodiak bears than Kodiak cattle; a bear was still worth more per head to Alaska than a steer; there were more guides and outfitters dependent on bears than Kodiak farmers dependent on cattle; the range was no better than it had been for cattle; the average size of the ranches affected by bears was still huge—more than 20,000 acres. None of those realities prevented the state from hiring a president of the ranchers' association, who had been a military fighter pilot, to hunt brown bears in a Piper airplane equipped with automatic firepower. Farther north, the ancient conflict between settler and wildlife took a novel form. Transplanted bison began to overrun the small clearings of more recently transplanted humans. One buffalo had a reputation for charging automobiles until a large truck sideswiped it. Would-be farmers in the area did not mourn the brave bull, whose species had served for a century as an example of how not to treat wildlife.[27] Elsewhere, predation control remained controversial, especially the reduction of wolf populations in areas where the numbers of moose had declined.[28]

New roads, vehicles capable of traveling off the road in summer or winter, the rapid growth of older transportation technologies, especially airborne, an expanding wood pulp industry, military defense construction, and developments associated with oil production are technologies and man-made habitat changes that cramp the wild animals' freedom and well-being. Some of the more massive projects have been forestalled. The Atomic Energy Commission at one time wanted to blast a harbor on the Arctic Ocean with nuclear weapons, as an experiment. Governor Gruening, as U.S. senator, proposed a huge hydroelectric dam at Rampart, on the Yukon River, that would cover 10,000 square miles and create a reservoir 10 percent larger than Lake Erie, flooding a giant wildlife habitat on which interior Natives depended.[29] Both government projects were abandoned under pressure from Natives, sportsmen, and environmentalists. Private proposals for development that threaten wildlife are less easily shot down, though federal and state governments have achieved some success in regulating them.

Man the hunter is still accused by preservationists of endangering the survival of species. The criticism becomes more stinging as hunting technologies improve and the hunt becomes less a fair chase and more a sure thing requiring little wilderness wisdom and sometimes very little exertion. The airplanes, autos, snowmobiles, all-terrain vehicles, two-way radios, and fancy, manufactured camping gear have made the term "roughing it" almost obsolete. Some Alaskans still get personal satisfaction from an old-style, legal hunt requiring exercise and skill, and many white residents still supplement their income by bringing home wild meat. In 1973 game meats were consumed at the per capita rate of more than seventeen pounds per Anchorageite, which represents 10 percent of all the red meat consumed that year by each person in Alaska's most urbanized region.[30]

After statehood, Alaskans were still amused by the big game hunter from outside who took his trophy home after a hunt that required very little of his time or muscle, only his money. Toward the end of the sixties, guided nonresidents on 600 or 700 hunts killed 5 percent or less of the big game taken each year. Some of the prestige enjoyed by guides under the game commission had eroded by 1968. Accusations that guides used airplanes illegally, pampered customers, and wasted wildlife were heard more frequently.[31]

Many Natives still rely on subsistence hunting but many also lean heavily for their livelihood on wages, craftsmanship, welfare, and business ventures. Open criticism by whites of the Natives' impact on wildlife populations and their relative immunity to regulation has become more common. In the spring of 1975 northern Eskimos were charged with the major responsibility for an alarming decline in the size of the Arctic caribou herd; the Eskimos had different explanations for the decline.[32] Since the comprehensive Native land claim settlement, the Natives' right to wildlife and their need for it have been debated hotly.

In the future, perhaps, Alaskan hunting will level off while nature watching increases, a trend visible in the other states after 1965. One thing appears to be certain, all others being equal: the demands by people for outdoor recreation will increase, placing additional pressures on big game. The latter will lose unless balanced, scientific relationships between man and animal are written into law and enforced. It comes down mainly to leaving enough territory for the beasts. To that end, Alaskan refuges have been created and enlarged, and more are planned by both the state and the federal government.[33]

The problems and conditions affecting Alaska's big game today are similar to those that faced the animals before General Buckner went to court, but the scale and the pace of change are different. Today Alaska is in the environmental spotlight because it's there, because historical events left more of nature more intact in Alaska than elsewhere under the Stars and Stripes, and because Americans invented conservation as a national political principle. But not as much remains, and what does has been modified by man and accelerating demographic, technological, and economic changes begun during the Second World War. The Buckner case was a symbolic incident that signaled the end of frontier Alaska. The episode was a fire siren in the night because big game, roaming wild, is the most vulnerable characteristic of a country's frontier personality, the true sign that natural environments do in fact exist next to people.

What personality changes are in store for Alaska? The question needs more study than it has received from economists balancing the future books, fast-buck "development" artists, weekend journalists, and enthusiastic young cheechakos posing as hardy pioneers. One vision dated 1975 sees Alaska as America's survival kit, as America's Ark, or, as Charles Hallock phrased it in 1908, "our cache near the Pole."[34] Those who view Alaska and its resources merely as a bailer for the prodigal American sailor, as the nation's ark, should be reminded what Noah took aboard his boat: "Of clean beasts, and of beasts that are not clean, and of fowls, and of every thing that creepeth upon the earth, there went in two and two unto Noah into the ark." Noah did not take into his ark two machine guns, two snowmobiles, and two barrels of gas.

Afterword:
A Big Game Plan

Historical relations between big game animals and people in Alaska suggest patterns and generalizations that are worth isolating, repeating, and comparing with what happened in other places.

Wealth from land and natural resources was the fundamental determinant of American growth and power, although (as a prominent economic historian has admitted) economic theory usually slights the role of natural resources to emphasize capital, labor, or entrepreneurship, when the causes of economic growth are weighed.[1] Apparently no investigator has looked closely enough at the economic significance of game meat to the earliest settlers on all American frontiers. Its availability, if Alaska is at all typical, must have been very important, perhaps critical, to the pace and character of human settlement. Game animals were a principal source of food consumed by the first immigrants, who harvested other, salable wildlife, especially fur-bearing animals and fish. The fishery and the fur trade preceded the development of other enterprises in the New World and were sometimes the source of capital for newer industries.

In most of the United States the big game disappeared quickly, by a historian's timetable. The noisy controversies of later decades were over land, water, timber, and minerals, not game animals (except for the uproar over birds). In Alaska the arguments were over land, minerals, and timber too, but the wildlife was still there when conservation became a national policy, and game was at the center of the debate over conservation because it was the most emotional environmental issue. Aspiring Alaskan frontier entrepreneurs used the game, especially the brown bear, as the rallying cry of pioneer democrats against wealthy urban sportsmen, just as middle-class Englishmen had earlier made hunting the emotional center of their battle against the privileged and landed aristocracy.[2] In recent controversies over the classification of federal lands in Alaska, hunting and game animal policy remain a focal point in the debate over other natural resources.[3]

For students of the social history of American science, the story of Governor Riggs's quarrel with the Bureau of Biological Survey challenges the conventional wisdom in the secondary historical literature that opposition to scientific conservation was only the selfish bleating of unscientific Western bumpkins. Sometimes the science was less than adequate. Biologists were influential in establishing policies for the conservation of brown bears, and for the implementation of those policies, at a time when large-animal mammalogy was not scientific enough in the matter of speciation. Events in the United States at about this time in reclamation engineering and forestry seem to parallel the brown bear's scrape with the law.[4] If this was a period of emerging scientific expertise in government, as some historians of the Progressive era of American political history believe, it seems clear that specialists in the conservation sciences were not yet very expert. And Samuel Hays's view that localism hampered comprehensive resource planning by experts, though supported by the Alaskan bear affair, should be elaborated to include the observation that poor science and inexpertise might be the weakness of centralized planning that locals indicted most effectively.[5]

The Alaskan experience also reveals an antagonism between West and East that parallels the abrasive regionalism plainly visible in the general history of American westward expansion. As Gene Gressley observes, "The American West has had a long tradition of protest against economic and cultural exploitation by the East."[6] The Alaskan record reads more precisely as the hostility of an undeveloped territory toward developed regions, for Alaskan verbal assaults were as frequently directed against exploitation by San Francisco and Seattle as by New York and Washington, D.C.

The anticonservation sentiment heard from Alaska did not reflect every Alaskan's opinion. Many residents lived in the Territory because they liked Alaska as it was. Opposition to game conservation dominated public utterances because it tended to come from businessmen and lawyers who controlled the communication media and public offices. Not all Alaskans shared the views of their newspaper editors, who usually demanded that big game be sacrificed if it stood in the way of economic development. The same appears to have been true in the general history of American conservation in the West. The anticonservationists were more vocal, not necessarily more numerous.[7]

Not all businessmen and professionals were opposed to the conservation of game animals. Some were members of sportsmen's clubs that actively supported the game commission. From the documentary record it is not even possible to conclude that most Alaskans favoring economic development and population growth opposed vigorous wildlife conservation. George Folta supported big game protection on a sustained yield basis and said in 1921 that he was "not able to regret our failure to increase in population"; Will Chase, a medical practitioner, ardent hunter, and supporter of wildlife conservation, participated in the Cordova Coal Party to protest Progressive measures conserving Alaskan coal. Thomas Riggs thought later in his life that Alaska should not be developed too rapidly.[8] Nor were Alaskan newspapers consistent in their opposition to conservation before 1941. When President Harding was in Seattle on his way back from Alaska he delivered a speech that told "get-rich-quick" and "fly-by-night" operators expecting to exploit the Territory's riches to forget it. Alaska would be "sanely developed for the benefit of Alaskans." Alaskans, he reported, were busily mining coal under existing laws and did not think forest conservation there was too drastic. Harding did not expect rapid development. The Fairbanks *News-Miner-Citizen* applauded: "The cries the States hear regarding Alaskan problems are the howls of the wolves who wish to feast off the richest public domain the United States ever owned."[9] The opinion was expressed a scant five years after the Sulzer bill was defeated.

All that can be said to describe an Alaskan opponent of wildlife conservation (to 1941) is that he was probably a businessman or lawyer, that he probably favored rapid economic development of Alaska, and that his opinion was the Alaskan opinion heard in public. He was in a minority, if one assumes that most Natives and most white resident hunters were big game conservationists of the utilitarian variety.

Another observation about the history of wildlife and people in Alaska deserves emphasis. The continual squabbling of Alaskan entrepreneurs and political leaders with conservationists and federal bureaucrats resembles a quarrel over territoriality and resources of the kind ethologists and sociobiologists have noted among animals. The persistent Alaskan dislike of transients who hunted is part of the same conflict, with another human trait noted by anthropologists thrown in: the distrust that aboriginal peoples and some animals have of strangers. Perhaps historians should consider more seriously the possibility that human history and natural history are not far apart, and that social history might be better understood if the premises were more animalistic. In the meantime, a useful analytical framework can be constructed from the Alaskan evidence.

Four main variables appear to have determined how big game animals survived the impact of man on the natural environment in Alaska. The first is the population ratio of hunters to game animals in a given region. The second is the demand or market for the meat, hides, or heads. The third is the effectiveness of available hunting technologies, broadly construed. The fourth is a combination of all the attitudes that would tend to preserve animals, including the Natives' magico-religious conservation beliefs and white political conservation policies and philosophies.

Obviously, other, secondary factors come into play. For example, the population ratio is affected by the stamina and vision of the hunter, the defensive mechanisms of the hunted, and the reproductive vigor of the species. The effect of the market can be modified by the psychology and industry of the hunter and trader. The technology variable is affected by weather. Attitudes do not count for much unless some form of enforcement is at work, such as a superstitious fear of violating codes of behavior or a real fear of arrest and imprisonment. Personality differences can modify each variable. Conservation sentiment, or the reverse, when advocated by a commanding personality like Simon Buckner, is more likely to succeed than when preached by Mr. Milktoast. Conservation as a national policy got powerful support during the presidency of Theodore Roosevelt, who was no shrinking violet. But the four primary variables can be controlled crudely to clarify what happened to wildlife in the past, and even, perhaps, to predict what may happen in the future.

Before the Alaskan gold rushes, until about 1890, the ratio of hunters to animals was in general low in the country and favorable to the continued existence of game. There were not enough hunters in the field to threaten the animals, no matter how effective the available technologies. The demand for game was weak. Native conservation attitudes were not yet tested. White attitudes were not yet clearly formulated; American conservation did not become a significant factor until the late nineteenth and early twentieth centuries. Exceptions could be found near towns and villages where there were more hunters, where the market was stronger and game was in fact depleted, or along the coasts, where transportation technologies enlarged the market for marine and terrestrial mammals and made access to them easier. For example, in the mid-1890s as many as fifteen whaling ships might winter at Herschel Island on the Arctic Coast, just east of the Alaska-Canada boundary. The crew of each vessel could consume 10,000 pounds of caribou meat annually, not to mention moose meat, sheep meat, and ptarmigan killed and sold by ambitious Natives.[10]

Beginning with the first gold rush, the ratio of hunters to animals increased dramatically in most parts of Alaska, and the demand for wild meat increased accordingly. Breech-loading, repeating firearms with fixed cartridges were available to Native and white alike at low cost, as was mechanized transportation for use on the sea, rivers, or lakes. The conservationist attitudes attributed to Natives appear not to have prevented them from threatening future supplies of game, while at the same time in 1902 and 1908, white conservationists outside secured the passage of Alaska's first comprehensive game laws to protect the animals. If the adoption of a law is sufficient evidence, whites in the States were more conservation minded than Alaskan Natives; within Alaska both whites and Natives wasted wildlife because enforcement was poor or indifferent until 1925.

Enforcement is one measure of how deeply a positive attitude toward conservation is held. Policymakers believed correctly that white conservation sentiment was not strong enough to endorse firm implementation of those early laws, and they staked the future of Alaskan game on what they expected after the initial gold fever to be a low hunter / animal ratio that would pose no danger even with the new technologies, and on strict control of the market. The lawmakers expected no profound conservationism in Alaska, among Native or white, and found very little, except as it reflected individual self-interest. The strategy worked as a temporary effort to save Alaska's big game from the fate of so many species in the nineteenth-century American West. Until the period beginning with the establishment of the game commission in 1925, the attitudinal and technological variables were much less important in the preservation of game than a weak market and a low ratio of hunters to animals.

The game commission's firm commitment to enforcement and to the encouragement of conservation attitudes through education began to pay off in the thirties. This development was extremely important because new technologies—better guns, highways, and autos, a railroad, motorboats, and airplanes—made the small number of hunters more of a threat to the game supply. The possibility raised by the Buckner case that hunting pressures could triple disturbed the commission greatly and explains its dilatory—sometimes intransigent—behavior. The commission wanted time to revise its entire system of regulation to accommodate safely the higher hunter / animal ratio that the new military establishment might introduce. Wartime realities rather than major policy and regulation changes mitigated the pressure on game animals until the last few months of the war, when what the commission had feared most happened: an orgy of killing by a large, transient population. Thereafter, hunting pressure increased, until statehood, though not as much as the population increases might indicate, for population gains were largely urban. A key to the survival of game animals in the period prior to the Second World War, along with strong conservationist attitudes encouraged by education and enforcement of the laws, was the successful near-elimination of the market. For all practical purposes, the demand for game was limited to an insignificant amount of nonresident trophy hunting and local hunting for food.

Through all periods, Natives were exempt from the game laws, either in fact or in spirit. They formed about half or more of the population and a larger percentage of the hunters, but they still represented a low hunter / animal ratio. For that reason they apparently did not threaten game species except locally, though abundant evidence exists that they probably wasted game as much as did white hunters. There is reason to believe that aboriginal ecological understanding and practice may be greatly overrated.

How can this analytical framework be used to plan the future of wildlife? All four variables can be manipulated consciously. People deliberately migrate, buy, and invent, and they adopt attitudes by persuasion. They can also impede immigration of their fellows to certain areas, such as animal refuges and parks, and in other ways lower the hunter / animal ratio. They can keep certain animal products off the market by law, including trophy heads. They can require that less efficient technologies be employed in the hunt, if it is necessary to preserve game. They can educate other people in the desirability of conserving game and implement that attitude with laws that are enforced. All these techniques are rational, practical instruments that have been used in game management. Whether they will be employed forcefully will probably depend upon the strength of conservationist sentiment—the attitudinal variable; the strength of it, in turn, will probably depend upon whether it can be demonstrated convincingly that the animals are important to the survival and health of our species, and therefore deserve their own territory and resources. Their abundance and variety remain a barometer of the planet's health, even in modern, postfrontier Alaska.

Abbreviations Used in the Notes

AGC	Alaska Game Commission
AR	Annual Report
AR AGC	Annual Report of the Alaska Game Commission to the Secretary of Interior
AR BBS SA	*Annual Report of the Chief, Bureau of Biological Survey, to the Secretary of Interior*
AR EO	Annual Report of the Executive Officer to the Alaska Game Commission
AR F&WS	*Annual Report of the Director, Fish and Wildlife Service, to the Secretary of Interior*
AR GA SA	*Annual Report of the Governor of Alaska to the Secretary of Agriculture*
AR GA SI	*Annual Report of the Governor of Alaska to the Secretary of Interior*
AR SI	*Annual Report of the Secretary of Interior*
BBS	Bureau of Biological Survey
CJS	*Corpus Juris Secundum*
DAB	*Dictionary of American Biography*
F&WS	Fish and Wildlife Service
GA GC	Governor of Alaska, General Correspondence, 1909–1958
GC BBS	General Correspondence, Bureau of Biological Survey
LC	Library of Congress
QR EO	Quarterly Report of the Executive Officer, Alaska Game Commission, to the Director, Fish and Wildlife Service
RG	Record Group, in the National Archives
SF&W	Sport Fisheries and Wildlife
Stat. L.	U.S. Statutes at Large

Notes

Chapter 1

1. *Simon Bolivar Buckner, Jr.*, v. *Frank Dufresne* and *Jack O'Connor* of the Alaska Game Commission, at Anchorage, Alaska, Court Record No. A–2671, U.S. District Court for the Territory of Alaska, Third Judicial Division, Alaska (hereafter cited as Buckner Case, A–2671), pp. 5, 13, 14; in Federal Archives and Records Center, Seattle. The case is summarized in *Alaska Reports*, vol. 10, pp. 121–28. See also O'Connor to Dufresne, 26 August 1941, "Licenses," SF&W, F&WS Records, NA RG 22, Washington, D.C.

2. O'Connor to Dufresne, 26 August 1941, "Licenses," SF&W, RG 22. In court, O'Connor repeated the polar bear story: Buckner Case, A–2671, p. 13.

3. O'Connor to AGC, Juneau, 25 August 1941, "Licenses," SF&W, RG 22.

4. Dufresne to Buckner, 2 September 1941, "Licenses," SF&W, RG 22.

5. Informal interview with Mrs. W. N. Cuddy, 2 August 1975, Anchorage.

6. Folta, Memo for Dufresne, 9 September 1941, "Licenses," SF&W, RG 22.

7. Buckner to Dufresne, 15 September 1941, "Licenses," SF&W, RG 22.

8. Editors of *Time*, "Buck's Battle," *Time* 45 (16 April 1945): 35. Biographical data were culled from this source and from W. H. Lawrence, "Buckner, Okinawa Commander Killed," *New York Times*, 19 June 1945, pp. 1, 7; S. T. Williamson, "Eight U.S. Commanders on Our Far-Flung Fronts," *New York Times Magazine* (17 May 1942): 15; D. G. Wittels, "These Are the Generals—Buckner," *Saturday Evening Post* 215 (8 May 1943): 17, 102.

9. Joseph Driscoll, *War Discovers Alaska*, p. 102. Ernest Gruening, *Many Battles*, pp. 308, 323.

10. For Anchorage's early years, see W. H. Wilson, "The Founding of Anchorage," *Pacific Northwest Quarterly* 58 (July 1967): 130–41; Evangeline Atwood, *Anchorage: All-American City*. M. E. Carberry, *Patterns of the Past: An Inventory of Anchorage's Heritage Resources*.

11. G. W. Rogers and R. A. Cooley, *Alaska's Population and Economy*, vol. 2, pp. 7, 8, 20, 36. M. S. Watson, *The War Department, Chief of Staff: Prewar Plans and Preparations*, p. 457. The Rogers and Cooley estimate of 8,000 servicemen for 1941 is apparently incorrect. The number of big game hunting licenses issued by year is in AR AGC to Secretary of Interior, 1959, AGC Records, microfilm, Alaska State Library, Juneau.

12. Informal interview with James O'Connor, 4 June 1976, Juneau.

13. AR EO, 1 November 1932–31 October 1933, AGC Records.

14. Informal interview with Sam O. White, 14 June 1976, Fairbanks.

15. AGC Minutes, 27 November 1931, AGC Records.

16. AR EO, 1 December 1935–31 October 1936, AGC Records. Other violations are reported in AR EO for 1937 and 1938. See also Orlando W. Miller, *The Frontier in Alaska and the Matanuska Colony*, pp. 29–32, 92, 100. For more about the colony see Evangeline Atwood, *We Shall Be Remembered*.

17. QR EO, 8 April 1941, AGC Records.

18. Jenks Cameron, *The Bureau of Biological Survey: Its History, Activities and Organization*, pp. 112–15. E. P. Walker, "Alaska Wild Life Protection," 1925–?, GC BBS, RG 22.

19. Frank Dufresne, *Alaska's Animals and Fishes*, p. xv.

20. Frank Dufresne, *My Way Was North*, pp. 11–27, 35, 36, 264. His other books are *Alaska's Animals and Fishes* and *No Room for Bears*. His wife, Klondy Nelson (Dufresne), wrote her autobiography with Corey Ford, entitled *Daughter of the Gold Rush*.

21. *My Way Was North*, p. xi.

22. Dufresne to Nelson, 9 June 1923, "Game Acts," GC BBS, RG 22.

23. Dufresne to Nelson, 1 March 1924, "Alaska General to Alaska Reports," GC BBS, RG 22.

24. Nelson to Dufresne, 3 February 1923, "Game Acts"; Nelson to Dufresne, 7 February 1923, "Alaska Reports"; Dufresne to Nelson, 17 September 1923, "Alaska General to Alaska Reports"; E. P. Walker to Nelson, 30 September 1925, and Walker to Chief, BBS, 14 October 1925, "Prohibition Enforcement to Alaska Reports"; all GC BBS, RG 22.

25. "Alaska General to Alaska Reports," GC BBS, RG 22.

26. Gabrielson to the author, 9 May 1976.

27. Dufresne, *My Way Was North*, p. 272.

28. Gabrielson to the author, 9 May 1976.

29. Ickes did interfere sometimes; see *The Secret Diary of Harold L. Ickes*, vol. 3: *The Lowering Clouds, 1939–1941*, p. 321. H. H. Hilscher, "Is Ickes Back of This Too?" *Alaska Life* 4 (December 1941): 3, 26–28. Editorials, *Anchorage Daily Times*, 8 October 1941 and 9 December 1943.

30. Jean Potter, *Alaska under Arms*, p. 126.

31. C. E. Gillham, "Andy Simons, Alaska's Number 1 Guide," *Alaska* 30 (April 1964): 14–16. Dufresne, *No Room for Bears*, pp. 208, 209.

32. *CJS*: "Game," vol. 38, pp. 2, 4, 8; "Property in Wild Animals," vol. 3A, p. 477; "Domicile," vol. 28, pp. 1–49.

33. See, e.g., A. A. Bailey, *Field Work of a Museum Naturalist*.

34. Folta to Nelson, 10 May 1921, "Game Acts," GC BBS, RG 22.

35. AR EO, 1 November 1931–31 October 1932, AGC Records. AGC Minutes, 15 December 1934, AGC Records.

36. *Empire*, 9 September 1949, "Alaska File, A–Z," SF&W, RG 22. *Empire*, 7 June 1950, with G. W. Folta "Clippings," in the possession of R. N. DeArmond, Juneau.

37. Hellenthal to A. J. Dimond, 24 November 1943, Dimond Papers, University of Alaska Archives, Fairbanks.

38. Dimond to Homer Cummings, U.S. Attorney General, 12 April 1933, Dimond Papers.

39. Dimond to W. Stanley, 11 July 1933; and J. W. Troy to Dimond, telegram, 17 May 1933, Dimond Papers.

40. Harding to the Attorney General, 25 May 1927, Folta Appointment File, Office of the Attorney General.

41. Typescript address of James Wickersham, 5 November 1932; address of Dimond, 1932; Democratic Platform, 23 January 1932; all "Campaign 32," Dimond Papers.

42. A book-length treatment of the episode is J. L. Penick, *Progressive Politics and Conservation: The Ballinger–Pinchot Affair*. For the Alaskan reaction, see H. Slotnick, "The Ballinger–Pinchot Affair in Alaska," *Journal of the West* 10 (April 1971): 337–47; L. E. Janson, *Copper Spike*, pp. 109–34; and *Alaska-Yukon Magazine* 9 (May 1910) for several articles.

43. *Melodrama*, p. 194. For evidence of Hellenthal's orations, see unidentified newspaper clippings dated 1906 and 1921, Mr. and Mrs. John A. Hellenthal, "Scrapbook," in the possession of Mr. and Mrs. John S. Hellenthal, Anchorage, pp. 12 and 16.

44. *Melodrama*, pp. 149, 161, 195, 235–37. J. A. Hellenthal, "Why Not Go Modern on Conservation?" *Alaska Life* 4 (January 1941): 3, 28, 30.

45. *Melodrama*, p. 283.

Chapter 2

1. L. White, Jr., "Historical Roots of Our Ecologic Crisis," *Science* 155 (10 March 1967): 1203–07. Aldo Leopold, *Game Management*, pp. 4, 5–12. The present study was in preparation when Thomas A. Lund was writing his legal history, *American Wildlife Law*, and I did not have an opportunity to correlate his classification scheme with mine.

2. Cameron, *Bureau of Biological Survey*, p. 4.

3. T. S. Palmer, *Chronology and Index of the More Important Events in American Game Protection, 1776–1911*, pp. 9, 10. T. S. Palmer, *Hunting Licenses: Their History, Objects, and Limitations*, pp. 10–14, 36.

4. R. H. Connery, *Governmental Problems in Wildlife Conservation*, pp. 204, 205.

5. For the story of the seal and otter, see J. R. Gibson, *Imperial Russia in Frontier America: The Changing Geography of Supply of Russian America, 1784–1867*; Francis Riley, *Fur Seal Industry of the Pribilof Islands*; C. L. Andrews, *The Story of Alaska*; S. G. Fedorova, *The Russian Population in Alaska and California, Late 18th Century–1867*.

6. Herbert quoted in T. W. Cart, "The Struggle for Wildlife Protection in the United States, 1870–1900: Attitudes and Events Leading to the Lacey Act" (Ph.D. diss.), p. 86.

7. Ibid., pp. 78, 79, 86, 90. P. J. Schmitt, *Back to Nature: The Arcadian Myth in Urban America*, pp. 7–14. J. F. Reiger, *American Sportsmen and the Origins of Conservation*, pp. 25, 31, 39, 105, 119.

8. Reiger, *American Sportsmen*, pp. 71, 32, 82, 121. Cart, "Struggle," p. 80.

9. Cart, "Struggle," p. 82.

10. Reiger, *American Sportsmen*, p. 31. Hallock's opinions of Alaska can be read in his *Our New Alaska*, published in 1886, and in his *Peerless Alaska, Our Cache near the Pole*, published in 1908.

11. Palmer, *Chronology and Index*, p. 8. The Bureau of Biological Survey, in 1900, listed as game (other than game birds): ruminants and peccaries (Ungulata), bears and raccoons (Carnivora), rabbits and squirrels (Rodentia), opossums (Marsupialia).

12. J. B. Trefethen, *Crusade for Wildlife*, pp. 18, 21. Reiger, *American Sportsmen*, pp. 119, 120.

13. Cameron, *Bureau of Biological Survey*, pp. 8–11, 111.

14. Cart, "Struggle," p. 111. Trefethen, *Crusade for Wildlife*, pp. 64, 65.

15. T. S. Palmer, "A Review of Economic Ornithology in the United States," in *Yearbook of the United States Department of Agriculture, 1899*, pp. 268, 269. Trefethen, *Crusade for Wildlife*, p. 163. Cart, "Struggle," pp. 9–13, 30, 181. C. W. Buchheister and Frank Graham, "From the Swamp and Back: A Concise and Candid History of the Audubon Movement," *Audubon* 75 (January 1973): 8, 10.

16. Palmer, *Chronology and Index*, p. 8. Cameron, *Bureau of Biological Survey*, p. 77 and notes.

17. Morgan Sherwood, "Science in Russian America, 1741–1865," *Pacific Northwest Quarterly* 58 (January 1967): 33–39. Morgan Sherwood, *Exploration of Alaska, 1865–1900*. Rogers and Cooley, *Alaska's Population*, vol. 2, p. 28.

18. Editors of *Forest and Stream*, "The Great Duck Egg Fake," *Forest and Stream* 44 (22 June 1895): 503, 504.

19. F. J. Turner, "The Significance of the Frontier in American History," in his *Frontier in American History*, pp. 1–38; originally presented in 1893.

20. U.S. Congress, Senate, *Congressional Record*, 53d Cong., 3d Sess., 26 January 1895, pp. 1407, 1408. U.S. Congress, Senate, "Joint Resolution of the General Assembly of the State of Oregon Asking Legislation to Protect the Eggs of Wild Fowls," *Senate Miscellaneous Document 142* (28 February 1895), 53d Cong., 3d Sess. (serial 3281).

21. Morgan Sherwood, "The Great Duck Egg Fake," *Alaska Journal* 7 (Spring 1977): 88–94.

22. Cameron, *Bureau of Biological Survey*, p. 83 and note; act of 25 May 1900 (31 Stat. L., 187), reprinted in Cameron, pp. 259, 260. Act of 6 June 1900 (31 Stat. L., 321, 322, 332) is also reprinted in Cameron, *Bureau of Biological Survey*, pp. 260, 261, as is 32 Stat. L., 285.

23. Act of 7 June 1900 (32 Stat. L., 327), reprinted in Cameron, *Bureau of Biological Survey*, pp. 262, 263.

24. T. S. Palmer, *Legislation for the Protection of Birds Other than Game Birds*, pp. 10–13.

25. Trefethan, *Crusade for Wildlife*, p. 174. D.C. Swain, *Federal Conservation Policy, 1921–1933*, pp. 32, 33.

26. For bear stories as literature see, e.g., *Alaska Magazine, Subject Index to Alaska Magazine* (formerly *The Alaska Sportsman*) *1935–1972*, pp. 37–39, 73, 74. For the "cache" in Alaskan art see, e.g., R. L. Shalkop, *Sidney Laurence (1865–1940), An Alaskan Impressionist*, pp. 14, 19, 29, 30, 34, 43, 44. One painter of Alaskan scenes even signed his work with a crude line drawing of a cache; R. L. Shalkop, *Eustace Ziegler, A Retrospective Exhibition*, p. 5.

27. Rogers and Cooley, *Alaska's Population*, vol. 2, p. 7.

28. Gibson, *Imperial Russia*, p. 48. But more recently Gibson reports that Tlingits supplied Sitka with an average of eleven tons of "mutton" each year in the 1840s, and with wildfowl meat and eggs. See Gibson's "Old Russia in the New World," in *European Settlement and Development in North America*, ed. J. R. Gibson, p. 54.

29. Bancroft Scraps, vol. 81, pp. 17, 18, 106–07. For a portrait of early Sitka, see T. C. Hinckley, *The Americanization of Alaska, 1867–1897*, pp. 29–65.

30. W. W. Greener's *The Gun* quoted in Trefethen, *Crusade for Wildlife*, pp. 128, 133.

31. Trefethen, *Crusade for Wildlife*, pp. 40, 134, 135.

32. Robert Stein, "The Gold Fields of Alaska," *Review of Reviews* 13 (June 1896): 699.

33. De Weese to the President, 1 December 1901, in U.S. Congress, House, "Game Law in Alaska," *House Report 951* (14 March 1902), 57th Cong., 1st sess. (serial 4402), pp. 3, 6.

34. W. H. Osgood and L. B. Bishop, *Results of a Biological Reconnaissance of the Yukon River Region*, pp. 23, 24. W. H. Osgood, *Natural History of the Queen Charlotte Islands, British Columbia; Natural History of the Cook Inlet Region, Alaska*, p. 61.

35. J. A. Loring, "Notes on the Destruction of Animal Life in Alaska," *Annual Report of the New York Zoological Society, 1901*, pp. 142, 143.

36. Act of 7 June 1902 (32 Stat. L., 327), reprinted in Cameron, *Bureau of Biological Survey*, pp. 262, 263.

37. Trefethen, *Crusade for Wildlife*, p. 134. Cameron, *Bureau of Biological Survey*, pp. 111, 112.

38. Andy Simons, "Hunting the Alaska Brown Bear," in Boone and Crockett Club, *North American Big Game*, p. 378.

39. T. M. Taylor, "Vanished Monarch of the Sierra," *The American West* 13 (May / June 1976): 36–38. J. M. Holzworth, *The Wild Grizzlies of Alaska*, pp. 223–32.

40. Frank Dufresne, "North America's Grouchiest Beast," *Alaska* 29 (December 1963): 24. Lewis Regenstein, in *The Politics of Extinction*, quotes George Goodwin on the influence of the repeating rifle.

41. Holzworth, *Wild Grizzlies of Alaska*, pp. 223–41. See also Taylor, "Vanished Monarch," pp. 36, 59.

42. Holzworth, *Wild Grizzlies of Alaska*, p. 220. Boone and Crockett Club, *North American Big Game*, p. 513. Also, Frank Dufresne, *Mammals and Birds of Alaska*. The natural history of the brown, or grizzly, bears is summarized from the following sources: W. H. Burt, *A Field Guide to the Mammals*, 2d ed., pp. 48–51; R. W. Manville and S. P. Young, *Distribution of Alaskan Mammals*, p. 43; Robert Rausch, "On the Status of Some Arctic Mammals," *Arctic* 6 (July 1953): 97, 98. See also R. Rausch, "Geographic Variation in Size in North American Brown Bears, Ursus Arctos L., as Indicated by Condylobasal Length," *Canadian Journal of Zoology* 41 (January 1963): 33–45.

43. "Second Set of Data for NRC," Dufresne to Chief, Bureau of Biological Survey, 14

October 1937, "Alaska File A–Z," SF&W, RG 22. Dufresne, *Mammals and Birds*, p. 6. R. N. De Armond, "A Northern Notebook," *Alaska Daily Empire*, 10 May 1951. D. R. Klein, W. Troyer, and R. A. Rausch, "The Status of the Brown Bear in Alaska," *Proceedings of the Ninth Alaskan Science Conference, 1958*, pp. 21–24.

44. Trefethen, *Crusade for Wildlife*, pp. 136–37.

45. Ibid., pp. 137, 138. D. J. Orth, *Dictionary of Alaska Place Names*, p. 272. The proposal was Senate Bill No. 4166, introduced 8 February 1904 by Dillingham's colleague, Redfield Proctor.

46. Kidder to M. Grant, 4 April 1904; Loring to Grant, 17 March 1904; Stone to Grant, 11 March 1904; all in Box 1, Charles Sheldon Papers, University of Alaska Archives, Fairbanks. Stone is quoted in Trefethen, *Crusade for Wildlife*, p. 139. W. H. Osgood, *A Biological Reconnaissance of the Base of the Alaska Peninsula*, p. 28. W. H. Osgood, *Biological Investigations in Alaska and Yukon Territory*, pp. 18–19.

47. The letter, Wadsworth and Grant to Dillingham, 23 March 1904, is reprinted in full in Trefethen, *Crusade for Wildlife*, p. 141.

48. 35 Stat. L., 102, reprinted in Cameron, *Bureau of Biological Survey*, pp. 265–68; also, pp. 112, 113. U.S. Congress, House, "Law for Protection of Wild Game Animals and Birds in Alaska . . .," *House Report 989* (5 June 1924), 68th Cong., 1st sess. (serial 8229), p. 2. *AR GA SI 1909*, p. 513.

49. Madison Grant, "Condition of Wildlife in Alaska," in *Hunting at High Altitudes*, ed. G. B. Grinnell, pp. 369–74.

50. *AR GA SA 1911*, p. 5. *AR GA SA 1912*, p. 7. *AR GA SI 1915*, pp. 486, 487. *AR GA SA 1910*, p. 4. *AR GA SI 1910*, p. 251. U.S. Congress, House, "Protection of Game in Alaska," *House Report 2010* (28 January 1911), 61st Cong., 3d sess. (serial 5847), p. 1. *AR GA SI 1911*, pp. 371, 386.

51. Section 3 of the Organic Act of 1912 (37 Stat. L. 512). The best history of political events leading to the act of 1912 is still J. P. Nichols, *Alaska: . . . Its First Half Century under the Rule of the United States*, originally published in 1924, but the politics of big game play no role in her narrative.

52. Grant, "Condition of Wildlife," pp. 386–92.

53. J. B. Trefethen, *An American Crusade for Wildlife*, pp. 164, 177, 180. The quotation is from Hornaday to C. L. Andrews, 8 March 1904, in Andrews Collection, University of Oregon, Eugene; research note courtesy of Ted C. Hinckley.

54. *Our Vanishing Wild Life*, p. 269; italics in the original. For an official Alaskan attitude, see *AR GA SI 1916*, pp. 433, 434.

55. Trefethen, *Crusade for Wildlife*, pp. 206–08.

56. U.S. Congress, House, "To Regulate the Killing and Sale of Certain Game Animals in Northern Alaska," *Hearings*, Part 1, Committee on Territories, 65th Cong., 2d sess., 1918, U.S. Senate Library, vol. 215, no. 4, pp. 3, 5, 18, 33. R. S. McDonald to Governor Strong, 20 May 1917, GA GC, Roll 42. A detailed account of the Sulzer bill's history is in Trefethen, *Crusade for Wildlife*, pp. 208–17.

57. Reiger, *American Sportsmen*.

58. Trefethen, *Crusade for Wildlife*, pp. 211–16. T. Riggs to T. Roosevelt, 29 March 1918, Thomas C. Riggs, Jr., Papers, LC, Washington, D.C. See also "Confidential to Defenders of Big Game," by W. T. Hornaday, 4 March 1918, Riggs Papers, LC.

59. Riggs to Roosevelt, 29 March 1918; Riggs to Senator G. P. McLean, 29 March 1918, Riggs Papers, LC.

60. *AR GA SI 1920*, p. 47. A. M. Bailey to Nelson, 30 April 1920, GC BBS, RG 22. Trefethen, *Crusade for Wildlife*, p. 218.

61. Georgeson to W. H. Evan, 20 July 1915, "Bears," SF&W, RG 22. Georgeson, *Information for Prospective Settlers in Alaska*, pp. 19, 20.

62. A. M. Bailey Report to the Bureau of Biological Survey, n.d.; G. Folta to Nelson, 10

May 1921; J. A. Bourke, "special officer," to Governor Riggs, 8 July 1920; all with "Bears," SF&W, RG 22.

63. Rex Beach, "The Chronicle of a Chromatic Bear Hunt," in Beach, *Oh Shoot! Confessions of an Agitated Sportsman*, pp. 39–43, 50, 75.

64. Folta to Nelson, 10 May 1921, "Game Acts," GC BBS, RG 22. A. C. Bonebrake, "An Instance of Unprovoked Attack by a Brown Bear," *Journal of Mammalogy* 3 (August 1922): 185, 186. Charles Sheldon, "The 'Unprovoked' Attack by a 'Brown' Bear," in *Journal of Mammalogy* 4 (February 1923): 51, 52. G. B. Grinnell, "The 'Unprovoked' Attack by a Bear," in *Journal of Mammalogy* 4 (February 1923): 52, 53.

65. Dufresne tells the story of the rogue bear in "Grouchiest Beast," pp. 25, 45.

66. Ohmer's response is dated 16 October 1920; the completed forms are in "Alaska Reports," GC BBS, RG 22.

67. Riggs to Grinnell, 25 June 1919, Riggs Papers, LC.

68. *AR GA SI 1919*, pp. 460–61.

69. Merriam, *Review of the Grizzly and Big Brown Bears of North America*.

70. Memorandum from H. W. Henshaw to Secretary of Agriculture, 2 February 1915, "Regulations to Alaska Game Law," GC BBS, RG 22. Bailey's Report to the Bureau of Biological Survey, 1920, "Bears," SF&W, RG 22. Miscellaneous newspaper clippings, GA GC, Roll 73. That Hornaday's constituency were "women and children" was Grinnell's opinion, used without his permission; see Grinnell to Riggs, 9 March 1920 and 15 November 1920, GA GC, Roll 73; Grinnell to Nelson, 22 March 1921, and Riggs to Nelson, 15 February 1921, "Game Acts," GC BBS, RG 22.

71. (35 Stat. L., 102). Junius Henderson and E. L. Craig, *Economic Mammalogy*, p. 200. Riggs to M. Grant, 4 June 1920, Roll 73; Riggs to Secretary of Agriculture, 28 June 1918, Roll 48; E. Steffen to Riggs, 16 September 1919, Roll 61; all rolls in GA GC.

72. *AR GA SI 1919*, p. 460. Riggs to J. C. Murphy, Attorney General of Alaska, 2 January 1920, Roll 73, GA GC. Riggs to H. Christoffers, Bureau of Fisheries in Seattle, 30 October 1919; Riggs to Nelson, 13 November 1919; both in "Game Acts," GC BBS, RG 22.

73. Nelson to Humphrey, 28 November 1919; Humphrey to Nelson, 26 November 1919; Nelson to Riggs, 28 November 1919; all "Game Acts," GC BBS, RG 22.

74. Riggs to Nelson, 9 February 1920, enclosing a copy of Riggs's letter to the attorney general of Alaska, "Game Acts," GC BBS, RG 22. J. W. Troy, Collector, to Governor, 17 December 1919, Roll 61, GA GC.

75. Nelson to Sheldon, 22 March 1920, "Game Acts," GC BBS, RG 22.

76. Nelson to Grinnell, 26 March 1920, "Game Acts," GC BBS, RG 22.

77. Nelson to Grinnell, 22 March 1920; Nelson to Grinnell, 29 March 1920; both in "Game Acts," GC BBS, RG 22.

78. Copy of solicitor's case with Secretary of Agriculture to U.S. Attorney General, n.d., "Game Acts," GC BBS, RG 22.

79. Riggs to Grinnell, 23 May 1920; Riggs to Grinnell, 25 November 1920; Riggs to M. Grant, 4 June 1920; all Roll 73, GA GC.

Chapter 3

1. Riggs to B. Browne, 11 April 1918, Riggs Papers, LC. Trefethen, *Crusade for Wildlife*, pp. 186–91, 216.

2. R. F. Griggs, "The Valley of Ten Thousand Smokes," *National Geographic Magazine* 31 (January 1917): 12–68. Trefethen, *Crusade for Wildlife*, p. 221.

3. P. E. Rich and A. R. Tussing, *The National Park System in Alaska: An Economic Impact Study*, p. 34.

4. Riggs to Belmore Browne, 20 July 1918, Riggs Papers, LC. Riggs to Nelson, 13 June 1921, "Prohibition Enforcement to Alaska Reports," GC BBS, RG 22.

5. Cameron, *Bureau of Biological Survey*, p. 131.

6. Riggs to Nelson, 13 June 1921, GC BBS, RG 22.

7. I. Gabrielson to A. J. Dimond, 15 October 1940, Roll 277, GA GC.

8. E. W. Nelson, "The Emperor Goose," in *Alaskan Bird-Life as Depicted by Many Writers*, ed. Ernest Ingersoll, p. 61.

9. Riggs to Belmore Browne, 20 July 1918, Riggs Papers, LC. *AR GA SA 1918*, p. 9.

10. Nelson to Governor Scott Bone, 22 April 1922, "Prohibition Enforcement to Alaska Reports," GC BBS, RG 22.

11. Riggs to Nelson, 13 June 1921, "Prohibition Enforcement to Alaska Reports," GC BBS, RG 22.

12. Nelson to Riggs, 28 May 1921, "Game Acts," GC BBS, RG 22.

13. Walker to Nelson, 18 August 1921, GC BBS, RG 22.

14. Memorandum, Nelson to Secretary of Agriculture, 18 January 1924, "Alaska File, A–Z," SF&W, RG 22.

15. Riggs to C. J. Todd, 20 July 1918, Roll 48; Petition to Governor Clark, October 1909, Roll 1; both GA GC.

16. W. D. Mclaughlin to Nelson, 5 June 1921, "Game Acts," GC BBS, RG 22.

17. Bone to Nelson, 19 November 1921, "Prohibition Enforcement to Alaska Reports," GC BBS, RG 22. Murie to Nelson, 5 November 1921, Box 4, Olaus J. Murie Papers, University of Alaska Archives, Fairbanks.

18. Stowe to Messrs. Sproule and Burtness, Members of the congressional party visiting Alaska, ca. 1923; Nelson to Stowe, 28 June 1923; both "Game Acts," GC BBS, RG 22.

19. Ericson to Strong, December 1917, Roll 42, GA GC.

20. H. Alheidt to Governor Strong, 22 October 1913, Roll 12; Strong to Alheidt, 13 September 1913, Roll 19; Strong to Alheidt, 27 September 1913, Roll 19; Petition to Dimond, Roll 19; P. Ericksen to Strong, 1 June 1915, Roll 25; all GA GC.

21. Warden to Strong, 1 December 1913, Roll 12; R. E. Steel to Strong, 22 June 1917, Roll 42; both GA GC.

22. J. A. Baugham to Governor Riggs, 1 November 1918, Roll 49; Baugham to Governor Strong, 30 November 1915, Roll 25; both GA GC.

23. Riggs to J. A. Baugham, 8 January 1918, Roll 49, GA GC. Murie to Nelson, 12 March 1921; Murie to Nelson, 7 January 1922; both in "Alaska Reports," GC BBS, RG 22.

24. Stephen R. Capps, "A Game Country without Rival in America. . . ," *National Geographic Magazine* 31 (January 1917): 81. R. S. McDonald to Strong, 20 May 1917, Roll 42, GA GC.

25. R. F. Scott, E. F. Chatelain, and W. A. Elkins, "The Status of the Dall Sheep and Caribou in Alaska," *Transactions of the North American Wildlife Conference, 1950*, p. 615.

26. Crossley to Governor Clark, received 21 June 1912, Roll 7; W. Loyd to Clark, 5 September 1912, Roll 7; Governor Strong to Secretary of Interior, 13 February 1917, Roll 42; R. R. McDonald to Strong, 16 October and 27 June 1917, Roll 42; all GA GC.

27. D. M. Lynch to J. A. Baugham, with Baugham to Riggs, 14 May 1919, Roll 61; Riggs to Secretary of Agriculture, 20 March 1918, Roll 48; both GA GC.

28. McDonald to Strong, 1 March and 1 August, 1917, Roll 42; GA GC.

29. R. L. Steavens report, October 1924, "Alaska Reports," GC BBS, RG 22.

30. Anonymous (signed "An Alaskan"), "The Moose Butchers of Kenai," *American Forestry* 29 (December 1923): 719, 720, 750. F. M. Goodwin, Assistant Secretary of Interior, to Bone, 20 February 1924, Roll 112; Bone to E. C. Peterson, 10 March 1924, Roll 112; both GA GC.

31. Rogers and Cooley, *Alaska's Population*, vol. 2, pp. 17, 18, 30. Rogers and Cooley do not claim more stability for the population in that period. The conclusion that permanent white residents began to outnumber transients in the 1920s must be considered a tentative hypothesis until census manuscripts can be analyzed.

32. Ibid., vol. 2, p. 33. U.S. Bureau of the Census, *Thirteenth Census . . . 1910*, vol. 4: *Population . . . Occupational Statistics*, pp. 96–108, table 2; *Fourteenth Census . . . 1920*, vol. 4, pp. 1264, 1265; *Fifteenth Census . . . 1930—Outlying Territories and Possessions*. G. C. Martin et. al., *Mineral Resources of Alaska . . . 1918*, pp. 15, 18, 24, 37, 41. Philip S. Smith, *Mineral Industry of Alaska in 1939*, p. 85. K. H. Stone, "Populating Alaska: The United States Phase," *Geographical Review* 42 (July 1952): 399, 402.

33. See, e.g., J. E. Barrett to Strong, 18 October 1913, Roll 12; Irons to the Governor, 4 February 1912, Roll 7; both GA GC. E. P. Walker to Nelson, 9 March 1923; Lomen et al. to Nelson, 4 October 1921; Parks to Nelson, 3 October 1921; Walker to Story, 16 February 1923, copy; all "Game Acts," GC BBS, RG 22.

34. Riggs to W. A. Hesse, Roll 23; J. P. Hubrick to Governor Bone, 11 December 1923, Roll 112; both GA GC.

35. Materials in "Alaska Reports," GC BBS, RG 22, including a clipping from the *Daily Empire* of Juneau, 24 July 1923.

36. Slip dated 1922, 1923, 1924, Roll 112, GA GC. W. H. Chase to Nelson, 13 January 1923; Nelson to Dufresne, 3 February 1923; Nelson to Chase, 25 January 1923; all "Game Acts," GC BBS, RG 22.

37. Ernest Gruening, *The State of Alaska*, pp. 201–06.

38. Unidentified newspaper clipping, 1921, probably the *Daily Empire* of Juneau; Parks to Nelson, 9 March 1921; Bailey to Nelson, 21 March 1921; all "Game Acts," GC BBS, RG 22. Governor's secretary to W. A. Watts, 16 June 1924, Roll 112, GA GC.

39. House Joint Memorial No. 12, 1923, "Game Acts," GC BBS, RG 22. Territory of Alaska, *Journal of the House of Representatives, Sixth Session, 1923*, pp. 184, 198. For more about the role of experts, see Samuel P. Hays, *Conservation and the Gospel of Efficiency*.

40. Hornaday to Nelson, 19 January 1921 and 15 March 1921, "Game Acts," GC BBS, RG 22.

41. E. P. Walker to Nelson, 27 June 1923 and 9 March 1923, "Game Acts," GC BBS, RG 22. Riggs to Nelson, 13 June 1921, "Prohibition Enforcement to Alaska Reports," GC BBS, RG 22. U.S. Congress, House, "To Provide that Powers be Transferred," *House Report 989* (5 June 1924), 68th Cong., 1st sess. (serial 8229), pp. 1–3. U.S. Congress, House, "To Establish Alaska Game Commission," *House Report 993* (5 June 1924), 68th Cong., 1st sess. (serial 8229), pp. 1–5. U.S. Congress, House, "To Establish Alaska Game Commission," *Hearings*, Committee on Agriculture, 68th Cong., 1st sess. (1924), U.S. Senate Library vol. 215, no. 17.

42. Riggs to Nelson, 22 September 1924, "Game Acts," GC BBS, RG 22.

43. See, e.g., Swain, *Federal Conservation Policy, 1921–1933*, pp. 37, 38. See also Margaret Lantis, "Edward William Nelson," *Anthropological Papers of the University of Alaska* 3 (December 1954): 3–16; and Sherwood, *Exploration of Alaska*, pp. 94–97.

44. Alaska Game Commission, *Laws and Regulations Relating to Game, Land, Fur-bearing Animals and Birds in Alaska*, for 1928 and for 1929. *AR BBS SA, 1928*, p. 19. *AR BBS SA, 1929*, p. 33. See also AGC Minutes, 17 January 1927 and 3 November 1928, AGC Records.

45. Gibson, *Imperial Russia*, pp. 94–107; Gibson does not mention bears. Fedorova, *Russian Population in Alaska*, pp. 197, 198.

46. T. C. Hinckley and C. Hinckley, eds., "Ivan Petroff's Journal of a Trip to Alaska in 1878," *Journal of the West* (January 1966): 24.

47. C. V. Piper, *Grasslands of the South Alaska Coast*, pp. 22, 23.

48. Cameron, *Bureau of Biological Survey*, p. 315. T. W. Cart, " 'New Deal' for Wildlife: A Perspective on Federal Conservation Policy, 1933–40," *Pacific Northwest Quarterly* 63 (July 1972): 114.

49. Georgeson, *Information for Settlers*, pp. 19, 20. *AR GA SI, 1915*, pp. 486, 487. Strong to Secretary of Commerce, 27 February 1915, Roll 25, GA GC.

50. (44 Stat. L. 1452–1455). During the first year of the law, action was taken on sixty-three cases; three leases were issued; see *AR SI, 1928*, p. 48. *AR SI, 1933*, p. 61, states that eleven leases to graze cattle, horses, and sheep were in force.

51. Janson, *Copper Spike*, pp. 39, 82. *Ketchikan Chronicle*, 25 November 1928, with "Clipping File, 1908–1930," Daniel A. Sutherland Papers, University of Alaska Archives, Fairbanks. AGC Minutes, 12 November 1928, AGC Records.

52. The number 500 is mentioned in Holzworth, *Wild Grizzlies of Alaska*. The town's population in 1920 and 1930 was 374 and 442; Rogers and Cooley, *Alaska's Population*, vol. 2, p. 27. Also, J. S. Long with G. D. McCord, *McCord of Alaska: Statesman for the Last Frontier*.

53. AR EO, 1 November 1928–31 October 1929, AGC Records. H. E. Smith, "Jack Thayer was Killed by a Bear," *Alaska* 37 (August 1971): 62, 63. Harry McGuire, "The Last Stand of the Bear," *Outdoor Life* article reprinted in Holzworth, *Wild Grizzlies of Alaska*, pp. 345–47.

54. AGC, *Laws and Regulations* for 1930.

55. *Wild Grizzlies of Alaska*, pp. ix–xi.

56. Pp. 5, 213, 214.

57. AR EO, 1 November 1929–31 October 1930, AGC Records. John Holzworth to Congresswoman Caroline O'Day, 15 April 1936, "Admiralty-Bears," SF&W, RG 22.

58. *Seward Gateway* article, 8 November 1930, in "Regulations to Alaska Game Law," GC BBS, RG 22. *Seward Gateway* article, 30 May 1931, in "Bears," SF&W, RG 22.

59. AR EO, 1932, AGC Records. AR EO, 1930, AGC Records.

60. AGC, *Laws and Regulations* for 1933 and for 1935. AGC Minutes, 6 December 1930, AGC Records.

61. AGC Minutes, 2 August 1931 and 28 November 1931, AGC Records. Senator F. W. Walcott to H. W. Terhune, 15 October 1931; Terhune to Chief, BBS, 2 November 1931; P. Reddington, Memo for Secretary of Agriculture, 22 May 1933; all "Bears," SF&W, RG 22. *Alaska Weekly*, 11 July 1924, with Daniel Sutherland Papers, University of Alaska Archives. M. L. Wilson, Acting Secretary of Agriculture, to Secretary of Interior, 24 July 1937, "Admiralty–Bears," SF&W, RG 22.

62. The quickest and most pleasant way to learn about the island is to examine "Admiralty, Island in Contention," a special issue of *Alaska Geographic* 3 (Summer 1973).

63. AR EO, 1932, AGC Records. *AR BBS SA, 1932*, p. 30, and *1933*, p. 32. M. L. Wilson, Acting Secretary of Agriculture, to Secretary of Interior, 24 July 1937, "Admiralty–Bears," SF&W, RG 22.

64. In 1932, 109 nonresident big game licenses were issued, 52 were issued in 1933, and 64 in 1934. The number had increased earlier: 90 in 1929, 120 in 1930, and 105 in 1931. It may be that Biological Survey Chief Paul Reddington had these increases in mind, but they were not impressive and represented no threat to the bear. AR AGC, 1959, appendix, AGC Records.

65. Proposal, with White to J. N. Darling, 4 October 1934; Ickes to White, 18 October 1934; both "Admiralty–Bears," SF&W, RG 22. Ickes, *Secret Diary*, vol. 3, p. 654. Gruening, *Many Battles*, pp. 258, 270.

66. AR EO, 1 November 1929–31 October 1930, 1 November 1930–31 October 1931, 1 November 1932–31 October 1933, AGC Records.

67. Folder labeled "Campaign 1932," A. J. Dimond Papers. U.S. Congress, House, *Congressional Record*, 74th Cong., 1st sess., 3 January 1935, 79, pt. 1: 46. *Daily Alaska Empire*, Juneau, 28 January 1935. Territory of Alaska, *Journal of the House of Representatives, 1935*, pp. 8–10, 109, 129. Territory of Alaska, *Journal of the Senate, 1935*, pp. 84, 85, 99.

68. Emory Tobin to the author, 28 December 1976, with memoranda and clippings. Circulation reached 10,000 in four years; most of the subscribers lived in the States. The first editorial in the January 1935 issue was reprinted in the January 1950 issue.

69. Cart's " 'New Deal' for Wildlife," pp. 113–20, summarizes these events and forces at the national level.

70. Dufresne to Gabrielson, 19 August 1937; Dufresne to Gabrielson, 21 September 1937, and 5 December 1938; all "Bears," SF&W, RG 22. AGC Minutes, 19 February 1938, 22 February 1938, and 11 January 1939, AGC Records.

71. Dimond's comments are in the *Seward Gateway*, 5 November 1938. Kodiak Commissioner to Secretary of Agriculture, 2 December 1938, "Bears," SF&W, RG 22. Sarber, "Report of the Kodiak Brown Bear Control Project, Kodiak Island, Alaska, March–July 1939," p. 36, also "Bears," SF&W, RG 22 (hereafter Sarber, "Report, 1939").

72. W. E. Crouch to AGC, 8 March 1939; Order of Secretary of Agriculture, 14 June 1939; Sarber to Dufresne, 14 June 1939; all "Bears," SF&W, RG 22. Sarber, "Report, 1939," pp. 8, 10.

73. Sarber, "Report, 1939" pp. 13–15, 18, 24–26, 33, 34. Sarber to Dufresne, 25 August 1939; Sarber to Dufresne, 14 June 1939; both "Bears," SF&W, RG 22.

74. Ickes to Secretary of Agriculture, 3 March 1939; Report of E. I. Rowland to A. C. Kinsley, February–August 1940, pp. 1, 15, 16; Ohmer to C. Rhode, 10 July 1952; all "Bears," SF&W, RG 22.

75. AGC Minutes, 17 January 1939, AGC Records. The Kodiak refuge is described, as of 1960, in U.S. Fish and Wildlife Service, Bureau of Sport Fisheries and Wildlife, *Kodiak National Wildlife Refuge*. Kay Kennedy, "Twelve Brown Bear Men," *Alaska* 6 (February 1940): 16–18, 20, 21.

Chapter 4

1. Burt, *Field Guide*, 2d ed., p. 12. Dufresne, *Alaska's Animals and Fishes*, pp. 48, 37, 38. Manville and Young, *Distribution*, pp. 67, 62. AR EO, 1 January 1943–30 November 1943, AGC Records.

2. Ernest P. Walker, *Mammals of the World*, vol. 2, p. 1471. Dufresne, *Alaska's Animals and Fishes*, p. 46. P. C. Lent, "Muskox Management Controversies in North America," *Biological Conservation* 3 (July 1971): 255–59.

3. O. E. Burris and D. E. McNight, *Game Transplants in Alaska*, p. 1.

4. Morgan Sherwood, "Science in Russian America," *Pacific Northwest Quarterly* 58 (January 1967): 33–36. A biography of Steller is Leonhard Stejneger, *Georg Wilhelm Steller: The Pioneer of Alaskan Natural History*. See also Alexander Vucinich, *Science in Russian Culture: A History to 1860*.

5. Sherwood, *Exploration of Alaska*, pp. 18–56, 70–75, 93–97, 182–86. T. W. Crouch, "Frederick Funston in Alaska, 1892–1894," *Journal of the West* 10 (April 1971): 273–306. Jed Dannenbaum, "John Muir and Alaska," *Alaska Journal* 2 (Autumn 1972): 14–20.

6. Osgood, "The Game Resources of Alaska," *U.S. Department of Agriculture Yearbook, 1907*, pp. 469–82. See the Bibliography for Osgood's other publications.

7. Examples: Wood, "Among the Thlinkets in Alaska," *Century* 24 (July 1882): 323–39; Muir, "Letters from Alaska," *San Francisco Daily Bulletin*, 6, 23, 27 September, 29, 30 October, 8, 12 November, all in 1879; Seton-Karr, *Shores and Alps of Alaska*; Kidder, "Hunting Sheep in Western Alaska," *Outing* 43 (October 1903): 50–54; De Weese, "A Red Letter Day with Alaskan Big Game," *Field and Stream* 2 (February 1898): 253–56; Stone, "Explorer-Naturalist in the Arctic," *Scribner's Magazine* 33 (April 1903): 438–49; Loring, "The Quest for Ovis Dalli," *Outdoor Life* 14 (September 1904): 549–58; Cane, *Summer and Fall in Western Alaska*; Sheldon, *The Wilderness of Denali*; Browne, "In the Caribou Country," *Outing* 56 (June 1910): 259–69. For a more complete listing of this type of literature, see James Wickersham, *A Bibliography of Alaskan Literature, 1724–1924*.

8. W. H. Osgood, "Clinton Hart Merriam, 1885–1942," *Journal of Mammalogy* 24 (17 November 1943): 426. Keir B. Sterling, *Last of the Naturalists: The Career of C. Hart Merriam*, p. 204, note. Remington Kellogg, "A Century of Progress in Smithsonian Biology," *Science*

104 (9 August 1946): 132–41. Lawrence Badash, "The Completeness of Nineteenth-Century Science," *Isis* 63 (March 1972): 48–58.

9. Rausch, "Status of Some Arctic Mammals," p. 97.

10. On the "species problem" I follow, mainly: Ernst Mayr, *Animal Species and Evolution*; Mayr, "Species Concepts and Definitions," in *The Species Problem*, ed. Mayr; Mayr, "Illiger and the Biological Species Concept," *Journal of the History of Biology* 1 (Fall 1968): 163–68. Also, Mayr, "Evolution," *Scientific American* 239 (September 1978): 47–55.

11. *Journal of Mammalogy* 1 (November 1919): 47. Osgood, "Merriam," p. 426. See also W. J. Hamilton, Jr., "Mammalogy in North America," in California Academy of Sciences, *A Century of Progress in the Natural Sciences, 1853–1953*, pp. 661–88.

I have made no systematic study of the social origins of mammalogists, although such an investigation should be welcomed by historians of biology. The five men are Madison Grant, George Bird Grinnell, Charles Sheldon, Edward W. Nelson, and C. Hart Merriam. Sheldon, Grant, and Grinnell graduated from Yale, where they were probably exposed to some undergraduate biology. Grant's specialized training was in law, but he is best remembered for his activities as secretary and president of the New York Zoological Society. Sheldon, a railroad executive, retired early to devote his life to natural history. Grinnell eventually received a doctorate under O. C. Marsh, the paleontologist, but he is best remembered as the publisher of *Forest and Stream*, founder of the Audubon Society and the Boone and Crockett Club, and as a biological generalist and conservationist rather than as a mammalogist specifically. Grinnell, Sheldon, and Grant were gentlemen naturalists who exercised immense influence in the establishment of policy for Alaskan game. Merriam and Nelson were the senior bureaucrats involved. Both had some biological training, but Merriam first went into medicine and Nelson's scientific training came mainly through apprenticeship and self-education. Merriam was an ornithologist before he was a mammalogist and Nelson's interest in mammalogy was only part of his interest in natural history generally. For Grant, *DAB, Supplement Two*, p. 256; for Grinnell, *DAB, Supplement Two*, pp. 571, 572; for Merriam, *DAB, Supplement Three*, pp. 517–19; for Sheldon, *Who Was Who in America*, vol. 1: *1897–1942*, p. 1112; for Nelson, *DAB Supplement One*, pp. 571, 572.

12. Robert K. Merton, "Priorities in Scientific Discovery," *American Sociological Review* 22 (December 1957): 635–59.

13. Stone, "Explorer Naturalist," p. 448. Stone, "Some Results of a Natural History Journey to Northern British Columbia, Alaska, and the Northwest Territory . . . ," *Bulletin of the American Museum of Natural History* 13 (1900): 32–36.

14. Osgood, "Merriam," pp. 429, 434, 436. Merriam, "Criteria for the Recognition of Species and Genera," *Journal of Mammalogy* 1 (November 1919): 6–9. Sterling, *Last of the Naturalists*, is a full biography of Merriam. The Simpson quote is in his *Principles of Classification and a Classification of Mammals*, p. 225.

15. Swain, *Federal Conservation Policy*, p. 40.

16. Bailey, *Field Work*, pp. 5–9, 57. Bailey to E. W. Nelson, 21 March 1921, "Game Acts," GC BBS, RG 22.

17. *Mammals of the World*. The quote is in Walker's report, 21 November 1939, with "Admiralty–Bears," SF&W, RG 22.

18. *American Men of Science* (1938), p. 1079. Seymour Hadwen and L. J. Palmer, *Reindeer in Alaska*, p. 3. Palmer, *Progress of Reindeer Grazing Investigations in Alaska*, pp. 23, 29. Box 1, L. J. Palmer Collection, University of Alaska Archives, Fairbanks. O. J. Murie, "Planning for Alaska's Big Game," in *Science in Alaska, 1950*, ed. H. B. Collins, p. 261. A. Starker Leopold and F. Fraser Darling, *Wildlife in Alaska: An Ecological Reconnaissance*, pp. 57–73.

19. O. J. Murie, *Journeys to the Far North*, pp. 247–49. Murie to Nelson, 5 November 1921, Box 4, O. J. Murie Papers. O. J. Murie, *Alaska–Yukon Caribou*. Also, M. E. Murie (Mrs. Olaus Murie), *Two in the Far North*. Robert Marshall, *Alaska Wilderness: Exploring the Central Brooks Range*.

20. Adolph Murie, *The Wolves of Mount McKinley*. Adolph Murie, *A Naturalist in Alaska*.

21. For O. Murie, *American Men of Science* (1938), p. 1023; for Osgood, *World Who's Who in Science* (1968), p. 1291; for A. Murie, *American Men of Science* (1944), p. 1275; for Bailey, *American Men and Women of Science: Physical and Biological Sciences* (1971), p. 23; for Walker, *American Men of Science* (1938), p. 1481; for Palmer, *American Men of Science* (1938), p. 1079; and for Hadwen, see Hadwen and Palmer, *Reindeer in Alaska*, p. 3.

22. *AR BBS SA, 1930*, pp. 67, 68. AR AGC, 1948 and 1949, AGC Records.

23. Richard A. Cooley, *Politics and Conservation: The Decline of the Alaska Salmon*, pp. xiv, xv, is a handy source for the annual size of the salmon pack from 1941 to 1959; see p. 118 for illegal fishing at Karluk. *Commercial Appeal*, Memphis, with "Wildlife Refuges–Bears," RG 22. Webster K. Clark, "Kodiak Bear–Red Salmon Relationships at Karluk Lake, Alaska," *Transactions of the North American Wildlife Conference, 1959*, p. 337. For more about the early Karluk fishery, see Jefferson F. Moser, *The Salmon and Salmon Fisheries of Alaska*, pp. 144–57.

24. Carlson quoted in Bob DeArmond, "A Northern Notebook," *Daily Empire*, Juneau, 10 May 1951, with "Wildlife Refuges–Bears," RG 22.

25. Materials with "Wildlife Refuges–Bears," RG 22.

26. Long with McCord, *McCord of Alaska*, p. 14, and caption for photo following p. 124. Excerpt from Thomas's broadcast, 20 February 1951; H. H. Rochelle to Regional Director, F&WS, Juneau, telegram, 14 February 1951; both "Wildlife Refuges–Bears," RG 22.

27. Memorial No. 6, "Wildlife Refuges–Bears," RG 22.

28. "Kodiak Bear Management Plan," p. 46, "Wildlife Refuges–Bears," RG 22. AR AGC, 1952, AGC Records.

29. Dufresne, *My Way Was North*, pp. 204–06, 209, 210.

30. Hellenthal, "Why Not?" p. 19. Hellenthal, *Melodrama*, p. 281.

31. U.S. Congress, House, "To Regulate the Killing and Sale," *Hearings* (1918), pp. 46–51.

32. Cart, " 'New Deal' for Wildlife," p. 113, for the quotation.

33. *AR GA SI, 1919*, p. 461. Riggs to Col. McGuire, 5 January 1920, Roll 61, GA GC.

34. AGC Minutes, 1 December 1930, 22 February 1938, 25 February 1938, 26 February 1938, AGC Records. AR AGC, 1940, AGC Records.

35. Bernard Brodie and Fawn Brodie, *From Crossbow to H-Bomb*, pp. 71–81, 131–35. Trefethen, *American Crusade*, pp. 59, 146, 176.

36. Cameron, *Bureau of Biological Survey*, pp. 262, 266, 293, 294.

37. AR EO, 1931, AGC Records. *AR F&WS, 1941*, p. 403.

38. *Alaska Railroad Record*, 16 January 1917, p. 78. Edwin F. Fitch, *The Alaska Railroad*, pp. 9–12, for the story of the unlucky cow moose. A general history of the railroad, to 1945, is William H. Wilson, *Railroad in the Clouds: The Alaska Railroad in the Age of Steam, 1914–1945*.

39. AR EO, 1928, and AR EO, 1 November 1936–31 December 1937, AGC Records.

40. U.S. Congress, House, "To Regulate the Killing and Sale of Certain Game Animals," *Hearings*, pt. 1, Committee on Territories, 65th Cong., 2d sess. (1918), U.S. Senate Library vol. 215, no. 4., p. 21.

41. Murie, *Journeys*, p. 114.

42. The minister is quoted in T. C. Hinckley, "Alaska and the Emergence of America's Conservation Consciousness," *The Prairie Scout* 2 (1974): 88.

43. White, informal conversation, June 14, 1976. S. Jensen, "Early Alaska Bush Pilot Interviews—Sam O. White," 2 December 1961, typescript pp. 3, 4, University of Alaska Archives, Fairbanks. AR EO, 1935, AGC Records, confirms the use of private airplanes by wardens without compensation. White's account of his career that is of interest here is in: "Sam White, Alaskan, Part 3," *Alaska* 31 (February 1965): 47–52; "Part 4" (March 1965): 48–53; "Part 5" (May 1965): 54, 57; "Part 6" (June 1965): 56–59. AR EO, 1941, AGC Records. Frank Dufresne, "The Game and Fur Belong to All the People," *Alaska* 10 (April 1944): 18.

44. Gelles to Reddington, 9 August 1928, "Alaska Hunting to Alaska Game Laws," GC BBS, RG 22. AR EO, 1928, AGC Records.

45. Solicitor, U.S. Department of Agriculture, to Reddington, 18 October 1928; H. Terhune to BBS, wire, 16 November 1928; both "Solicitor's Opinions," SF&W, RG 22.

46. QR EO, 31 January 1945, AGC Records, urges enactment of rules against driving game. AR EO, 1946, AGC Records, mentions driving game to hunters on the ground, and shooting at hunters from the air. AR AGC, 1944, AGC Records, mentions the number of airplanes operating out of Anchorage; AR AGC, 1946, mentions the public's annoyance with air hunts; AR AGC, 1956, mentions the relative success of airborne hunters. Recent conditions are described in Jim Rearden, "State of Alaska's Guides," *Alaska* 34 (November 1968): 8.

47. Jay Hammond, "Tarnished Trophies," *Alaska* 35 (July 1969): 15.

48. Russell Annabel, "Trouble in Alaska's Game Lands," *Saturday Evening Post* 221 (1 January 1949): 34, 48.

Chapter 5

1. U.S. F&WS, *Big-Game Resources of the United States, 1937–1942*, pp. ii, 14, and *AR F&WS, 1941*, p. 335, for the discrepant totals. The Alaskan data are in Dufresne, *Mammals and Birds*, pp. 6–15; second set of data for the National Resources Committee in Dufresne to Chief, BBS, 14 October 1937, "Alaska File A–Z," SF&W, RG 22; and, Scott et al., "Status of Dall Sheep and Caribou," pp. 612–26.

2. Albert W. Erickson, *The Black Bear in Alaska*, p. 3. Boone and Crockett Club, *North American Big Game*, p. 522. Hereafter in this chapter, general information about the animals will be drawn, without page citations, from the following reference books: W. H. Burt, *A Field Guide to the Mammals*, 3d ed.; Frank Dufresne, *Alaska's Animals and Fishes*; Ira N. Gabrielson and F. C. Lincoln, *The Birds of Alaska*; Richard H. Manville and Stanley P. Young, *Distribution of Alaskan Mammals*; and Ernest P. Walker, *Mammals of the World*, vol. 2.

3. AR EO, 1 January 1938–30 November 1938, AGC Records.

4. Edward F. Chatelain, "Bear–Moose Relationships on the Kenai Peninsula," *Transactions of the North American Wildlife Conference, 1950*, p. 226.

5. AR EO, 1 December 1935–31 October 1936, and 1 November 1932–31 October 1933, AGC Records.

6. A. Starker Leopold and F. Fraser Darling, "Effects of Land Use on Moose and Caribou in Alaska," *Transactions of the North American Wildlife Conference, 1953*, p. 553. Lawrence J. Palmer, "Food Requirements of Some Alaskan Game Mammals," *Journal of Mammalogy* 25 (15 February 1944): 49, 50.

7. T. S. Palmer to William Hornaday, 26 June 1909, "Regulations to Alaska Game Law, 1922," GC BBS, RG 22. AR AGC, 1942, AGC Records. AGC, *Laws and Regulations, 1944–45*, p. 22. David L. Spencer and Edward F. Chatelain, "Progress in the Management of the Moose of South Central Alaska," *Transactions of the North American Wildlife Conference, 1953*, p. 551.

8. Spencer and Chatelain, "Progress in Management of Moose," pp. 550, 551.

9. AR EO for the following periods: 1 January 1938–30 November 1938; 1 December 1938–31 December 1939; 1 January 1941–31 December 1941; 1 January 1942–30 November 1942; 1 January 1943–30 November 1943; all AGC Records. For examples of poaching, see Governor's secretary to Herbert Lee, 16 July 1917, Roll 42, and Frank Aldrich to Governor Riggs, 30 April 1918, Roll 49, both GA GC. And AR AGC, 1940, AGC Records.

10. Leopold and Darling, *Wildlife in Alaska*, pp. 12, 13, 50–52. L. J. Palmer, "Food Requirements," pp. 49, 50, 53.

11. Interpretations in the text above are from my reading of the documents and of D. J. Ray's conclusions in *The Eskimos of Bering Strait, 1650–1898*, pp. 226–40, including notes.

Textual information above and below has been taken from Ray, and from the following: Margaret Lantis, "The Reindeer Industry of Alaska," *Arctic* 3 (April 1950): 27–44; Palmer, *Progress in Reindeer Investigations*; Jack R. Luick, "The Cantwell Reindeer Industry, 1921–1928," *Alaska Journal* 3 (Spring 1973): 107–13; James and Catherine Brickley, "Reindeer, Cattle of the Arctic," *Alaska Journal* 5 (Winter 1975)· 16–24; Leopold and Darling, *Wildlife in Alaska*, pp. 47–82; Scott et al., "Status of Dall Sheep and Caribou," pp. 617–25. The white herder's side is in Carl J. Lomen, *Fifty Years in Alaska*.

12. Luick, "Cantwell Reindeer Industry," p. 110. Scott et al., "Status of Dall Sheep and Caribou," p. 625.

13. Ray, *Eskimos of Bering Strait*, p. 240, note.

14. Lantis, "Reindeer Industry," p. 34.

15. O. J. Murie to Edward W. Nelson, 1 April 1922, "Alaska General to Alaska Reports," GC BBS, RG 22. AR EO, 1930, and 1 January 1938–30 November 1938, with AGC Records.

16. AR EO, 1 November 1936–31 December 1937, AGC Records. Scott et al., "Status and Management of the Polar Bear and Pacific Walrus," *Transactions of the North American Wildlife Conference, 1959*, pp. 367–70. Jim Rearden, "Aerial Polar Bear Hunt," *Alaska* 37 (August 1971): 14. Second set of NRC data, Dufresne to Chief, BBS, 14 October 1937, "Alaska File, A–Z," SF&W, RG 22. Wolfgang Ullrich, *Endangered Species*, pp. 41, 42.

17. Boone and Crockett Club, *North American Big Game*, p. 490. Scott et al., "Status of Dall Sheep and Caribou," p. 615; the documentary record does not support the authors' contention that hunting for meat never had any appreciable effect on the numbers of sheep. Dufresne to Chief, BBS, 14 October 1937, "Alaska File, A–Z," SF&W, RG 22.

18. L. J. Palmer, "Food Requirements," pp. 49, 50, 54.

19. Wickersham to Nelson, 6 August 1925; Nelson to Wickersham, 17 August 1925; both GC BBS, RG 22.

20. *AR F&WS, 1944*, p. 226. Dufresne to Chief, BBS, 14 October 1937, "Alaska File, A–Z," SF&W, RG 22. AR AGC, 1949 and 1950, AGC Records.

21. John L. Buckley, "Animal Population Fluctuations in Alaska—A History," *Transactions of the North American Wildlife Conference, 1954*, pp. 342, 252–54.

22. National Research Council, Committee on Agricultural Land Use and Wildlife Resources, *Land Use and Wildlife Resources*, p. 31. For more detail and debate on this issue see P. S. Martin and H. E. Wright, eds., *Pleistocene Extinctions, the Search for a Cause*.

23. T. S. Palmer, "Extermination of Noxious Animals by Bounties," *Yearbook of the Department of Agriculture, 1896*, pp. 55, 64. Cameron, *Bureau of Biological Survey*, p. 44 note.

24. The bureau's role, to 1929, is discussed in Cameron, *Bureau of Biological Survey*, pp. 42–65, 173–85.

25. Palmer, "Extermination of Noxious Animals," pp. 55, 59, 68.

26. A special symposium on predation held by the American Society of Mammalogists in 1930 is illustrative of the evidence and disagreements; see *Journal of Mammalogy* (August 1930): 325–401. Cameron, *Bureau of Biological Survey*, pp. 190, 191. Vingenz Ziswiler, *Extinct and Vanishing Animals*, p. 73. Trefethen, *Crusade for Wildlife*, pp. 298, 299.

27. For data on bounties, see Dufresne to Harry Liek, 25 November 1938, and M. Burge to S. P. Young, n.d. (probably December 1938); with "Predatory–Alaska and Arizona," GC BBS, RG 22. AGC Minutes, 14 November and 15 November 1928, AGC Records, for the special prize money.

28. Memo for Gabrielson from S. P. Young, 28 February 1936; R. N. White to H. W. Terhune, 8 April 1932; both "Predatory–Alaska and Arizona," GC BBS, RG 22. AR EO, 1933, AGC Records, for the Nenana letter.

29. QR EO, 1 April 1939, AGC Records. Leopold and Darling, *Wildlife in Alaska*, p. 59.

30. *Wolves of Mount McKinley Park*, pp. xvi–xviii, 230, 231.

31. Leopold and Darling, *Wildlife in Alaska*, p. 63, and their "Effects of Land Use on Moose and Caribou in Alaska," pp. 553–55.

32. E. A. Goldman, "The Coyote–Archpredator," *Journal of Mammalogy* 11 (August 1930): 327. Dufresne to E. Gruening, 3 January 1941, Roll 277, GA GC. AR AGC, 1952, AGC Records.

33. AR EO, 1931, AGC Records.

34. AR AGC, 1952, AGC Records.

35. Edward O. Wilson, *Sociobiology: The New Synthesis*, p. 509.

36. The Kenai incidents are: J. A. Bourke to Governor Strong, 15 February 1917, Roll 42; Wardens' Reports, J. Tolman to Governor Clark, 12 September 1912, Roll 7; both GA GC.

37. Ralph H. Imler and E. R. Kalmbach, *The Bald Eagle and Its Economic Status*, pp. 9, 10, 12, 27. Richard H. Pough, *Audubon Western Bird Guide*, pp. 55, 56.

38. Ingersoll, *Alaskan Bird-Life*, p. 31, for Nelson's early opinion.

39. Gruening to Speaker of the House, Nineteenth Territorial Legislature, 21 March 1949, Roll 277, GA GC; also printed in Territory of Alaska, *Journal of the House* (22 March 1949), pp. 1030–35.

40. Bailey, *Field Work*, p. 31. Imler and Kalmbach, *Bald Eagle*, pp. 2, 8. E. R. Kalmbach to Dufresne, 7 January 1941, Roll 277, GA GC.

41. Governor Bone to Strong, n.d., Roll 112; H. A. Wade to Bone, 24 October 1923, Roll 102; Bone to Wade, 18 December 1923, Roll 102; all GA GC.

42. William Sulzer to Gruening, 24 February 1941, Roll 277, GA GC.

43. Gruening to Speaker of the House, 21 March 1949, Roll 277, GA GC.

44. Territory of Alaska, *Journal of the Senate* (16 March 1949), p. 675. Names checked in Atwood and De Armond, *Who's Who in Alaskan Politics*.

Chapter 6

1. My points of departure in the discussion of the motives of both conservationists and hunters are David R. Klein, "The Ethics of Hunting and the Antihunting Movement," *Transactions of the North American Wildlife and Natural Resources Conference, 1973*, pp. 256, 257, and R. D. Guthrie, "The Ethical Relationship between Humans and Other Organisms," *Perspectives in Biology and Medicine* 11 (Autumn 1967): 52–62. Darling's comment is in "Man's Responsibility for the Environment," *Biology and Ethics*, ed. F. G. Ebling, p. 121. For the "rights of rocks" see Roderick Nash, "American Environmental History," *Pacific Historical Review* 41 (August 1972): 367, 371.

2. AR EO, 1939, AGC Records, for reported takes.

3. AR EO, 1 January 1942–30 November 1942, AGC Records. The first estimate allowed 100 pounds for dressed deer, 600 for a moose, 200 for a caribou, 150 each for a sheep and a goat. The estimate for 1943 is in Dufresne, "Game and Fur Belong to All," p. 18. One estimate of the amount of game used as food in the States is in Albert M. Day, "Wartime Uses of Wildlife Products," *Transactions of the North American Wildlife Conference, 1943*, p. 46.

4. AR AGC, 1948, AGC Records. Miller, *Frontier in Alaska*, p. 210.

5. The continued reliance on game is clear from Rogers and Cooley, *Alaska's Population*, vol. 2, pp. 165–69; Robert D. Arnold et al., *Alaska Native Land Claims*, pp. 268, 269, 286, 287; W. A. Elkins, "Pressing Problems in Administration of Wildlife Resources in Alaska," *Science in Alaska, 1950*, pp. 277, 278; David R. Klein, "Waterfowl in the Economy of the Eskimos on the Yukon-Kuskokwim Delta, Alaska," *Arctic* 19 (December 1966): 319–36; Yupiktak Bista, *A Report on Subsistence and the Conservation of Yupik Life-Style*.

6. Questionnaires, with analysis, including a summary in the Juneau *Empire*, 24 July 1923, and editorial, 26 July 1923, in "Alaska Reports," GC BBS, RG 22.

7. John L. Buckley, *Wildlife in the Economy of Alaska*.

8. The industry at that time is described by T. C. Hinckley in "The Inside Passage: Popular Gilded Age Tour," *Pacific Northwest Quarterly* 56 (April 1965): 67–74.

9. AR AGC, 1940, AGC Records.

10. Aldo Leopold, *A Sand County Almanac*, pp. 167, 200.

11. A. Koch and W. Peden, eds., *The Life and Selected Writings of Thomas Jefferson*, p. 488; Jefferson used the phrase to express his concern (in a letter to Madison dated 6 September 1789) about national debts, not natural resources.

12. Walker, "Circular Letter to Fur Wardens," April 1921, "Alaska Reports," GC BBS, RG 22. Dufresne, "What of Tomorrow?" *Alaska* 3 (April 1937): 9.

13. Dufresne, *Alaska's Animals and Fishes*, pp. 296, 297. Leopold, *Sand County Almanac*, p. 149.

14. Dufresne, *Alaska's Animals and Fishes*, pp. 3, 4. Dufresne, "What of Tomorrow?" p. 9. Leopold, *Sand County Almanac*, pp. 196, 268; parentheses were removed from the last quotation.

15. Grant, "Condition of Wildlife," p. 370. The Dufresne quotation is from "What of Tomorrow?" p. 9.

16. Carl O. Sauer, "Theme of Plant and Animal Destruction in Economic History," in his *Land and Life*, p. 149.

17. Susan Flader, *Thinking Like a Mountain*, p. 31. Leopold, *Sand County Almanac*, pp. 177, 236.

18. Ramón Mârgôlef, *Perspectives in Ecological Theory*, p. 50. Charles W. Fawcett, "Comments: Vanishing Wildlife and Federal Protective Efforts," *Ecology Law Review* 1 (Summer 1971): 558. Rudy R. Lachenmeier, "The Endangered Species Act of 1973: Preservation or Pandemonium," *Environmental Law* 5 (Fall 1974): 31.

19. White, "An Emergency," pp. 213, 214. Krutch, "The Sportsman or the Predator? A Damnable Pleasure," *Saturday Review* (17 August 1957): 8.

20. Muir, *Travels in Alaska*, pp. 187, 18. There is some confusion on one small point: whether Muir ate wild meat after someone else had shot and prepared it. S. Hall Young, in his *Alaska Days with John Muir*, p. 171, says that Muir did. Here, we take Muir's word that he did not. McConnell, "The Conservation Movement–Past and Present," *Western Political Quarterly* 7 (September 1954): 465.

21. See, e.g., reactions at the Symposium on Predatory Animal Control held in May 1930 and reported in the *Journal of Mammalogy*, pp. 325–401.

22. See, e.g., Robert C. Lucas, "The Contribution of Environmental Research to Wilderness Policy Decisions," *Journal of Social Issues* 22 (October 1966): 118, and Mârgôlef, *Perspectives in Ecological Theory*, p. 50.

23. A. D. Graham, *The Gardeners of Eden*, p. 139.

24. Roosevelt, Grinnell, and Kent are quoted in Roderick Nash, *Wilderness and the American Mind*, pp. 152, 153. See also Klein, "Ethics," p. 261.

25. Pp. 59, 137, 54.

26. Leopold, *Sand County Almanac*, p. 210. Krutch, "Sportsman or Predator?" p. 9.

27. S. L. Washburn and C. S. Lancaster, "The Evolution of Hunting," in *Man the Hunter*, ed. R. B. Lee and I. DeVore, p. 293.

28. Dubos, *Beast or Angel?* p. 44. Ethological writing in this vein includes: Konrad Z. Lorenz, *On Aggression*; Robert Ardrey, *The Territorial Imperative*; Lionel Tiger and Robin Fox, *The Imperial Animal*. The leading advocate of sociobiology and the biological origins of social behavior is Edward O. Wilson; see his *Sociobiology*.

29. In the first issue of *Alaska* (then called *The Alaska Sportsman*) 1 (January 1935): 3.

30. *AR GA SA, 1916*, p. 2.

Chapter 7

1. Waldemar Jochelson, *History, Ethnology and Anthropology of the Aleut*, pp. 41–57. Wendell H. Oswalt, *Alaskan Eskimos*, pp. 119, 120. Robert F. Spencer, *The North Alaskan Eskimo*, p. 268.

2. Murie, *Alaska-Yukon Caribou*, pp. 2, 3. A small sample of Tanaina hunting practices, extracted from Cornelius Osgood, *Ethnography of the Tanaina*, appears in *The Cook Inlet Collection*, ed. Morgan Sherwood, pp. 11–18.

3. Frederica de Laguna, *Under Mount St. Elias: The History and Culture of the Yakutat Tlingit*, vol. 1, pp. 364–73. Aurel Krause, *The Tlingit Indians*, pp. 125, 132.

4. Ray, *Eskimos of Bering Strait*, p. 194. Ivan Petroff, "Population, Resources, etc., of Alaska [Tenth Census, 1880]," in *Compilation of Narratives of Explorations of Alaska*, pp. 133, 134.

5. The size and value of the fur trade is in U.S. Census Office, *Report on Population and Resources of Alaska at the Eleventh Census: 1890*, p. 215. Turner, *The Character and Influence of the Indian Trade in Wisconsin*, ed. D. H. Miller and W. W. Savage, pp. xviii, 77. Anthropologists writing since Turner have noted the effects of the fur trade; a recent example is James W. Van Stone, *Athapaskan Adaptations: Hunters and Fishermen of the Subarctic Forests*, pp. 101–04.

6. Arnold, *Alaska Native Land Claims*, pp. 25, 66, 69, 70. The Alaska law is 15 Stat. L. 240–242. Nichols, *Alaska*, p. 47.

7. Arnold, *Alaska Native Land Claims*, pp. 80–83. Gruening, *State of Alaska*, p. 362. Kent Sturgis, "Native Claims Act," *Anchorage Daily News*, 22 December 1971.

8. Stanton Patty, ed., "A Conference with the Tanana Chiefs," *Alaska Journal* 1 (Spring 1971): 2–18. An earlier conference over the rights of Natives in southeastern Alaska was held in 1898; see T. C. Hinckley, " 'The Canoe Rocks–We Do Not Know What Will Become of Us,' " *Western Historical Quarterly* 1 (July 1970): 265–90.

9. For the laws, see Cameron, *Bureau of Biological Survey*, pp. 262, 265. E. W. Nelson to Gov. Riggs, 14 February 1921, "Solicitor's Opinions," SF&W, RG 22. Bailey to Nelson, 9 February 1921, "Alaska Reports," GC BBS, RG 22.

10. Nelson to A. M. Bailey, 23 February 1921; Riggs to Nelson, 15 February 1921; both "Game Acts," GC BBS, RG 22.

11. Cameron, *Bureau of Biological Survey*, p. 294.

12. Cameron, *Bureau of Biological Survey*, pp. 99–103, for treaty. Yupiktak Bista, *Report on Subsistence*, pp. 46–53.

13. Solicitor to Nelson, 3 March 1925, "Solicitor's Opinions," SF&W, RG 22. Conversation with Sam White.

14. Cameron, *Bureau of Biological Survey*, p. 295. Solicitor to Reddington, 3 May 1930, "Solicitor's Opinions," SF&W, RG 22.

15. AGC Minutes, 14 January 1939, AGC Records.

16. Dall, "Travels on the Yukon," in *Yukon Territory*, ed. F. M. Trimmer, p. 135.

17. S. Hall Young, *Hall Young of Alaska*, pp. 170, 171.

18. Muir, *Travels in Alaska*, p. 235.

19. U.S. Congress, House, "Game Law in Alaska," *House Report 951* (1902), 57th Cong., 1st sess. (serial 4402), pp. 3, 4, 8. See also T. C. Hinckley, "Conservation Consciousness," p. 89.

20. William Paul to BBS, 22 November 1939, GC BBS, RG 22.

21. See above, chap. 2.

22. De Weese to the President, 1 December 1901, in U.S. Congress, *House Report 951*, p. 6. Osgood, *Alaska Peninsula*, pp. 28, 29.

23. Some examples are mentioned in G. H. Peterson to Gov. Clark, 24 October 1912, Roll 7; Judge Peter Overfield to George Cantwell of Seward, 11 March 1913, Roll 19; Charles Madsen to Gov. Strong, 2 April 1917, Roll 42; J. A. Baugham to Gov. Strong, 5 March 1917, Roll 42; all GA GC.

24. The idea can be traced back to some of the earliest observations by Europeans of Indian–animal relations, and was probably reinforced in the eighteenth century by Rousseau's writings on the "noble savage." It became firmly established among intellectuals in the 1930s, thanks to its adoption and propagation by Aldo Leopold; see his *Game*

Management, p. 5. Statements in support of the conclusion that American Natives were conservation-minded include: N. B. Johnson, "The American Indian as Conservationist," *Chronicles of Oklahoma* 30 (Autumn 1952): 333–40; Robert F. Heizer, "Primitive Man as an Ecologic Factor," *Kroeber Anthropological Society Papers* 13 (Fall 1955): 1–31; Fred Fertig, "Child of Nature, the American Indian as an Ecologist," *Sierra Club Bulletin* 55 (August 1970): 4–7; Wilbur R. Jacobs, "Frontiersmen, Fur Traders, and Other Varmints: An Ecological Appraisal of the Frontier in American History," *A.H.A. Newsletter* 8 (November 1970): 5–11; idem, "The Indian and the Frontier in American History–A Need for Revision," *Western Historical Quarterly* 4 (January 1973): 43–56; idem, "The Grand Despoliation . . . ," *Pacific Historical Review* 47 (February 1978): 1–26. The conclusion was shared by two secretaries of the interior: Stewart L. Udall, *The Quiet Crisis*, and Walter J. Hickel, *Who Owns America?* p. 179.

Evidence against all or parts of the doctrine is in, among other places: Anthony Netboy, "The Indian and the Forest," *American Forests* 60 (October 1954): 24, 25, 63; A. W. F. Banfield, "Plight of the Barren Ground Caribou," *Oryx* 4 (April 1957): 5–20; H. J. Lutz, *Aboriginal Man and White Man as Historical Causes of Fires in the Boreal Forest, with Particular Reference to Alaska*; Daniel A. Guthrie, "Primitive Man's Relationship to Nature," *BioScience* 21 (July 1971): 721–25; W. H. Hutchinson, "The Remaking of the Amerind," *Westways* 64 (October 1972): 18–21, 94. Excepting the Lutz work, these writers do not deal with Alaskan Natives. Insofar as I know, no investigator has told the story of wasteful market hunting in Alaska by Natives or tried to explain it.

Two other authors survey the subject as a topic in American intellectual and social history: Douglas Hillman Strong, "The Indian and the Environment," *Journal of Environmental Education* 5 (Winter 1973): 49–51; and C. Martin, "The Indian and the Ecology Movement," in Martin, *Keepers of the Game*, pp. 157–88.

25. Wildlife management during the period is documented in GA GC. Patty, "Conference with Tanana Chiefs," p. 18. Walker to Nelson, 11 April 1922, "Alaska Reports," GC BBS, RG 22.

26. Olaus Murie said that interior Indians along the Tanana River never seemed to waste wild meat; at the same time, he said they were fond of unborn moose and caribou calves, and that each family kept too many dogs, feeding them perhaps as many as twenty-five caribou a summer. Murie to Nelson, 21 May 1921, "Alaska Reports," GC BBS, RG 22. Osgood, *Biological Investigations*, pp. 28, 29. Leopold and Darling, *Wildlife in Alaska*, pp. 39, 42, 45, is a later book but is relevant because the Eskimos described had not entirely abandoned subsistence hunting.

27. Robert F. Scott, "Wildlife in the Economy of the Alaska Natives," *Transactions of the North American Wildlife Conference, 1951*, p. 520. Walker to Nelson, 11 April 1922, "Alaska Reports," GC BBS, RG 22.

28. Knight, "A Re-examination of Hunting, Trapping, and Territoriality among the Northeastern Algonkian Indians," in *Man, Culture, and Animals: The Role of Animals in Human Ecological Adjustments*, ed. A. Leeds and A. P. Vayda, pp. 27–42.

29. Murie, *Alaska–Yukon Caribou*, pp. 2, 3.

30. VanStone, *Athapaskan Adaptations*, pp. 59, 65. Spencer, *North Alaskan Eskimo*, p. 264. Philip Drucker, *Indians of the Northwest Coast*, p. 155.

31. See Klein, "Ethics," p. 257, and Boyce Rensburger, *The Cult of the Wild*, pp. 1–27.

32. Darling, "Man's Responsibility," p. 118.

33. Spencer, *North Alaskan Eskimo*, pp. 267, 268, 270. It should be repeated that Spencer does not take the leaps of logic mentioned above, and that what may be true of one group of Alaskan Natives may not be true of another; the examples are intended only to demonstrate how easily the anthropological evidence can be misinterpreted.

34. Federal Field Committee for Development Planning in Alaska, *Economic Development in Alaska: A Report to the President*, p. 8.

35. Yupiktak Bista, *A Report on Subsistence*, pp. 51–53.

36. Spencer, *North Alaskan Eskimo*, pp. 267, 268. Ivan Petroff (Polaris), "Gold Seeking in the Regions of Perpetual Snow," *San Francisco Sunday Chronicle*, 26 December 1876, reprinted partially in Sherwood, *Cook Inlet Collection*, p. 86.

37. E.g., John Chapman, Anvik, to Secretary of Interior, 10 December 1917, Roll 48, GA GC; Leopold and Darling, *Wildlife in Alaska*, p. 39.

38. Washburn, "Ethnohistory: History 'In the Round,'" *Ethnohistory* 7 (Winter 1961): 35, 36. Spencer, *North Alaskan Eskimo*, p. 272.

39. Washburn, *The Indian in America*, pp. 56, 11, 12.

40. Jacobs, "Indian and Frontier," p. 50. Jacobs, "Great Despoliation," p. 5.

41. H. F. Dobyns, "An Appraisal of Techniques with a New Hemispheric Estimate," *Current Anthropology* 7 (October 1966): 395–416. Driver, *Indians of North America*, pp. 63–65.

42. Two new but already classic "anthropomedical" studies that deal with the effects of disease in history are Alfred W. Crosby, *The Columbian Exchange*, and William H. McNeill, *Plagues and People*.

43. Martin, *Keepers of the Game*.

44. Burch, *Daydreams and Nightmares: A Sociological Essay on the American Environment*, p. 49.

45. Turner, *Character and Influence of the Indian Trade*.

46. I risk criticism in using the term "petty." The Russian American Company and the Alaska Commercial Company (or the Hudson's Bay Company or John Jacob Astor's organization) were hardly "petty" capitalistic institutions. I mean only that on the trading frontier business relations between races were personalized.

47. For an excellent survey of the status of theoretical work on the subject, see Calvin Martin, *Keepers of the Game*, pp. 1–21.

48. Yi-Fu Tuan, "Our Treatment of the Environment in Ideal and Actuality," *American Scientist* 58 (May-June 1970): 244–49.

Chapter 8

1. Governor Parks to E. W. Nelson, 20 February 1926, "Game Acts," GC BBS, RG 22.

2. Population figures are from Rogers and Cooley, *Alaska's Population*, vol. 2, unless stated otherwise. License statistics from 1926 to 1959 (here and below) are in AR AGC, 1959, AGC Records.

3. *AR GA SI, 1911*, pp. 371, 372. Bailey, "Notes on Game Conditions in Alaska," 1 January 1921; Murie to Nelson, 12 March 1921; both "Alaska Reports," GC BBS, RG 22. W. A. Elkins, "Pressing Problems," p. 276.

4. E.g., E. P. Walker, "Circular Letter to Fur Wardens," April 1921, "Alaska Reports," GC BBS, RG 22.

5. AR AGC, 1959, AGC Records.

6. Riggs to Nelson, 13 June 1921, "Prohibition Enforcement," GC BBS, RG 22. Patty, "Conference with Tanana Chiefs," p. 8.

7. Rogers and Cooley, *Alaska's Population*, vol. 2, pp. 7, 32.

8. Ibid., vol. 2, p. 68. Buckner is quoted in Driscoll, *War Discovers Alaska*, pp. 320, 321.

9. T.S. Palmer, *Hunting Licenses*, pp. 10–14.

10. The prospector is quoted in Murie to Nelson, 10 August 1921, "Alaska Reports," GC BBS, RG 22. Riggs to Edmund Seymour, 12 October 1920, Roll 73, GA GC. The *Outdoor Life* article is from a clipping sent by J. A. McGuire to Riggs, in 1919, Roll 61, GA GC.

11. See, e.g., Riggs to McGuire, 17 July 1919, Roll 73, GA GC; *AR GA SI, 1919*, p. 461; Burnham to Nelson, 28 December 1920, "Game Acts," GC BBS, RG 22.

12. Based upon licenses issued; AR AGC, 1959, AGC Records. The pre–World War I figure is a guess based upon data for six years only: in 1900, 9 nonresidents were licensed;

in 1910, 23; in 1911, 25; in 1914, 21; in 1915, 22; in 1919, 9. See C. C. Shea to Governor's Secretary, 1 December 1911, Roll 7, GA GC; *AR GA SA, 1910* and *1911* and *1915*, and *AR GA SI, 1919*.

13. AR EO, 1939, AGC Records. Seventy to 75 percent of the nonresidents reported.

14. Cameron, *Bureau of Biological Survey*, pp. 266, 267, 295–98.

15. *AR GA SA, 1911*, p. 5. "Regulations Related to Licensed Guides and Packers," on Roll 112, GA GC. AR AGC, 1959, AGC Records.

16. AGC, "Information on Examination for Registered Guides" (Juneau), "Hunting and Fishing Miscellaneous," Vertical File, University of Alaska Archives, Fairbanks. AGC Minutes, 7 September 1931, AGC Records.

17. AGC Minutes, 27 November, 28 November, 1 December, 2 December, all 1931, AGC Records. Miscellaneous Report of the Executive Officer to AGC, 1 November 1936–31 December 1937, AGC Records.

18. AR EO, 1928 and 1933, AGC Records.

19. C. Madison to Governor, 11 February 1918, Roll 48; E. A. Axelson to U.S. Marshal, Juneau, 18 January 1924, Roll 112; both GA GC. See also AGC Minutes, 28 February 1938, AGC Records; *AR GA SA, 1918*, p. 3.

20. J. E. Pegues, "Alaska's Brownies," *Field and Stream* 35 (December 1930): 36. Nelson to E. P. Walker, 7 June 1922, "Game Acts," GC BBS, RG 22. Cameron, *Bureau of Biological Survey*, p. 295.

21. For examples of the wardens' enforcement of the firearm prohibition, see AR EO, 1927 and 1931, AGC Records. Dufresne's observation about Filipinos is in AR EO, 1932, AGC Records. M. G. White to Gabrielson, 31 January 1936, "Solicitor's Opinions, SF&W, RG 22. Rupert Emerson, Director, Division of Territories and Island Possessions, to Gruening, 23 August 1940, Roll 277, GA GC. *CJS* 38 (1943): 8. AR AGC, 1959, AGC Records.

22. M. A. Jones, *American Immigration*, is a survey of the subject. Hornaday's comments were in the *New York Times*, 24 April 1898, p. 11. Trefethen, *Crusade for Wildlife*, p. 176. R. G. Williams, *Game Commissions and Wardens: Their Appointment, Powers, and Duties*, pp. 98, 99.

23. Pp. 13–24, 73, 81, 263. Informal conversation, Mr. and Mrs. John S. Hellenthal.

24. U.S. Bureau of the Census, *Fourteenth Census . . . 1920*, vol. 3, pp. 1158–60. William R. Cashen, *A Brief History of Fairbanks*, p. 4. Simons's status is mentioned in G. Cotter to Governor Scott Bone, 22 December 1923, Roll 102, GA GC. Strong's background is documented in the John W. Troy Papers, Bancroft Library, University of California, Berkeley; this thin, microfilmed collection consists almost entirely of such documentation.

25. Muir, *Cruise of the Corwin*, pp. 161, 162. Examples of other complaints against the Coast Guard are E. P. Walker to Chief, BBS, 8 March 1924, "Game Acts," GC BBS, RG 22, and AGC Minutes, 26 November 1932, AGC Records.

26. Riggs to E. Seymour, 12 October 1920, Roll 73; Deputy Marshal, Sitka, to Secretary of War, copy, 4 November 1922, Roll 102; both GA GC. D. Hotovitsky to Walker, 8 February 1924, "Game Acts," GC BBS, RG 22.

27. Strong to Secretary of War, 3 September 1915, Roll 25; Acting Secretary of War to Strong, 2 October 1915, Roll 25; Strong to A. E. Light, 18 May 1917, Roll 42; all GA GC. U.S. Army Alaska, *Building Alaska with the U.S. Army*, pp. 53, 54.

28. C. Madison to the Governor, 11 February 1918, Roll 48, GA GC. AR EO, 1935, AGC Records.

29. AR EO, 1935; QR EO to Chief, BBS, 6 October 1936; AGC Minutes, 13 December 1935, 4 March 1937, and 14 January 1939; all AGC Records.

30. Dufresne to Gabrielson, 5 November 1940, "Solicitor's Opinions," SF&W, RG 22.

31. W. E. Crouch to Dufresne, 14 November 1940; Dufresne to Director, F&WS, 10 December 1940; both "Solicitor's Opinions," SF&W, RG 22.

Chapter 9

1. QR EO, 7 July 1941, AGC Records. Folta to Dufresne, 2 November 1940, "Alaska File," SF&W, RG 22. See also *CJS* 28 (1941): 28.

2. QR EO, 7 July 1941, AGC Records. Dufresne to Buckner, 20 September 1941, telegraph and letter, "Licenses," SF&W, RG 22.

3. Cashen, *Brief History of Fairbanks*, pp. 11–13. Gaffney to Commanding General, 7 August 1941, "Licenses," SF&W, RG 22.

4. Gaffney to C. G., 22 July 1941; White to Dufresne, 9 July 1941; both "Licenses," SF&W, RG 22.

5. Dufresne to Buckner, 11 July 1941; Dufresne to White, 11 July 1941; Buckner to Dufresne, 17 July 1941; Gaffney to Buckner, 22 July 1941; Gaffney to Buckner, 7 August 1941; Buckner to Dufresne, 7 August 1941; all "Licenses," SF&W, RG 22.

6. Dufresne to Buckner, 26 August 1941, "Licenses," SF&W, RG 22.

7. Walseth to AGC, 24 July 1941; Walseth to Dufresne, wire, 20 August 1941; Walseth to Dufresne, 21 August 1941; Dufresne to Walseth, wire, 26 August 1941; all "Licenses," SF&W, RG 22.

8. Gaffney to Dufresne, 11 August 1941; Gaffney to Dufresne, 29 August 1941; both "Licenses," SF&W, RG 22.

9. Mrs. Buckner to the author, 11 October 1975.

10. Memo for Dufresne from Folta, 9 September 1941, "Licenses," SF&W, RG 22.

11. *Anchorage Daily Times*, 12, 15, and 18 September 1941.

12. Ibid., 19 and 20 September 1941. Also, *Fairbanks Daily News Miner*, 27 September 1941.

13. Hereafter the court record will be used extensively: Buckner Case, A–2671. Judge Hellenthal's name will be substituted for the designation "Court" in the transcript.

14. The author was Eva Greenslit Anderson.

15. Atwood, *Anchorage*, p. 33.

16. *Anchorage Daily Times*, 23 September 1941. Romig, *The Wild Game Dinner or Pioneer Thanksgiving*, p. 6; pamphlet in the possession of John S. Hellenthal, Anchorage.

17. The telephone conversation is quoted in the court record, Buckner Case, A–2671.

18. Hellenthal quoted in the *Anchorage Daily Times*, 27 September 1941; not all of Hellenthal's words are in the court record, which documents only the fact that the judge did so order.

19. Buckner Case, A–2671, and *Anchorage Daily Times*, 27 September 1941.

20. The decision is summarized in print in *Alaska Reports* 10: 121–28.

21. *Anchorage Daily Times*, 3, 4, 6, 7 October 1941.

22. Ibid., 7, 8 October 1941. According to Buckner's diary, while in Hawaii in early 1944 the general was visited by a representative of the army's inspector general. Secretary Ickes had brought charges against Buckner, claiming the general had violated game laws protecting walruses. The Department of the Interior wanted Buckner returned to Alaska within three years for punishment. Buckner thought the action was spiteful. S. B. Buckner, diary, 13–16 February 1944, in the possession of William C. Buckner.

23. *Anchorage Daily Times*, 17 October 1941.

Chapter 10

1. Excerpt from a diary with the Gruening Papers, University of Alaska Archives, Fairbanks; copy courtesy of Renee Blahuta.

2. Driscoll, *War Discovers Alaska*, p. 153.

3. QR EO, 6 April 1942, AGC Records. Dufresne to Editor, *Kodiak Bear*, 16 November 1942, "Legislation," SF&W, RG 22.

4. Dufresne to Buckner, 6 August 1942; Buckner to Dufresne, 21 November 1942; both "Legislation," SF&W, RG 22.

5. I examined Pearson's column in the 24 September 1942 issue of the *Sacramento Union*, on microfilm, University of California, Davis, Shields Library. *Kodiak Bear*, 12 October 1942; newspaper clipping in the possession of William C. Buckner, Kansas City, Missouri.

6. Dufresne to Editor, *Kodiak Bear*, 16 November 1942; Gabrielson to K. Roosevelt, 29 October 1942; Craft to Dufresne, 4 December 1942; all "Legislation," SF&W, RG 22.

7. Gabrielson to the author, 9 May 1976. AR EO, 1945, AGC Records.

8. AGC to Carl Hayden, telegram, 17 November 1942, "Legislation," SF&W, RG 22. *Congressional Record* (1943), vol. 89, pt. 1, p. 1421, and pt. 5, p. 7041.

9. A copy of the general order, from headquarters, Alaska Defense Command, dated 19 July 1943 and signed for Buckner by General E. D. Post, is with "Alaska File," SF&W, RG 22.

10. Fortas to Henry L. Stimson, 15 October 1943, "Alaska File," SF&W, RG 22.

11. "Buck's Battle," *Time* 45 (16 April 1945): 36.

12. Watson, *Chief of Staff: Prewar Plans*, pp. 454–57. Maurice Matloff, *The War Department: Strategic Planning for Coalition Warfare, 1943–1944*, p. 398. K. J. Rohfleisch, "Drawing the Battle Line in the Pacific," in *The Army Air Forces in World War II*, ed. W. F. Craven and J. L. Cate, vol. 1, pp. 464, 467. E. Kathleen Williams, "Deployment of the AAF on the Eve of Hostilities," in *Army Air Forces*, ed. Craven and Cate, vol. 1, pp. 166–68. Harry L. Coles, "The Aleutian Campaign," in *Army Air Forces*, ed. Craven and Cate, vol. 1, p. 359.

13. Coles, "Aleutian Campaign," pp. 381, 383, 394. U.S. Army, Alaska, *Building Alaska*, pp. 88, 89. Samuel Eliot Morison, *Aleutians, Gilberts and Marshalls, June 1942–April 1944*, vol. 7: *History of United States Naval Operations in World War II*, pp. 59–63.

14. *Anchorage Daily Times*, 21 August and 2 October 1943.

15. AR AGC, 1943, AGC Records.

16. AR AGC, 1945 and 1946; AR EO, 1945; all AGC Records.

17. See, e.g., E. L. Bartlett to his office, telegram, 1 September 1949, regarding a bombing range in bison country, and Rhode to Director, F&WS, 10 August 1949, regarding military fish camps; both "Alaska File," SF&W, RG 22. Niska Elwell, "Wrong Target," *Alaska* 15 (October 1949): 14, 15, describes how two soldiers shot at two girls near Seward. J. Rearden, "Clarence Rhode," *Alaska* 46 (January 1980): 14, mentions Rhode's unofficial expression of disgust at the establishment of a hunting camp for generals.

18. George O. Van Orden, "Retraining the Returned G.I. to Shoot Safely," *Transactions of the North American Wildlife Conference, 1945*, pp. 57, 58. Elkins, "Pressing Problems," p. 276.

19. AR AGC, 1952, AGC Records. Executive Vice President, Bell Aircraft Corporation, to Rhode, 3 October 1953, "Alaska File," SF&W, RG 22. Charles J. Keim, "Conservation Comes North," *Alaska* 23 (November 1957): 14, 15, 42–45. Perry H. Davis, "Alaska Conservation—G.I. Style," *Alaska* 27 (July 1961): 14–17, 41–43.

20. Statistics are from AR AGC, 1959, AGC Records.

21. Gene Wilkinson, "Hosea's Last Hunt," *Alaska* 25 (January 1959): 10. Rearden, "Clarence Rhode."

22. Lawrence, "Okinawa Commander Killed," pp. 1, 7.

23. T. C. Price, President, Anchorage Bar Association, to Dimond, 26 July 1943; B. Perrine to Dimond, 27 December 1943; both in Box 25, Dimond Papers. Anchorage Bar Association to Attorney General, telegram, 30 September 1943; Resolution No. 6, Third Divisional Democratic Convention, Anchorage, 13 December 1943; R. E. Baumgartner to the Attorney General, 18 September 1943; all in Appointment File–Hellenthal, Attorney General's Office, Washington. A *Times* editorial of 9 December 1943 is with the Dimond Papers and also in the Appointment File.

24. Dimond to E. L. Bartlett, 17 November 1943; L. V. Ray to Dimond, 1 December

1943; H. Lyng to Dimond, 18 December 1943; Dimond to Lyng, 3 January 1944; G. B. Grigsby to Dimond, 18 December 1943; Hellenthal to Dimond, telegram, 1 October 1943; Buckner to Dimond, 28 October 1943; Francis Biddle to Dimond, 15 December 1943; Dimond to the President, 12 January 1944; all in box 25, Dimond Papers.

25. Julius Krug to Attorney General, 24 July 1946; Folta to Attorney General, 18 June 1946; *Anchorage Daily Times* clipping, 8 October 1951; Bartlett to J. Howard McGrath, 27 April 1951; Director, FBI, to Deputy Attorney General, 29 September 1951; all in Appointment File–Folta, U.S. Attorney General's Office. The *Empire* was dated 17 October 1951; newspaper clipping with other clippings about Folta, in the possession of R. N. De Armond, Juneau.

26. M. F. Jensen to U.S. Attorney General Herbert Brownell, 28 June 1955, Appointment File–Folta, U.S. Attorney General's Office.

27. Wayne E. Burton, *Creating a Northern Agriculture: Historical Perspectives in Alaskan Agriculture*, p. 8. Jim Rearden, "The Kodiak Bear War," *Outdoor Life* (August 1964): 17–19, 70–74. Lewis D. Harmon, "The Plight of the Bison," *Alaska* 27 (November 1961): 19.

28. See, e.g., David R. Klein, "Problems in Conservation of Mammals in the North," *Biological Conservation* 4 (January 1972): 99; Chuck Gray, "The Truth about the Moose / Wolf Controversy," *Alaska Pipeline Worker's Handbook*, pp. 155–58; and all of *Alaska Wildlife Digest* 2 (Spring 1975).

29. Paul Brooks and J. Foote, "The Disturbing Story of Project Chariot," *Harper's* 224 (April 1962): 60–62, 65–67. Gruening, *Many Battles*, pp. 497, 498. For two views of the Rampart project, see Arthur T. George, "Alaska Ponders: How Long Do We Wait?" *Construction Craftsman* 5 (March 1966): 10–12, and Paul Brooks, "The Plot to Drown Alaska," *Atlantic* 215 (May 1965): 53–59.

30. W. C. Thomas, C. F. Marsh, and C. A. Stephens, *Economic Analysis of Red Meat, Fish, Poultry and Wild Game Consumption Patterns in Anchorage, Alaska*, p. i.

31. See Rearden, "State of Alaska's Guides," pp. 6–10, 52, 53.

32. A recent study of one Native village in southwestern Alaska concluded that "traditional foods" could be equal in value to one-fourth of a family's income; see Michael Novak, "The Economics of Native Subsistence Activities in a Village of Southwestern Alaska," *Arctic* 30 (December 1977): 225. For all sides of the caribou question, see articles by James Greiner, Jim Rearden, Lael Morgan, and S. I. Sage in *Alaska* 42 (May 1976). A good recent survey of the issues surrounding the subject of Native subsistence is Jim Rearden, "Subsistence: A Troublesome Issue," *Alaska* 44 (July 1978): 4–6, 84–88.

33. Hugh A. Johnson and Harold T. Jorgenson, *The Land Resources of Alaska*, pp. 342–44, 447. Rich and Tussing, *National Park System in Alaska*. Editors of *Alaska Geographic*, "The Land–Eye of the Storm," *Alaska Geographic* 3 (1975).

34. Larry Pryor, "Alaska Could Well Become the Nation's Survival Kit," *San Francisco Sunday Examiner and Chronicle*, 28 December 1975.

Afterword

1. Douglass C. North, "International Capital Flows and the Development of the American West," *Journal of Economic History* 16 (December 1956): 493, 494.

2. Chester Kirby, "The Attack on the English Game Laws in the Forties," *Journal of Modern History* 4 (March 1932): 18–37. Kirby, "The English Game Law System," *American Historical Review* 38 (January 1933): 240–62.

3. See, e.g., Rearden, "Subsistence," pp. 4–6, 84–88.

4. E.g., Mary Ellen Glass, "The Newlands Reclamation Project: Years of Innocence, 1903–1907," *Journal of the West* 7 (January 1968): 58, 61; Conner Sorensen, "Federal Reclamation on the High Plains: The Garden City Project," *Great Plains Journal* 15 (Spring 1976): 114–33; Ashley L. Schiff, *Fire and Water: Scientific Heresy in the Forest Service*. The

point made in my text is not emphasized by these sources, but they provide information suggesting that poor science and science administration help to explain anticonservation sentiment. John M. Townley, "Soil Saturation Problems on the Truckee-Carson Project, Nevada," *Agricultural History* 52 (April 1978): 280–91, makes the point emphatically.

5. See the new preface in Hays, *Conservation and the Gospel of Efficiency*, Athenaeum edition, 1969.

6. Gressley, "Colonialism: A Western Complaint," *Pacific Northwest Quarterly* 54 (January 1963): 1.

7. The point is made in, e.g., McCarthy, *Hour of Trial: The Conservation Conflict in Colorado and the West, 1891–1907*.

8. Folta to E. W. Nelson, 10 May 1921, "Game Acts," GC BBS, RG 22. Janson, *The Copper Spike*, p. 124. Chase also wrote *Alaska's Mammoth Brown Bears*. Riggs's comment is in his manuscript reply to a request for information from the National Resources Committee, with Riggs Papers, LC.

9. "Alaska's Problem as President Harding Saw It," *Literary Digest* 78 (18 August 1923): 17, 18.

10. John R. Bockstoce, *Steam Whaling in the Western Arctic*, pp. 42, 43.

Bibliography

Special Sources

Alaska Cooperative Wildlife Research Unit. *Publications Available*. University of Alaska, Fairbanks: A.C.W.R.U., October 22, 1973.

Alaska Game Commission Records:

1. Annual Report of the Alaska Game Commission to the Secretary of the Interior, 1940–59 (first to twentieth). Microfilm, Alaska State Library, Juneau.

2. Annual Report of the Executive Officer to the Alaska Game Commission, 1925–48 (1944 missing). Microfilm, Alaska State Library, Juneau.

3. Quarterly Report of the Executive Officer, Alaska Game Commission, to Director, Fish and Wildlife Service, 1 July 1936 to 30 September 1946 (July–September 1941 and October–December 1943 missing). Microfilm, Alaska State Library, Juneau.

4. Minutes of the Meetings of the Alaska Game Commission, 1925–39. Microfilm, Alaska State Library, Juneau.

Alaska, Governor of. General Correspondence, 1909–58. Microfilm no. M939, Federal Archives and Records Center, Seattle, Washington. Appropriate files on the following rolls were examined: 1, 2, 7, 11, 12, 19, 25, 26, 33, 34, 42, 48, 49, 61, 62, 72, 73, 82, 83, 93, 94, 101, 102, 111–113, 121, 134, 146, 156, 168, 180, 190, 277, 280.

Alaska Railroad Record, 1916–18. Alaska Railroad Headquarters, Anchorage; courtesy of Louise Brenner.

Bancroft Scraps, vol. 81: "Alaska Miscellaneous." Bancroft Library, University of California, Berkeley.

Baugh, Virgil E. Memo to E. G. Campbell, Assistant Archivist, "List of Archival Materials on Cook Inlet, Alaska." April 29, 1968, National Archives.

Cart, Theodore Whaley. "The Struggle for Wildlife Protection in the United States, 1870–1900: Attitudes and Events Leading to the Lacey Act." Ph.D. dissertation, University of North Carolina, Chapel Hill, 1971.

Dimond, Anthony J. Papers. Boxes 24, 25, 29, University of Alaska Archives, Fairbanks.

Gruening, Ernest. Excerpts (30 July 1941 to 6 April 1943) from his diaries. With Gruening Papers, University of Alaska Archives; excerpts selected by Renee Blahuta.

Hellenthal, Mr. and Mrs. John A. "Scrapbook." In the possession of Mr. and Mrs. John S. Hellenthal, Anchorage.

Hill, Edward E., comp. "Preliminary Inventory of the Records of the Fish and Wildlife Service, National Archives, Record Group 22." Washington, D.C.: National Archives, June 1965; mimeographed.

Hornaday, William T., to C. L. Andrews, 8 March 1904. With Andrews Collection, University of Oregon, Eugene; note courtesy of Ted C. Hinckley.

"Hunting and Fishing Miscellaneous." One folder, vertical file, University of Alaska Archives, Fairbanks.

Murie, Olaus J. Papers, 1920–1946. Box 4, University of Alaska Archives, Fairbanks.

Palmer, Lawrence J. Collection. Box 1, University of Alaska Archives, Fairbanks.

179

Pearson, Drew. "Washington Merry-Go-Round." *Sacramento Union*, 24 September 1942; microfilm, University of California, Davis, Library.

Reiger, John F. "George Bird Grinnell and the Development of American Conservation, 1870–1901." Ph.D. dissertation, Northwestern University, 1970.

Riggs, Thomas C., Jr. Papers. Library of Congress, Washington, D.C.

Romig, J. H. *The Wild Game Dinner or Pioneer Thanksgiving* (presumably published in Anchorage by the author, 1947). In the possession of John S. Hellenthal, Anchorage.

Sheldon, Charles. Papers, selected folders. Correspondence File, Boxes 1 and 2, University of Alaska Archives, Fairbanks.

Sutherland, Daniel A. Papers, 1908–1931, "Clipping File, 1908–1930." University of Alaska Archives, Fairbanks.

Troy, John W. Papers. Bancroft Library, University of California, Berkeley; consists almost entirely of filmed statements about Governor J. F. A. Strong's citizenship.

U.S. Attorney General, Office of the. Copies of materials in the appointment files of George W. Folta and Simon Hellenthal. Washington, D.C.

U.S. District Court, Third Judicial Division, Alaska. Simon Bolivar Buckner, Jr., Petitioner, v. Frank Dufresne as Executive Officer and Jack O'Connor as Licensing Officer of the Alaska Game Commission, at Anchorage, Alaska. Court Record, No. A–2671, District Court for the Territory of Alaska, Third Division, U.S.A.; in Federal Archives and Records Center, Seattle.

U.S. National Archives, "Materials in the National Archives Relating to Alaska." Washington, D.C.: National Archives, June 1942; mimeographed.

U.S. National Archives, Region 10, Seattle. "Preliminary Inventory and List of Records of the Office of the Governor of Alaska, 1884–1958." Seattle: 1959; mimeographed; a more complete inventory as computer printout now exists.

U.S. National Archives, Record Group 22. Fish and Wildlife Service Records, Washington, D.C.

1. Minutes of the Alaska Game Commission, 1945, 1947–49, 1951–53, with file entitled "Alaska–Commission."

2. General Correspondence, Bureau of Biological Survey, 1890–1944. Files, by title: Game Acts; Alaska Reports; Sheldon to Vreeland; Alaska General to Alaska Reports, O. Murie; Regulations to Alaska Game Law, 1922; Alaska Hunting to Alaska Game Laws; Prohibition Enforcement to Alaska Reports; Mammals to Mammals Distribution; Operations–Finance; Predatory.

3. Sports Fisheries and Wildlife. Files, by title: Alaska File, A–Z; Solicitor's Opinions, A–Z; Bears; Licenses; Admiralty–Bears; Alaska–Commission (see above, Minutes); Legislation; Alaska–Regulations; Station Reports.

4. Wildlife Refuges. Files by big game animal: Bear; Caribou; Dall Sheep; Moose; Mountain Goat.

5. Commercial Fisheries, File 86.

White, Sam O. "Early Alaska Bush Pilot Interviews," by Sandy Jensen, 2 December 1961. University of Alaska Archives, Fairbanks.

Printed Sources

Alaska Game Commission. *Laws and Regulations Relating to Game, Land, Fur-bearing Animals and Birds in Alaska, 1925–50*. Issued annually, with slightly varying titles, as Alaska Game Commission Circulars. Washington, D.C.

Alaska Geographic, Editors of. "Admiralty: Island in Contention." *Alaska Geographic* 1 (1973): 1–78.

————. "The Land—Eye of the Storm." *Alaska Geographic* 2 (1975): 1–64.

Alaska, Governor of. *Annual Report on the Alaska Game Law, to the Secretary of Agriculture, 1910–1912, 1917, 1919*. Printed as Bureau of Biological Survey Circular no. 7 (1910), no. 85 (1911), no. 90 (1912), or as Bureau of Biological Survey Document no. 105 (1917) and no. 110 (1919). Washington, D.C.

———. *Annual Report to the Secretary of Interior, 1909–1912, 1914–1917, 1919, 1920*. Washington, D.C.

Alaska Reports, Editors of. "Buckner v. Dufresne et al." *Alaska Reports* 10 (1946): 121–28.

Alaska, Territory of. *Journal of the Senate of the Territory of Alaska, 1923, 1935, 1949*. Juneau.

———. *Journal of the House of Representatives of the Territory of Alaska, Sixth Session, 1923, Twelfth Session, 1935, and Nineteenth Session, 1949*. Juneau.

Alaska Wildlife Digest 2 (Spring 1975): 1–24.

An Alaskan. "The Moose Butchers of Kenai." *American Forestry* 29 (December 1923): 719, 720, 750.

Anderson, Eva Greenslit. *Dog-team Doctor: The Story of Dr. Romig*. Originally published 1940. Caldwell, Idaho, 1947.

Andrews, C. L. *The Story of Alaska*. Originally published 1938. Caldwell, Idaho, 1947.

Annabel, Russell. *Hunting and Fishing in Alaska*. New York, 1948.

———. "Trouble in Alaska's Game Lands." *Saturday Evening Post* 221 (1 January 1949): 34, 35, 47, 48.

Arnold, Robert D., et al. *Alaska Native Land Claims*. Anchorage, 1976.

Atwood, Evangeline. *Anchorage: All-American City*. Portland, Oreg., 1957.

———. *We Shall Be Remembered*. Anchorage, 1966.

Atwood, Evangeline, and De Armond, Robert N. *Who's Who in Alaskan Politics: 1884–1974*. Portland, Oreg., 1977.

Badash, Lawrence. "The Completeness of Nineteenth Century Science." *Isis* 63 (March 1972): 48–58.

Bailey, Alfred A. *Field Work of a Museum Naturalist, 1919–1922*. Denver Museum of Natural History, Museum Pictorial no. 22. Denver, 1971.

Banfield, A. W. F. "Plight of the Barren Ground Caribou." *Oryx* 4 (April 1957): 5–20.

Beach, Rex. "The Chronicle of a Chromatic Bear Hunt." In his *Oh, Shoot! Confessions of an Agitated Sportsman*, pp. 39–104. New York, 1921.

Bockstoce, John R. *Steam Whaling in the Western Arctic*. New Bedford, Mass., 1977.

Bonebrake, A. C. "An Instance of Unprovoked Attack by a Brown Bear." *Journal of Mammalogy* 3 (August 1922): 185, 186.

Boone and Crockett Club. *North American Big Game*. New York, 1939.

Brickley, James, and Brickley, Catherine. "Reindeer, Cattle of the Arctic." *Alaska Journal* 5 (Winter 1975): 16–24.

Brodie, Bernard, and Brodie, Fawn. *From Crossbow to H-Bomb*. New York, 1962.

Brooks, Alfred H. *Mineral Resources of Alaska . . . 1921*. U.S. Geological Survey Bulletin no. 739. Washington, D.C., 1923.

Brooks, Paul. "The Plot to Drown Alaska." *Atlantic Monthly* 215 (May 1965): 53–59.

Brooks, Paul, and Foote, J. "The Disturbing Story of Project Chariot." *Harper's* 224 (April 1962): 60–62, 65–67.

Browne, Belmore. "In the Caribou Country." *Outing* 56 (June 1910): 259–69.

Buchheister, Carl W., and Graham, Frank. "From the Swamp and Back: A Concise and Candid History of the Audubon Movement." *Audubon* 75 (January 1973): 4–45.

Buckley, John L. "Animal Population Fluctuations in Alaska—A History." *Transactions of the North American Wildlife Conference, 1954*, pp. 338–57. Washington, D.C., 1954.

———. *Wildlife in the Economy of Alaska*. Biological Papers of the University of Alaska no. 1, revised. Fairbanks, 1957.

Burch, William R. *Daydreams and Nightmares: A Sociological Essay on the American Environment*. New York, 1971.

Burke, Janis, comp. *A Descriptive Bibliography of Historical Research Material in the Anchorage Area*. Anchorage, August 1973.

Burris, O. E., and McKnight, D. E. *Game Transplants in Alaska*. Alaska Department of Fish and Game Technical Bulletin no. 4. Juneau, December 1973.

Burt, William Henry. *A Field Guide to the Mammals*. 3d ed. Boston, 1976.

Burton, Wayne E. *Creating a Northern Agriculture: Historical Perspectives in Alaskan Agriculture*. University of Alaska Institute of Agricultural Sciences Bulletin no. 43. Fairbanks, July 1975.

Cameron, Jenks. *The Bureau of Biological Survey: Its History, Activities and Organization*. Baltimore, 1929.

Capps, Stephen R. "A Game Country without Rival in America: The Proposed Mount McKinley National Park." *National Geographic Magazine* 31 (January 1917): 69–84.

Carberry, Michael E. *Patterns of the Past: An Inventory of Anchorage's Heritage Resources*. Anchorage, 1979.

Cart, Theodore W. " 'New Deal' for Wildlife: A Perspective on Federal Conservation Policy, 1933–40." *Pacific Northwest Quarterly* 63 (July 1972): 113–29.

Chase, Will H. *Alaska's Mammoth Brown Bears*. Kansas City, 1947.

Chatelain, Edward F. "Bear–Moose Relationships on the Kenai Peninsula." *Transactions of the North American Wildlife Conference, 1950*, pp. 224–34. Washington, D.C., 1950.

Clark, Webster K. "Kodiak Bear–Red Salmon Relationships at Karluk Lake, Alaska." *Transactions of the North American Wildlife Conference, 1959*, pp. 337–45. Washington, D.C., 1959.

Coles, Harry L. "The Aleutian Campaign." In *The Army Air Forces in World War II*, vol. 1: *Plans and Early Operations, January 1939 to August 1942*, edited by W. F. Craven and J. L. Cate, pp. 359–401. Chicago, 1948.

Connery, Robert H. *Governmental Problems in Wildlife Conservation*. New York, 1935.

Cooley, Richard A. *Politics and Conservation: The Decline of the Alaska Salmon*. New York, 1963.

Corpus Juris Secundum. Vol. 38 (1943), "Game," pp. 1–29. Vol. 3A (1973), "Property in Wild Animals," pp. 477–80. Vol. 28 (1941), "Domicile," pp. 1–49. Brooklyn, N.Y.

Crosby, Alfred W., Jr. *The Columbian Exchange: Biological and Cultural Consequences of 1492*. Westport, Conn., 1972.

Crouch, Thomas W. "Frederick Funston in Alaska, 1892–1894: Botany above the Forty-ninth Parallel." *Journal of the West* 10 (April 1971): 273–306.

Dall, William Healey. "Travels on the Yukon and in the Yukon Territory in 1866." In *The Yukon Territory*, edited by F. M. Trimmer, pp. 1–242. London, 1898.

Dall, William Healey, and Baker, Marcus. "Partial List of Charts, Maps, and Publications Relating to Alaska and the Adjacent Region. . . ." In Dall's *Pacific Coast Pilot: Coasts and Islands of Alaska*, appendix 1: *Meteorology and Bibliography*, pp. 163–375. Washington, D.C., 1879.

Dannenbaum, Jed. "John Muir and Alaska." *Alaska Journal* 2 (Autumn 1972): 14–20.

Darling, F. Fraser. "Man's Responsibility for the Environment." In *Biology and Ethics*, edited by F. G. Ebling, pp. 117–22. London, 1969.

Davis, Perry H. "Alaska Conservation—G.I. Style." *Alaska* 27 (July 1961): 14–17, 41–43.

Davis, Phyllis, comp. *A Guide to Alaska's Newspapers*. Juneau, 1976.

Day, Albert M. "Wartime Uses of Wildlife Products." *Transactions of the North American Wildlife Conference, 1943*, pp. 45–54. Washington, D.C., 1943.

De Armond, Robert N. "A Northern Notebook." *Alaska Daily Empire*, Juneau, 10 May 1951.

de Laguna, Frederica. *Under Mount St. Elias: The History and Culture of the Yakutat Tlingit*, pt. 1. Smithsonian Institution Contributions to Anthropology vol. 7. Washington, D.C., 1972.

De Weese, Dall. "A Red Letter Day with Alaska Big Game." *Field and Stream* 2 (February 1898): 253–56.

Dobyns, Henry F. "An Appraisal of Techniques with a New Hemisphere Estimate." *Current Anthropology* 7 (October 1966): 395–416, 425–45.

Doughty, Robin W. *Feather Fashions and Bird Preservation*. Berkeley and Los Angeles, 1975.

Driscoll, Joseph. *War Discovers Alaska*. Philadelphia, 1943.

Driver, Harold. *Indians of North America*. Chicago, 1969.

Drucker, Philip. *Indians of the Northwest Coast*. Garden City, N.Y., 1963.

Dubos, René. *Beast or Angel?* New York, 1974.

Dufresne, Frank. *Alaska's Animals and Fishes*. New York, 1946.

———. "The Game and Fur Belong to All the People." *Alaska* 10 (April 1944): 16–18, 21.

———. *Mammals and Birds of Alaska*. U.S. Fish and Wildlife Circular no. 3. Washington, D.C., 1942.

———. *My Way Was North*. New York, 1966.

———. *No Room for Bears*. New York, 1965.

———. "North America's Grouchiest Beast." *Alaska* 29 (December 1963): 24, 25, 45.

———. "What of Tomorrow." *Alaska* 3 (April 1937): 9.

Dufresne, Klondy Nelson, with Ford, Corey. *Daughter of the Gold Rush*. New York, 1955.

Elkins, W. A. "Pressing Problems in Administration of Wildlife Resources in Alaska." In *Science in Alaska, 1950*, edited by H. B. Collins, pp. 268–81. Washington, D.C., 1952.

Elwell, Niska. "Wrong Target." *Alaska* 15 (October 1949): 14, 15, 23–26.

Emmons, G. T. "Report on the Condition and Needs of Natives of Alaska." U.S. Congress, Senate, *Senate Document 106* (January 1905), 58th Cong., 3d sess. (serial 4765).

Erickson, Albert W. *The Black Bear in Alaska*. Juneau, 1965.

Fawcett, Charles W. "Comments: Vanishing Wildlife and Federal Protective Efforts." *Ecology Law Review* 1 (Summer 1971): 520–60.

Federal Field Committee for Development Planning in Alaska. *Economic Development in Alaska: A Report to the President*. Washington, D.C., August 1966.

Fedorova, S. G. *The Russian Population in Alaska and California, Late 18th Century–1867*. Translated and edited by R. A. Pierce and A. A. Donnelly. Originally published in Moscow, 1971. Kingston, Ontario, 1973.

Fertig, Fred. "Child of Nature, the American Indian as an Ecologist." *Sierra Club Bulletin* 55 (August 1970): 4–7.

Fitch, Edwin M. *The Alaska Railroad*. New York, 1967.

Flader, Susan. *Thinking Like a Mountain: Aldo Leopold and the Evolution of an Ecological Attitude toward Deer, Wolves and Forests*. Columbia, Mo., 1974.

Forest and Stream, Editors of. "The Great Duck Egg Fake." *Forest and Stream* 44 (22 June 1895): 503–04.

Gabrielson, Ira N. "Alaskan Waterfowl and Their Management." In *Science in Alaska, 1950*, edited by H. B. Collins, pp. 292–305. Washington, D.C., 1952.

———. *Wildlife Conservation*. New York, 1941.

Gabrielson, Ira N., and Lincoln, F. C. *The Birds of Alaska*. Harrisburg, Pa., 1959.

George, Arthur T. "Alaska Ponders: How Long Do We Wait." *Construction Craftsman* 5 (March 1966): 10–12.

Georgeson, C. C. *Information for Prospective Settlers in Alaska*. Alaska Agricultural Experiment Stations Circular no. 1, revised. Washington, D.C., 1917.

Gibson, James R. *Imperial Russia in Frontier America: The Changing Geography of Supply of Russian America, 1784–1867*. New York, 1976.

———. "Old Russia in the New World." In *European Settlement and Development in North America*, edited by James R. Gibson, pp. 46–65. Toronto, 1978.

Gillham, C. E. "Andy Simons, Alaska's Number 1 Guide." *Alaska* 30 (April 1964): 14, 15, 42–44.

Glass, Mary Ellen. "The Newlands Reclamation Project: Years of Innocence, 1903–1907." *Journal of the West* 7 (January 1978): 55–63.

Goldman, E. A. "The Coyote—Archpredator." *Journal of Mammalogy* 11 (August 1930): 325–35.

Graham, A. D. *The Gardeners of Eden*. London, 1973.

Grant, Madison. "The Caribou." *Seventh Annual Report of the New York Zoological Society* (1902): 174–96.

———. *The Passing of the Great Race*. New York, 1916.

———. "Condition of Wildlife in Alaska." In *Hunting at High Altitudes*, edited by G. B. Grinnell, pp. 367–92. New York, 1913.

Gray, Chuck. "The Truth about the Moose / Wolf Controversy." *Alaska Pipeline Worker's Handbook* 1 (Summer 1975): 155–58.

Greiner, James. "Tomorrow Came Too Soon." *Alaska* 42 (May 1976): 4–8.

Gressley, Gene M. "Colonialism: A Western Complaint." *Pacific Northwest Quarterly* 54 (January 1963): 1–8.

Griggs, Robert F. "The Valley of Ten Thousand Smokes." *National Geographic Magazine* 31 (January 1917): 12–68.

Grinnell, George Bird. "The 'Unprovoked' Attack by a Bear." *Journal of Mammalogy* 4 (February 1923): 52, 53.

Gruening, Ernest. *Many Battles*. New York, 1973.

———. *The State of Alaska*. New York, 1954.

Guthrie, Daniel A. "Primitive Man's Relationship to Nature." *BioScience* 21 (July 1971): 721–25.

Guthrie, R. D. "The Ethical Relationship between Humans and Other Organisms." *Perspectives in Biology and Medicine* 11 (Autumn 1967): 52–62.

Hadwen, Seymour, and Palmer, L. J. *Reindeer in Alaska*. U.S. Department of Agriculture Bulletin no. 1089. Washington, D.C., September 1922.

Hallock, Charles. *Our New Alaska*. New York, 1886. Reprint. New York, 1970.

———. *Peerless Alaska, Our Cache near the Pole*. New York, 1908.

Hamilton, W. J., Jr. "Mammalogy in North America." In California Academy of Sciences, *A Century of Progress in the Natural Sciences, 1853–1953*, pp. 661–88. San Francisco, 1955.

Hammond, Jay. "Tarnished Trophies." *Alaska* 35 (July 1969): 14–16, 50.

Harmon, Lewis D. "The Plight of the Bison." *Alaska* 27 (November 1961): 19–21, 42–43.

Hays, Samuel P. *Conservation and the Gospel of Efficiency*. Originally published 1959. New York, 1969.

Heizer, Robert F. "Primitive Man as an Ecologic Factor." *Kroeber Anthropological Society Papers* 13 (Fall 1955): 1–31.

Hellenthal, J. A. *The Alaskan Melodrama*. New York, 1936.

———. "Why Not Go Modern on Conservation?" *Alaska Life* 4 (January 1941): 3, 13, 18, 19, 27, 28, 30.

Henderson, Junius, and Craig, E. L. *Economic Mammalogy*. Baltimore, 1932.

Hickel, Walter J. *Who Owns America?* Englewood Cliffs, N.J., 1971.

Hilscher, Herbert H. "Is Ickes Back of This Too?" *Alaska Life* 4 (December 1941): 3, 26–28.

Hinckley, Ted C. "Alaska and the Emergence of America's Conservation Consciousness." *The Prairie Scout* 2 (1974): 79–111.

———. *The Americanization of Alaska, 1867–1897*. Palo Alto, 1972.

———. " 'The Canoe Rocks—We Do Not Know What Will Become of Us.' " *Western Historical Quarterly* 1 (July 1970): 265–90.

———. "The Inside Passage: Popular Gilded Age Tour." *Pacific Northwest Quarterly* 56 (April 1965): 67–74.

Hinckley, Ted C., and Hinckley, C., eds. "Ivan Petroff's Journal of a Trip to Alaska in 1878." *Journal of the West* 5 (January 1966): 1–46.

Holzworth, John Michael. *The Wild Grizzlies of Alaska*. New York, 1930.

Hornaday, William T. *Our Vanishing Wild Life*. New York, 1913.

Hutchinson, W. H. "The Remaking of the Amerind." *Westways* 64 (October 1972): 18–21, 94.

Ickes, Harold L. *The Secret Diary of Harold L. Ickes*, vol. 3: *The Lowering Clouds, 1939–1941*. New York 1954.

Imler, Ralph H., and Kalmbach, E. R. *The Bald Eagle and Its Economic Status*. U.S. Fish and Wildlife Circular no. 30. Washington, D.C., 1955.

Ingersoll, Ernest, ed. *Alaskan Bird-Life as Depicted by Many Writers*. New York, 1914.

Jacobs, Wilbur R. "Frontiersmen, Fur Traders, and Other Varmints: An Ecological Appraisal of the Frontier in American History." *A.H.A. Newsletter* 8 (November 1970): 5–11.

———. "The Great Despoliation." *Pacific Historical Review* 47 (February 1978): 1–26.

———. "The Indian and the Frontier in American History—A Need for Revision." *Western Historical Quarterly* 4 (January 1973): 43–56.

Janson, Lone E. *The Copper Spike*. Anchorage, 1975.

Jochelson, Waldemar. *History, Ethnology and Anthropology of the Aleut*. Washington, D.C., 1933. Reprint. Oosterhout, N.B., Netherlands, 1966.

Johnson, Hugh A., and Jorgenson, Harold T. *The Land Resources of Alaska*. New York, 1963.

Johnson, N. B. "The American Indian as Conservationist." *Chronicles of Oklahoma* 30 (Autumn 1952): 333–40.

Jones, M. A. *American Immigration*. Chicago, 1960.

Keim, Charles J. "Conservation Comes North." *Alaska* 23 (November 1957): 14, 15, 42–45.

Kellogg, Remington. "A Century of Progress in Smithsonian Biology." *Science* 104 (9 August 1946): 132–41.

Kennedy, Kay. "Twelve Brown Bear Men." *Alaska* 6 (February 1940): 16–18, 20–21.

Kidder, James H. "Hunting Sheep in Western Alaska." *Outing* 43 (October 1903): 50–54.

Kirby, Chester. "The Attack on the English Game Laws in the Forties." *Journal of Modern History* 4 (March 1932): 18–37.

———. "The English Game Law System." *American Historical Review* 38 (January 1933): 240–62.

Klein, David R. "The Ethics of Hunting and the Antihunting Movement." *Transactions of the North American Wildlife and Natural Resource Conference, 1973*, pp. 256–67. Washington, D.C., 1973.

———. "Problems in Conservation of Mammals in the North." *Biological Conservation* 4 (January 1972): 97–101.

———. "Waterfowl in the Economy of the Eskimos of the Yukon-Kuskokwim Delta, Alaska." *Arctic* 19 (December 1966): 319–36.

Klein, David R., Troyer, W., and Rausch, R. A. "The Status of the Brown Bear in Alaska." *Proceedings of the Ninth Alaskan Science Conference, 1958*, pp. 21–24. College, Alaska, 1958.

Knight, Rolf. "A Re-examination of Hunting, Trapping, and Territoriality among the Northeastern Algonkian Indians." In *Man, Culture, and Animals: The Role of Animals in Human Ecological Adjustments*, edited by A. Leeds and A. P. Vayda, pp. 27–42. Washington, D.C., 1965.

Koch, A., and Peden, W., eds. *The Life and Selected Writings of Thomas Jefferson*. New York, 1944.

Krause, Aurel. *The Tlingit Indians*. Translated by Erna Gunther. Originally published 1885. Seattle, 1956.

Krutch, Joseph Wood. "The Sportsman or the Predator? A Damnable Pleasure." *Saturday Review*, 17 August 1957, pp. 8, 9, 39, 40.

Lachenmeier, Rudy R. "The Endangered Species Act of 1973: Preservation or Pandemonium?" *Environmental Law* 5 (Fall 1974): 29–83.

Lantis, Margaret. "Edward William Nelson." *Anthropological Papers of the University of Alaska* 3 (December 1954): 4–16.

———. "The Reindeer Industry in Alaska." *Arctic* 3 (April 1950): 27–44.

Lawrence, W. H. "Buckner, Okinawa Commander Killed. . . ." *New York Times*, 19 June 1945.

Lee, R. B., and De Vore, I., eds. *Man the Hunter*. Chicago, 1968.

Lent, Peter C. "Muskox Management Controversies in North America." *Biological Conservation* 3 (July 1971): 255–63.

Leopold, Aldo. *Game Management*. Originally published 1933. New York, 1947.

———. *A Sand County Almanac*. Originally published 1949. New York, 1966.

Leopold, A. Starker, and Darling, F. Fraser. "Effects of Land Use on Moose and Caribou in Alaska." *Transactions of the North American Wildlife Conference, 1953*, pp. 553–62. Washington, D.C., 1953.

———. *Wildlife in Alaska: An Ecological Reconnaissance*. New York, 1953.

Literary Digest, Editors of. "Alaska's Problem as President Harding Saw It." *Literary Digest* 78 (18 August 1923): 17, 18.

Lomen, Carl J. *Fifty Years in Alaska*. New York, 1954.

Long, John Sherman, with McCord, Grace Doering. *McCord of Alaska: Statesman for the Last Frontier*. Cleveland, 1975.

Lorenz, Konrad Z. *On Aggression*. New York, 1968.

Loring, J. Alden. "Notes on the Destruction of Animal Life in Alaska." *Annual Report of the New York Zoological Society, 1901* (1902): 141–44.

———. "The Quest for Ovis Dalli." *Outdoor Life* 14 (September 1904): 549–58.

Lucas, Robert C. "The Contribution of Environmental Research to Wilderness Policy Decisions." *Journal of Social Issues* 22 (October 1966): 116–28.

Luick, Jack R. "The Cantwell Reindeer Industry, 1921–1928." *Alaska Journal* 3 (Spring 1973): 107–13.

Lund, Thomas A. *American Wildlife Law*. Berkeley and Los Angeles, 1980.

Lutz, H. J. *Aboriginal Man and White Man as Historical Causes of Fires in the Boreal Forest, with Particular Reference to Alaska*. Yale University School of Forestry Bulletin no. 65. New Haven, 1959.

McCarthy, G. Michael. *Hour of Trial: The Conservation Conflict in Colorado and the West, 1891–1907*. Norman, Okla., 1977.

McConnell, Grant. "The Conservation Movement—Past and Present." *Western Political Quarterly* 7 (September 1954): 463–78.

McGuire, Harry. "The Last Stand of the Bear." *Outdoor Life*; reprinted in John Michael Holzworth, *The Wild Grizzlies of Alaska*, pp. 340–54. New York, 1930.

McNeill, William H. *Plagues and People*. Garden City, N.Y., 1976.

Manville, Richard W., and Young, S. P. *Distribution of Alaskan Mammals*. Bureau of Sport Fisheries and Wildlife Circular no. 211. Washington, D.C., 1965.

Mârgôlef, Ramón. *Perspectives in Ecological Theory*. Chicago, 1968.

Marshall, Robert. *Alaska Wilderness: Exploring the Central Brooks Range*. Berkeley and Los Angeles, 1956.

Martin, Calvin. *Keepers of the Game*. Berkeley and Los Angeles, 1978.

Martin, G. C., et al. *Mineral Resources of Alaska, 1918*. U.S. Geological Survey Bulletin no. 712. Washington, D.C., 1920.

Martin, P. S., and Wright, H. E., eds. *Pleistocene Extinctions, the Search for a Cause*. New Haven, 1967.

Matloff, Maurice. *The War Department. Strategic Planning for Coalition Warfare, 1943–1944*. U.S. Army in World War II, vol. 4, pt. 3:2. Washington, D.C., 1959.

Mayr, Ernst. *Animal Species and Evolution*. Cambridge, Mass., 1963.

———. "Evolution." *Scientific American* 239 (September 1978): 47–55.

———. "Illiges and the Biological Species Concept." *Journal of the History of Biology* 1 (Fall 1968): 163–78.

———. "Species Concepts and Definitions." In *The Species Problem*, edited by Ernst Mayr, pp. 1–22. Washington, D.C., 1957.

Merriam, C. Hart. "Bears—Description and Distribution." In Boone and Crockett Club, *North American Big Game*, pp. 371–78. New York, 1939.

———. "Criteria for the Recognition of Species and Genera." *Journal of Mammalogy* 1 (November 1919): 6–9.

———. *Review of the Grizzly and Big Brown Bears of North America*. U.S. Department of Agriculture, Bureau of Biological Survey North American Fauna no. 41. Washington, D.C., 1918.

Merton, Robert K. "Priorities in Scientific Discovery." *American Sociological Review* 22 (December 1957): 635–59.

Miller, Orlando W. *The Frontier in Alaska and the Matanuska Colony*. New Haven, 1975.

Morgan, Lael. "Caribou Kills—An Eskimo Report." *Alaska* 42 (May 1976): 8, 77, 78.

Morison, Samuel Eliot. *Aleutians, Gilberts and Marshalls, June 1942–April 1944*. History of United States Naval Operations in World War II, vol. 7. Boston, 1951.

Moser, Jefferson F. *The Salmon and Salmon Fisheries of Alaska*, pp. 1–178. Bulletin of the United States Fish Commission, vol. 18, 1898. Washington, D.C., 1899.

Muir, John. *The Cruise of the Corwin*. Boston, 1917.

———. "Letters from Alaska." *San Francisco Daily Bulletin*, 6, 23, 27 September; 29, 30 October; 8, 12 November; all 1879.

———. *Travels in Alaska*. Boston, 1913.

Murie, Adolph. *A Naturalist in Alaska*. New York, 1961.

———. *The Wolves of Mount McKinley*. U.S. National Park Service Fauna Series no. 5. Washington, D.C., 1944.

Murie, Margaret E. *Two in the Far North*. New York, 1957.

Murie, Olaus J. *Alaska-Yukon Caribou*. U.S. Department of Agriculture Bureau of Biological Survey, North American Fauna no. 54. Washington, D.C., 1935.

———. *Journeys to the Far North*. Palo Alto, 1973.

———. "Planning for Alaska's Big Game." In *Science in Alaska, 1950*, edited by H. B. Collins, pp. 258–67. Washington, D.C., 1952.

Nash, Roderick. "American Environmental History: A New Teaching Frontier." *Pacific Historical Review* 41 (August 1972): 362–72.

———. *Wilderness and the American Mind*. New Haven, 1967.

National Research Council, Committee on Agricultural Land Use and Wildlife Resources. *Land Use and Wildlife Resources*. Washington, D.C., 1970.

Nelson, Edward W. "The Emperor Goose." In *Alaskan Bird-Life as Depicted by Many Writers*, edited by Ernest Ingersoll, pp. 57–61. New York, 1914.

———. *Report upon Natural History Collections Made in Alaska between the Years 1877 and 1881*. Washington, D.C., 1887.

———. *Wild Animals of North America*. Washington, D.C., 1918.

Netboy, Anthony. "The Indian and the Forest." *American Forests* 60 (October 1954): 24, 25, 63.

Nichols, Jeannette Paddock. *Alaska . . . Its First Half Century under the Rule of the United States*. 1924. Reprint, New York, 1963.

North, Douglass C. "International Capital Flows and the Development of the American West." *Journal of Economic History* 16 (December 1954): 493–505.

Novak, Michael. "The Economics of Native Subsistence Activities in a Village of Southwestern Alaska." *Arctic* 30 (December 1977): 225–33.

Ortega y Gasset, José. *Meditations on Hunting*. Written in 1942. New York, 1972.

Orth, Donald J. *Dictionary of Alaska Place Names*. U.S. Geological Survey Professional Paper no. 567. Washington, D.C., 1967.

Osgood, Cornelius. *Ethnography of the Tanaina*. New Haven, 1937.

Osgood, Wilfred H. *Biological Investigations in Alaska and Yukon Territory*. U.S. Department of Agriculture, Bureau of Biological Survey North American Fauna no. 30. Washington, D.C., 1909.

———. *A Biological Reconnaissance of the Base of the Alaska Peninsula*. U.S. Department of Agriculture, Division of Biological Survey North American Fauna no. 24. Washington, D.C., 1904.

———. "Clinton Hart Merriam, 1855–1942." *Journal of Mammalogy* 24 (17 November 1943): 421–36.

———. "The Game Resources of Alaska." *U.S. Department of Agriculture Yearbook, 1907*, pp. 469–82. Washington, D.C., 1908.

———. *Natural History of the Queen Charlotte Islands, British Columbia; Natural History of the Cook Inlet Region, Alaska*. U.S. Department of Agriculture, Division of Biological Survey North American Fauna no. 21. Washington, D.C., 1901.

Osgood, Wilfred H., and Bishop, Louis B. *Results of a Biological Reconnaissance of the Yukon River Region*. U.S. Department of Agriculture, Division of Biological Survey North American Fauna no. 19, Washington, D.C., 1900.

Oswalt, Wendell H. *Alaskan Eskimos*. San Francisco, 1967.

Owings, Loren C. *Environmental Values, 1860–1972*. Detroit, 1976.

Palmer, Lawrence J. "Food Requirements of Some Alaskan Game Mammals." *Journal of Mammalogy* 25 (15 February 1944): 49–54.

———. *Progress of Reindeer Grazing Investigations in Alaska*. U.S. Department of Agriculture Bulletin no. 1423. Washington, D.C., October 1926.

Palmer, Theodore S. *Chronology and Index of the More Important Events in American Game Protection, 1776–1911*. U.S. Department of Agriculture, Bureau of Biological Survey Bulletin no. 41. Washington, D.C., 1912.

———. "Extermination of Noxious Animals by Bounties." *Yearbook of the Department of Agriculture for 1896*, pp. 55–68. Washington, D.C., 1897.

———. *Hunting Licenses: Their History, Objects, and Limitations*. U.S. Department of Agriculture, Bureau of Biological Survey Bulletin no. 19. Washington, D.C., 1904.

———. *Legislation for the Protection of Birds Other than Game Birds*. U.S. Department of Agriculture, Division of Biological Survey Bulletin no. 12. Washington, D.C., 1900.

———. "A Review of Economic Ornithology in the United States." *Yearbook of the United States Department of Agriculture, 1899*, pp. 259–92. Washington, D.C., 1900.

Patty, Stanton, ed. "A Conference with the Tanana Chiefs." *Alaska Journal* 1 (Spring 1971): 2–18.

Pegues, John F. "Alaska's Brownies." *Field and Stream* 35 (December 1930): 36, 37, 62.

Penick, James L. *Progressive Politics and Conservation: The Ballinger–Pinchot Affair*. Chicago, 1968.

Petroff, Ivan (Polaris). "Gold Seeking in the Regions of Perpetual Snow." *San Francisco Sunday Chronicle*, 26 December 1875.

———. "Population, Resources, etc., of Alaska [Tenth Census, 1880]." In *Compilation of Narratives of Explorations of Alaska*, pp. 55–285. Washington, D.C., 1900.

Phillips, John C., and Boone and Crockett Club. *American Game Mammals and Birds: A Catalogue of Books, 1582–1925, Including Sport, Natural History, and Conservation*. New York, 1930.

Piper, C. V. *Grasslands of the South Alaska Coast*. U.S. Department of Agriculture, Bureau of Plant Industry Bulletin no. 82.

Potter, Jean. *Alaska under Arms*. New York, 1942.

Pough, Richard H. *Audubon Western Bird Guide*. Garden City, N.Y., 1957.

Pryor, Larry. "Alaska Could Well Become the Nation's Survival Kit." *This World* of the *San Francisco Sunday Examiner and Chronicle*, 28 December 1975.

Rausch, Robert. "Geographic Variation in Size in North American Brown Bears, Ursus Arctos L., as Indicated by Condylobasal Length." *Canadian Journal of Zoology* 41 (January 1963): 33–45.

———. "On the Status of Some Arctic Mammals." *Arctic* 6 (July 1953): 91–148.

Ray, Dorothy Jean. *The Eskimos of Bering Strait, 1650–1898*. Seattle, 1975.

Rearden, Jim. "Aerial Polar Bear Hunt, Part 2." *Alaska* 37 (August 1971): 14–16.

———. "Clarence Rhode." *Alaska* 46 (January 1980): 11–14, 50–54.

———. "The Kodiak Bear War." *Outdoor Life* (August 1964): 17–19, 70–74.

———. "State of Alaska's Guides." *Alaska* 34 (November 1968): 6–10, 52, 53.

———. "Subsistence: A Troublesome Issue." *Alaska* 44 (July 1978): 4–6, 84–88.

———. "Ways of the Caribou." *Alaska* 42 (May 1976): 6, 7.

Regenstein, Lewis. *The Politics of Extinction*. New York, 1975.

Reiger, John F. *American Sportsmen and the Origins of Conservation*. New York, 1975.

Rensberger, Boyce. *The Cult of the Wild*. Garden City, N.Y., 1977.

Rhode, Clarence J., and Barker, Will. *Alaska's Fish and Wildlife*. U.S. Department of Interior, Fish and Wildlife Circular no. 17. Washington, D.C., 1953.

Rich, P. E., and Tussing, A. R. *The National Park System in Alaska: An Economic Impact Study*. College, Alaska, 1973.

Riley, Francis. *Fur Seal Industry of the Pribilof Islands*. U.S. Department of Interior, Fish and Wildlife Service Circular no. 275. Washington, D.C., October 1967.

Rogers, George W., and Cooley, Richard A. *Alaska's Population and Economy*. 2 vols. N.p. but probably Juneau, March 1962.

Rohfleisch, Kramer J. "Drawing the Battle Line in the Pacific." *The Army Air Forces in World War II*, vol. 1: *Plans and Early Operations, January 1939 to August 1942*, pp. 427–70. Edited by W. F. Craven and J. L. Cate. Chicago, 1948.

Sage, S. I. "The View from Kivalina." *Alaska* 42 (May 1976): 78.

Sauer, Carl O. "Theme of Plant and Animal Destruction in Economic History." In *Land and Life*, edited by Carl O. Sauer, pp. 145–54. Berkeley and Los Angeles, 1965; originally published in 1938.

Schiff, Ashley L. *Fire and Water: Scientific Heresy in the Forest Service*. Cambridge, Mass., 1962.

Schmitt, Peter J. *Back to Nature: The Arcadian Myth in Urban America*. New York, 1969.

Scott, Robert F. "Wildlife in the Economy of Alaskan Natives." *Transactions of the North American Wildlife Conference, 1951*, pp. 508–23. Washington, D.C., 1951.

Scott, Robert F., Chatelain, Edward F., and Elkins, W. A. "The Status of the Dall Sheep and Caribou in Alaska." *Transactions of the North American Wildlife Conference, 1950*, pp. 612–26. Washington, D.C., 1950.

Scott, Robert F., Kenyon, Karl W., Buckley, John L., and Olson, Sigurd T. "Status and Management of the Polar Bear and Pacific Walrus." *Transactions of the North American Wildlife Conference, 1959*, pp. 366–74. Washington, D.C., 1959.

Seton-Karr, H. W. *Shores and Alps of Alaska*. London, 1887.

Shalkop, Robert L. *Eustace Ziegler, A Retrospective Exhibition*. Anchorage, 1977.

———. *Sidney Laurence (1865–1940), An Alaskan Impressionist*. Anchorage, 1975.

Sheldon, Charles. "The 'Unprovoked' Attack by a 'Brown' Bear." *Journal of Mammalogy* 4 (February 1923): 51, 52.

———. *The Wilderness of Denali*. New York, 1930.

Sherwood, Morgan, ed. *The Cook Inlet Collection*. Anchorage, 1974.

———. *Exploration of Alaska, 1865–1900*. New Haven, 1965.

———. "The Great Duck Egg Fake." *Alaska Journal* 7 (Spring 1977): 88–94.

———. "Specious Speciation in the Political History of the Alaskan Brown Bear." *Western Historical Quarterly* 10 (January 1979): 49–60.

———. "Science in Russian America, 1741–1865." *Pacific Northwest Quarterly* 58 (January 1967): 33–39.

Simons, Andy. "Hunting the Alaska Brown Bear." In Boone and Crockett Club, *North American Big Game*, pp. 378–84. New York, 1939.

Simpson, George Gaylord. *Principles of Classification and a Classification of Mammals*. American Museum of Natural History Bulletin no. 85. New York, 1945.

Slotnick, Herman. "The Ballinger–Pinchot Affair in Alaska." *Journal of the West* 10 (April 1971): 337–47.

Smith, Harold E. "Jack Thayer Was Killed by a Bear." *Alaska* 37 (August 1971): 23, 62, 63.

Smith, Philip S. *Mineral Industry in Alaska in 1939.* U.S. Geological Survey Bulletin no. 926-A. Washington, D.C., 1941.

Sorensen, Conner. "Federal Reclamation on the High Plains: The Garden City Project." *Great Plains Journal* 15 (Spring 1976): 114–33.

Spencer, David L., and Chatelain, Edward F. "Progress in the Management of the Moose of South Central Alaska." *Transactions of the North American Wildlife Conference, 1953*, pp. 539–52. Washington, D.C., 1953.

Spencer, Robert F. *The North Alaskan Eskimo: A Study in Ecology and Society.* Smithsonian Institution Bureau of Ethnology Bulletin no. 171. Washington, D.C., 1959.

Stein, Robert. "The Gold Fields of Alaska." *Review of Reviews* 13 (June 1896): 697–99.

Stejneger, Leonhard. *Georg Wilhelm Steller: The Pioneer of Alaskan Natural History.* Cambridge, Mass., 1936.

Sterling, Keir B. *Last of the Naturalists: The Career of C. Hart Merriam.* New York, 1974.

Stone, Andrew J. "Explorer–Naturalist in the Arctic." *Scribner's Magazine* 33 (April 1903): 438–49.

———. "Some Results of a Natural History Journey to Northern British Columbia, Alaska, and the Northwest Territory. . . ." *Bulletin of the American Museum of Natural History* 13 (1900): 31–62.

Stone, Kirk H. "Populating Alaska: The United States Phase." *Geographical Review* 42 (July 1952): 384–404.

Strong, Douglas Hillman. "The Indian and the Environment." *Journal of Environmental Education* 5 (Winter 1973): 49–51.

Sturgis, Kent. "Native Land Claims Act: What Will It Mean to All Alaskans?" *Anchorage Daily News*, 22 December 1971.

Swain, Donald C. *Federal Conservation Policy, 1921–1933.* Berkeley and Los Angeles, 1963.

Taylor, Ted M. "Vanished Monarch of the Sierra." *The American West* 13 (May/June 1976): 36–38, 59.

Thomas, W. C., Marsh, C. F., and Stephens, C. A. *Economic Analysis of Red Meat, Fish, Poultry and Wild Game Consumption Patterns in Anchorage, Alaska.* University of Alaska Institute of Agricultural Sciences Research Report no. 73–4. Fairbanks, March 1973.

Tiger, Lionel, and Fox, Robin. *The Imperial Animal.* New York, 1972.

Time, Editors of. "Buck's Battle." *Time* 45 (16 April 1945): 32, 35, 36.

Tourville, Elsie A., comp. *Alaska, A Bibliography, 1570–1970, with Subject Index.* Boston, 1974.

Trefethen, James B. *An American Crusade for Wildlife.* New York, 1975.

———. *Crusade for Wildlife.* Harrisburg, Pa., and New York, 1961.

Tuan, Yi-Fu. "Our Treatment of the Environment in Ideal and Actuality." *American Scientist* 58 (May–June 1970): 244–49.

Turner, Frederick Jackson. *The Character and Influence of the Indian Trade in Wisconsin.* Edited by D. H. Miller and W. W. Savage. Originally published 1891. Norman, Okla., 1977.

———. "The Significance of the Frontier in American History." In Turner, *The Frontier in American History*, pp. 1–38. Originally presented in 1893. New York, 1950.

Udall, Stewart L. *The Quiet Crisis.* New York, 1963.

Ullrich, Wolfgang. *Endangered Species.* New York, 1972.

U.S. Army, Alaska. *Building Alaska with the U.S. Army.* Headquarters U.S. Army Alaska, Pamphlet 355–5. Anchorage, 10 August 1962.

U.S., Bureau of Biological Survey. *Annual Report of the Chief of the Bureau of Biological Survey to the Secretary of Agriculture*. Washington, D.C., 1908, 1909, 1911–1922, 1924, 1926–1940.

————. *National Bird and Mammal Reservations in Alaska in Charge of the U.S. Department of Agriculture*. U.S. Department of Agriculture Bureau of Biological Survey Circular no. 71. Washington, D.C., 11 April 1910.

————. *Service and Regulatory Announcements*. Washington, D.C., 1914–38.

U.S. Bureau of the Census. *Thirteenth Census of the United States, 1910*, vol. 4: *Population . . . Occupational Statistics*. Washington, D.C., 1914.

————. *Fourteenth Census of the United States, 1920*, vols. 3 and 4. Washington, D.C., 1923.

————. *Fifteenth Census of the United States: 1930—Outlying Territories and Possessions*. Washington, D.C., 1932.

————. *U.S. Census of Population: 1950*, vol. 2: *Characteristics of the Population*, pts. 51–54: *Territories and Possessions*. Washington, D.C., 1953.

U.S. Census Office. *Report on Population and Resources of Alaska at the Eleventh Census: 1890*. Washington, D.C., 1893.

U.S. Congress, House. "Game Law in Alaska." *House Report 951* (14 March 1902), 57th Cong., 1st sess. (serial 4402).

————. "Protection of Game in Alaska, etc." *House Report 7106* (1 February 1907), 59th Cong., 2d sess. (serial 5064).

————. "Protection of Game in Alaska." *House Report 2010* (28 January 1911), 61st Cong., 3d sess. (serial 5847).

————. "Protection of Fur Bearing Animals in Alaska." *Hearings*, Subcommittee on Alaskan Fur-Bearing Animals, of the Committee of Ways and Means, 63d Cong., 3d sess. (1915), U.S. Senate Library vol. 124, no. 4.

————. "To Regulate the Killing and Sale of Certain Game Animals in Northern Alaska." *Hearings*, pt. 1, Committee on Territories, 65th Cong., 2d sess. (1918), U.S. Senate Library vol. 215, no. 4.

————. "To Establish Alaska Game Commission. . . ." *Hearings*, Committee on Agriculture, 68th Cong., 1st sess. (1924), U.S. Senate Library vol. 336, no. 17.

————. "To Provide that Powers . . . Governor of Alaska under . . . Law for Protection of Wild Game Animals and Birds in Alaska Be Transferred to . . . Secretary of Agriculture." *House Report 989* (5 June 1924), 68th Cong., 1st sess. (serial 8229).

————. "To Establish Alaska Game Commission. . . ." *House Report 993* (5 June 1924), 68th Cong., 1st sess. (serial 8229).

U.S. Congress, Senate. "Destruction of Eggs of Gamefowl. . . ." *Senate Report 923* (12 February 1895), 53d Cong., 3d sess. (serial 3289).

U.S. Department of Interior. *Annual Report of the Secretary of Interior*. Washington, D.C., by fiscal year.

U.S. Fish and Wildlife Service. *Annual Report of the Director . . . to the Secretary of Interior*. Washington, D.C., 1941–46.

————. *Big-Game Resources of the United States, 1937–1942*. Fish and Wildlife Research Report no. 8. Washington, D.C., 1944.

————. Bureau of Sport Fisheries and Wildlife. *Kodiak National Wildlife Refuge*. Washington, D.C., 1960.

Van Orden, George O. "Retraining the Returned G.I. To Shoot Safely." *Transactions of the North American Wildlife Conference, 1945*, pp. 53–61. Washington, D.C., 1945.

Van Stone, James W. *Athapaskan Adaptations: Hunters and Fishermen of the Subarctic Forests*. Chicago, 1974.

Vucinich, Alexander. *Science in Russian Culture: A History to 1860*. Stanford, 1963.

Walker, Ernest P. *Mammals of the World*. vol. 1 of 2 vols. Baltimore, 1964.

Washburn, S. L., and Lancaster, C. S. "The Evolution of Hunting." In *Man the Hunter*, edited by R. B. Lee and I. De Vore, pp. 293–303. Chicago, 1968.

Washburn, Wilcomb E. "Ethnohistory: History 'In the Round,' " *Ethnohistory* 7 (Winter 1961): 31–48.

———. *The Indian in America*. New York, 1975.

Watson, Mark Skinner. *The War Department, Chief of Staff: Prewar Plans and Preparations*. U.S. Army in World War II, vol. 4, pt. 1. Washington, D.C., 1950.

White, Lynn, Jr. "The Historical Roots of Our Ecologic Crisis." *Science* 155 (10 March 1967): 1203–07.

White, Sam O. "Sam White, Alaskan." Pt. 3, *Alaska* 31 (February 1965): 47–52; pt. 4 (March 1965): 48–53; pt. 5 (May 1965): 54–57; pt. 6 (June 1965): 56–59.

White, Stewart Edward. "An Emergency is Declared to Exist." *Saturday Evening Post* 202 (12 April 1930): 5, 209, 210, 213, 214.

Wickersham, James. *A Bibliography of Alaskan Literature, 1724–1924*. College, Alaska, 1927.

Wilkinson, Gene. "Hosea's Last Hunt." *Alaska* 25 (January 1959): 10, 11, 41, 42.

Williams, E. Kathleen. "Deployment of the AAF on the Eve of Hostilities." In *The Army Air Forces in World War II*, vol. 1: *Plans and Early Operations, January 1939 to August 1942*, edited by W. F. Craven and J. L. Cate, pp. 151–93. Chicago, 1948.

Williams, R. G. *Game Commissions and Wardens: Their Appointment, Powers, and Duties*. U.S. Department of Agriculture Bureau of Biological Survey Bulletin no. 28. Washington, D.C., 1907.

Williamson, S. T. "Eight U.S. Commanders on Our Far-Flung Fronts." *New York Times Magazine*, 17 May 1942, p. 15.

Wilson, Edward O. *Sociobiology: The New Synthesis*. Cambridge, Mass., 1975.

Wilson, William H. "The Founding of Anchorage." *Pacific Northwest Quarterly* 58 (July 1967): 130–41.

———. *Railroad in the Clouds: The Alaska Railroad in the Age of Steam, 1914–1945*. Boulder, 1977.

Wittels, D. G. "These Are the Generals—Buckner." *Saturday Evening Post* 215 (8 May 1943): 17, 102.

Wood, C. E. S. "Among the Thlinkets in Alaska." *Century* 24 (July 1882): 323–39.

Yeager, Lee Emmett. *Thirty Years of Cooperative Wildlife Research Units, 1935–1965*. Bureau of Sport Fisheries and Wildlife Resources Bulletin no. 6. Washington, D.C., 1965.

Young, S. Hall. *Alaska Days with John Muir*. New York, 1915.

———. *Hall Young of Alaska*. New York, 1927.

Yupiktak Bista. *A Report on Subsistence and the Conservation of Yupik Life-Style*. N.p., 1974.

Zagoskin, L. A. *Lieutenant Zagoskin's Travels in Russian America, 1842–1844*. Edited by H. N. Michael; translated by Penelope Rainey. Toronto, 1967.

Ziswiler, Vingenz. *Extinct and Vanishing Animals*. New York, 1967.

Index